Facilitating Collaboration in Public Management

A Volume in
Research in Management Consulting

Series Editor:
Anthony F. Buono
Bentley University

Research in Management Consulting

Series Editor:
Anthony F. Buono
Bentley University

An Evolving Paradigm: Integrative Perspectives on Organizational Development, Change, Strategic Management, and Ethics (2012)
Edited by Anthony F. Buono

The Changing Paradigm of Consulting: Adjusting to the Fast-Paced World (2011)
Edited by Anthony F. Buono, Ralph Grossmann, Hubert Lobnig, and Kurt Mayer

Preparing Better Consultants (2011)
Edited by Susan Adams and Alberto Zanzi

The Qualimetrics Approach: Observing the Complex Object (2011)
By Henri Savall and Veronique Zardet

Consultation for Organizational Change (2010)
Edited by Anthony F. Buono and David W. Jamieson

Work and People: An Economic Evaluation of Job Enrichment (2010)
By Henri Savall

Board Members and Management Consultants: Redefining the Boundaries of Consulting and Corporate Governance (2009)
Edited by Pierre-Yves Gomez and Rickie Moore

Client-Consultant Collaboration: Coping with Complexity and Change (2009)
Edited by Anthony F. Buono and Flemming Poulfelt

Emerging Trends and Issues in Management Consulting: Consulting as a Janus-Faced Reality (2009)
Edited by Anthony F. Buono

Mastering Hidden Costs and Socio-Economic Performance (2008)
By Henri Savall and Veronique Zardet

Socio-Economic Intervention in Organizations: The Intervener-Researcher and the SEAM Approach to Organizational Analysis (2007)
Edited by Anthony F. Buono and Henri Savall

Creative Consulting: Innovative Perspective on Management Consulting (2006)
Edited by Anthony F. Buono

Challenges and Issues in Knowledge Management (2005)
Edited by Anthony F. Buono and Flemming Poulfelt

Enhancing Inter-Firm Networks & Interorganizational Strategies (2003)
Edited by Anthony F. Buono

Developing Knowledge and Value in Management Consulting (2002)
Edited by Anthony F. Buono

Current Trends in Management Consulting (2001)
Edited by Anthony F. Buono

Facilitating Collaboration in Public Management

Ralph Grossmann
University of Klagenfurt, Austria

Hubert Lobnig
Lemon Consulting

Klaus Scala
University of Graz, Austria

with the assistance of

Michael Stadlober
MelangeC Sustainable Consulting

IAP

INFORMATION AGE PUBLISHING, INC.
Charlotte, NC • www.infoagepub.com

Library of Congress Cataloging-in-Publication Data

Facilitating collaboration in public management / Ralph Grossmann ... [et al.].
p. cm. – (Research in management consulting)
Includes bibliographical references.
ISBN 978-1-61735-886-9 (pbk.) – ISBN 978-1-61735-887-6 (hbk.) – ISBN 978-1-61735-888-3 (e-book) 1. Public-private sector cooperation. 2. Interorganizational relations. 3. Strategic alliances (Business) 4. Business networks. 5. Business consultants. I. Grossmann, Ralph.
HD3871.F33 2012
658'.046–dc23

2012020192

Printed in the United States of America

CONTENTS

PREFACE

Anthony F. Buono

This volume represents another first for the *Research in Management Consulting* (*RMC*) series. As *RMC* has evolved over the past decade, there has been an explicit attempt to look backward as well as forward in examining trends, perspectives, and insights into the world of management consulting. As a way of enhancing our understanding of historic contributions to our thinking about intervening in organizations—especially from the vantage point of different countries and cultures—the series has reissued and updated several works previously available only in French by the noted management scientist Henri Savall, founder of ISEOR, the Institute for Socio-Economic Research in Organizations at the University Jean Moulin Lyon 3—*Mastering Hidden Costs and Socio-Economic Performance* (2008), *Work and People* (2010), and *The Qualimetrics Approach: Observing the Complex Object* (2011).

This volume is part of a parallel effort to continue to learn across cultural perspectives, focusing on current thinking in the European context. My involvement with the volume's authors began with our association through the Management Consulting (MC) Division of the Academy of Management. Working closely with Ralph Grossmann and Hubert Lobnig, the MC Division held its 2009 international conference in Vienna, Austria, a highly engaging and successful event that led to our co-edited volume, *The*

Facilitating Collaboration in Public Management, pages vii–ix

Changing Paradigm of Consulting (2011). As we continued to exchange information and our insights into the consultation process, I became increasingly intrigued by the Austrian approach to organizational intervention, especially in the context of interorganizational settings. Grossmann and his colleagues had been engaged in a series of consulting engagements and research projects with an array of Austrian organizations in the realm of public-private partnerships. While this topic has been explored in previous *RMC* books—most notably by German scholars Joerg Sydow and Arnold Windeler (2003) and French researcher Eric Davoine (2003) in a volume on *Enhancing Inter-firm Networks and Interorganizational Strategies*—those contributions were chapters in a larger collection. This volume is the first book length investigation of the potential and challenges inherent in collaborative ventures between for-profit enterprises, publicly-funded service organizations, and non-profit organizations. The focus is on the role that management consultants can play in facilitating such collaborative ventures. Especially within the European context, this particular organizational form is becoming an increasingly common and powerful type of organizational system, and, as such, interventions that can ease and expedite their performance demand our attention and scholarship.

As Grossmann and his colleagues skillfully document and illustrate, cooperative relationships and networks function according to their own underlying logic, which is typically grounded in a spirit of collaboration and negotiation. That spirit, however, can easily and unintentionally be undermined, which can unleash pressures and forces that can limit the potential involved. As they argue, the resulting dynamic reflects a different perspective on building interpersonal, intergroup, and interorganizational relationships, one that is removed from historic attempts at coordination through tight hierarchical control, which, as they argue, is often "inflexible, bureaucratic, and incapable" of achieving the level of commitment and dedication necessary for success.

Collaborative ventures involve goals that must be jointly pursued as they cannot be reached alone. Although partners will still pursue their own interests—which are often decidedly different across private sector and public sector lines—they also need to recognize and take into account the interests of others. As Grossmann and his colleague underscore, the extremes of "domination and subordination are simply out of place in this type of interorganizational structure," as the partnerships must strive for levels commitment, involvement, and motivation from their members that go well beyond those that hierarchical top-down structures typically provide.

As the volume clearly indicates, such high levels of collaboration do not emerge on their own. Mergers, acquisitions, joint ventures, partnerships, and strategic alliances are often launched with great fanfare, only to fall well short of pre-venture expectations. As my own work in this area has underscored (cf. Buono, 1997, 2005; Buono & Bowditch, 1989; Buono & Nurick, 1992), the challenges are significant. To truly work in practice, collaborative relationships and networks must be deliberately formed, developed, organized, and guided. Yet, as Grossmann and colleagues amply illustrate, the underlying process is infused with a number of tensions—from the challenge of balancing collaboration and competition, to the appropriate mix of loose-tight controls and linkages, to ensuring commitment from members to the partnership while they maintain allegiance to their primary organization. While these dynamics are examined within the field of public services, the concepts, ideas, and learnings in the volume have broad applicability to a wide range of organizations and sectors.

Drawing on their consulting and research experiences, the authors bring the field of transorganizational development to life through a series of practical examples and cases that depict the range of challenges involved. Building on a thoughtful blend of theory and practice, they provide ample insight and direction as to the types of structures, processes, and interventions that will go a long way toward providing the type of guidelines needed for both short- and long-term success. Grossmann and his colleagues are to be commended for their insightful exploration into this complex and evolving subject.

As with all volumes in the RMC series, my hope is that this book will stimulate the reader's thinking about the processes and structures that can facilitate the creation and long-term success of truly collaborative interorganizational ventures. Given the complexity of challenges we are currently facing, it is becoming increasingly clear that management consultants have a significant role to play in facilitating these ventures, helping to bridge the gap between the private and public sectors, facilitating collaboration between businesses and public services organizations that are capable of serving the greater good.

INTRODUCTION

Why Organizations Collaborate

**Ralph Grossmann, Hubert Lobnig,
Klaus Scala, and Michael Stadlober**

A federal ministry decides to promote new media at universities by forming an independent network that assigns substantial government funds autonomously. Hospitals and health providers form regional networks and systematically develop new patient care processes—beyond organizational boundaries. Several unions embark on a long course of decision-making, ending by forming a new combined union. Public sponsors ask cultural institutions to jointly conduct their upcoming film-related activities and create a new organization together. The networking of various national and regional political players as well as collaboration projects between insurance and social service companies results in sustained change in the treatment of the unemployed.

The list could easily continue as such collaborative relationships and inter-organizational networks are a part of the current trend in organizational life. This tendency is no coincidence—societies are increasingly developing into a coexistence of highly specialized systems and organizations, which can be very effective at doing what they do. The on-going differentiation of

Facilitating Collaboration in Public Management, pages xi–xiv organizations is especially obvious in the field of public services. In former days, public administration directly provided many services—but now these services are made available through a variety of specialized and independent enterprises. As part of this trend, the social and organizational capacity to handle problems has undoubtedly increased. Yet new concerns have also emerged, focusing on the challenge of dealing with interconnected issues that exceed existing organizational boundaries, competencies and professions. In fact, there are myriad questions as to how to even draw attention to these issues, prompting participants to pay attention in a substantial way.

A reality in today's complex environment is that most social issues—from climate protection, to health care, to education and migration policies—cannot be adequately handled by one organization alone. Collaboration between independent organizations offers an attractive way to deal with interrelated problems in a way that improves the quality of public services and fosters sustainable development. We all benefit from interorganizational collaboration, as when hospitals, doctors, and regional health care organizations coordinate their activities to simplify referral, admission, discharge and follow-up care, and reducing long waiting times and hospital stays in the process.

The public sector promotes collaborative relationships and networks in order to attract new resources and to outsource services from management. "Public-Private Partnerships," collaboration between for-profit enterprises, publicly-funded service organizations, and non-profit organizations, are an increasingly common and powerful type of organizational systems. Managers of organizations perceive collaboration as an opportunity for growth and innovation, as a means of exploiting synergies, and as a way to protect their own organizations when faced with a turbulent environment. The ability of an organization to collaborate with others and to participate in networks is increasingly becoming a strategic success factor: "The capability for inter-organizational collaboration will be the decisive factor for organizational success in the 21st Century" (Austin, 2000).

NEW CHALLENGES FOR MANAGEMENT CONSULTING AND ORGANIZATION DEVELOPMENT

Cooperative relationships and networks operate typically according to their own logic—collaboration through negotiation. This approach reflects a new concept of building relationships and differs from coordination through tight hierarchical control as well as from the loose seller-buyer relations inherent in the free market-economy. In public services the focus on profits produces undesirable side effects, like unequal access to public services and lack of services in unprofitable areas. Privatization shifts gains to the private owner, and risks and losses to the public. Hierarchical control also tends to be inflexible, bureaucratic and incapable of achieving gains through efficiency.

In collaborative ventures, there are goals jointly pursued that cannot be reached alone. Independent partners pursue their own interests, but recognize and take into account the interests of others. Domination and subordination are simply out of place in this type of interorganizational structure. At the same time, stronger bonds between the participants arise that go well beyond those in anonymous buyer-seller relationships, and more commitment and motivation emerges compared to hierarchical top-down structures.

Such collaboration, however, does not function by itself. Many collaborative relationships and networks are launched with great momentum, but without any true outcomes or intended effect. As our central thesis, collaborative relationships and networks must be deliberately formed, developed, organized and controlled. This is a new, very demanding task: how can binding structures of communications, work and decision-making *between* organizations be introduced? How can collaboration and competition be balanced? How loosely or tightly should collaborative ventures and networks be linked? What rules are needed? What are the conditions and skills needed within the organizations and by the persons involved, and how can they be developed? What role will the initiating political institutions play? How could cooperative mergers be set up?

The "Why" of this Volume

Organizational development (OD) of collaboration-based relationships and networks presents managers, staff workers and consultants with a new challenge that requires special and often underrated skills. The shift moves from the individual, vertically structured organization to a mix of horizontal organizational relationships such as networks, collaborative projects, clusters, joint ventures and public-private partnerships.

This book presents the basic foundation and methods of transorganizational development (Cummings, 1984) as well as what the important components of managing collaborative relationships. Founded on the theoretical basis of systems theory and organizational development, we illustrate the process design of collaborative relationships and networks. The book combines the close connection of 36 case studies, individual long-term consulting experiences, and a theoretical-conceptual framework to make our case for transorganizational development and collaborations.

Although we emphasize the field of public services, interested practitioners from the private sector also may benefit from the ideas and learning opportunities presented in the book.

Golden Thread

At the beginning of the book, we cite individual consulting experiences to trace how the collaboration of organizations recently has become an issue. At the same time, the development and professionalization of this aspect of OD becomes significant (Chapter 1). Chapter 2 is devoted to the trends in the organization of public services and the mix of specialized organizations with different tasks, success criteria and cultures, positioned between the market, state and civil society. We describe the multifaceted organizational landscape in the field of public services as a challenging and difficult starting point for collaboration. In Chapter 3 we lay out the conceptual guidelines for our understanding of OD as a special approach to change make clear which view we are taking when observing this situation and how we work as consultants and teachers. This perspective includes the theoretical foundations of our OD research and our approach for this book (Chapter 4).

In order to cover the full diversity and breadth of collaboration relationships and networks involved in the provision of public services, we outline several short, practical examples that reveal the challenges as well as the pitfalls experienced in this field (Chapter 5). Against this colorful background, the "network" is differentiated as an umbrella term used for many different forms of collaboration, and success criteria gained from research and transorganizational consulting are presented for organizing collaboration relationships (Chapter 6).

Using a detailed description and analysis of a few examples, we simultaneously provide a clear and comprehensive picture about how success criteria in specific processes can be considered and implemented (Chapters 7 & 8). In the final chapter, focused on collaborative mergers, the volume concludes with a discussion of a possible, but not absolutely necessary, endpoint for a collaboration relationship between organizations. A decision to merge cooperatively can offer some guidelines for managing other types of mergers.

ACKNOWLEDGEMENTS

Our thanks go out to those who have directly and indirectly participated in this project including: Helena Biritz, Marlies Garbsch, and Silvia Nossek from the research team. We also want to thank those we interviewed about their experiences: the managers, consultants and project managers from 36 collaborations and networks from Germany, Austria and Switzerland as well as the contractors of relevant consulting projects. For the preparation of the English text, we thank Tom Meyer and especially Beth Waitkus, who, through the combination of language and OD experience provided a crucial contribution to the editorial content of this book.

CHAPTER 1

FROM COMPETITION TO COOPERATION AND COMPETITION

Prerequisites for Successful Collaborative Ventures

Ralph Grossmann, Hubert Lobnig, and Klaus Scala

This chapter captures our practical experiences and the main conceptual framework that led us to our understanding of organizational networks and transorganizational collaboration. As a context for our work, the discussion revisits the most important stages of development of our central case—an institute referred to as iff—starting with its foundation over 20 years ago. Our focus on the emergence of the research and our consulting to organizational networks has intensified and changed over the years.

From a practical point of view, the projects realized over this long period of time clearly illustrate the emergence of organizational networks and trans-organizational collaboration in modern societies. From a theoretical point of view, we originally departed from traditional sociological concepts, proceeded to standard organization-development concepts and have now

Facilitating Collaboration in Public Management, pages 1–18

arrived at newer concepts of organizational networking and trans-organizational collaboration. Through this evolution, we have experimented with a number of innovative interventions guided by collaboration and networking concepts, which will be described in detail in the following chapter sections.

Our department at iff was founded under the name "Societal Learning: Work—Health—Environment" in 1984. In the first years, the main focus of iff's work was on workplace health promotion, where we carried out research activities and professional training. With time, we began to research the concept of and experiences with implementing health promotion in different areas. This work led to the insight that exceptional collaboration between professionals, organizations and different sectors of the society is a key criterion for success. As our fields of work emerged, we transferred our learning within the broad field of occupational health, health promotion and health and social services to other public service industry sectors.

OTTAWA CHARTER FOR HEALTH PROMOTION (1986)

In 1986, the World Health Organization (WHO) invited us to participate in and contribute our experiences to a working group called "Work and Health" in an Ottawa conference, which was a kick-off event for the upcoming health-promotion movement. The main outcome of the conference was the "Ottawa Charter for Health Promotion," that became the founding document of health promotion.

Even today, more than 20 years after the event, the principles formulated in the Ottawa Charter are still guiding health-promotion efforts throughout the world. According to the Ottawa Charter two major aspects must be considered: 1) health cannot be provided by health-care systems alone because health affects everyone in all parts of society; 2) the generation and maintenance of health depends on individual behavior and is influenced and determined by people's physical and social environments. Accordingly, the Ottawa Conference was focused how health as a major issue should be put on the agenda of organizations and networks of organizations in all parts of society. The Charter 'outlines a comprehensive strategy for health promotion through five interactive activities that cover the whole range of the new approach to health' (Grossmann & Scala, 1996, p. 17), which includes:

- Building healthy public policy
- Creating supportive environments
- Strengthening community action

- Developing personal skills
- Reorienting health services

Meeting the requirements developed in the Ottawa Charter has posed and is still posing a great challenge to the developmental intelligence of many types of organizations in all parts of society. It implicitly points out the importance of organizational development (OD) as one of the main Charter statements because a society cannot cope with its health issues successfully unless its various organizations continuously develop and cooperate. From our perspective, the programmatic concept of health promotion is closely related with the concept of OD, as well as inter-professional, cross-industrial, and trans-organizational work.

The Ottawa Charter was an excellent entry point for collaboration with experts from the WHO because our OD background allowed us to offer very practical and convincing suggestions about how to implement the Charter. Taking a close look at these programmatic streams of the Ottawa Charter, one could draw the conclusion that implementing such an approach towards health promotion requires much networking and collaboration which have to take place both individually—between certain experts and organizational players—as well as on the institutional or systems-level between different professional groups and organizations. For example, the implementation of public health policy cannot be realized by governments or public administration alone. To create environments supportive for health in a company, region, or city requires coordinated action of different organizations such as the public administration, schools, companies, and community groups (neighborhood communities, parents' initiatives, ecologically-oriented non-governmental organizations, self-help groups, etc.). Therefore, one of the key concepts explicitly communicated in the Ottawa Charter for putting health promotion into practice was the concept of building networks between different professional groups and organizations as well as between individuals and organizations.

HEALTH PROMOTION: THE SETTINGS APPROACH

The issue of health promotion requires that the targets of health-promotion interventions are to be defined. Conventionally, we think about how people should make positive lifestyle changes to counter unhealthy behavior patterns by receiving information, classes or individual counseling. However, focusing interventions on individuals alone leads to limited success, since the context of individual behavior, the environment, the social system, and organizational life may still remain untapped. Alternately, we have found that the "settings approach" is a useful solution to this problem.

Our definition of a "setting" is a social system that provides the context for an individuals' behavior. This approach, therefore, suggests that social systems and not individuals are the target of health-promotion interventions (see also Grossmann & Scala, 1996). Figure 1.1 illustrates the difference between the educational model addressing individuals and the systemic model addressing social systems or settings.

The settings approach has led to a general shift in thinking about the individual as the center of health-promotion activities to the environment being the major target of health-related interventions. When we first introduced the settings approach, it was quite a revolutionary concept because the majority of the health educators or prevention experts considered the individual as the intervention target. For example, anti-smoking campaigns aiming at proving that smoking is unhealthy could be translated as individually-centered messages like, "Smokers are stupid. Do you want to be stupid?"

The definition of a "setting" is a social system that is targeted by health-promotion activities. From the perspective of OD concepts and research, the term "setting" has a twofold meaning. It can be used in a more general sense—as has been defined by the WHO—such as social systems, com-

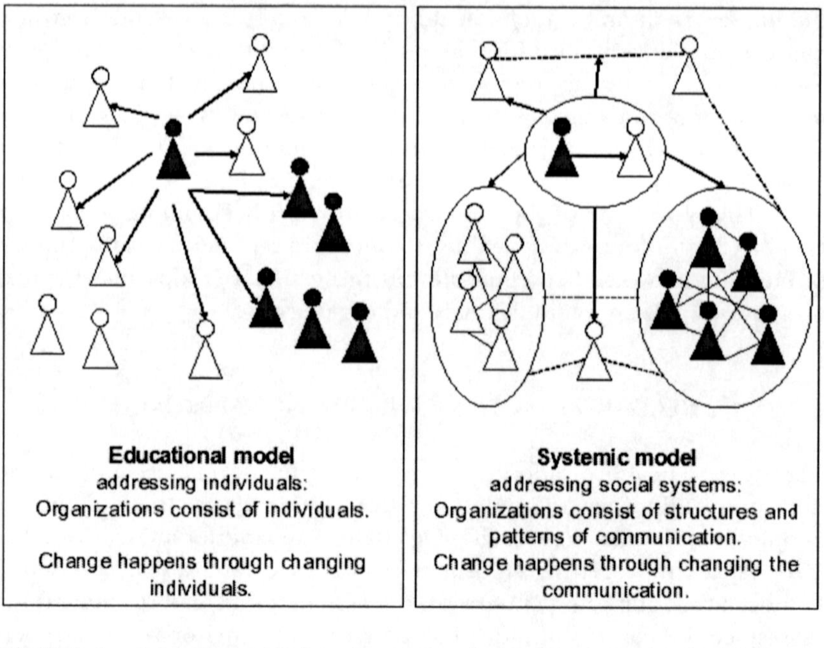

FIGURE 1.1. Educational Model versus Systemic Model as a Basis of Health-promotion Interventions (Adapted from Grossmann and Scala (1996, p.47)).

munities (as cities, regions) or organizations (cf. companies, schools) that influence people's daily well-being. More specifically, however, we call the system targeted with an intervention the "setting of the intervention." For example, a consultant who intends to intervene in a social system has first to decide who should actually be part of the target system. This target system—or setting of the intervention—comprises all people, groups, or organizations that are either affected by or involved in the intervention.

Having defined the target system, a change agent or consultant then has to ensure that these people, groups, or organizations become a social system by setting up their own communication structures. In essence, each intervention creates its own social system—it must be purposely and actively developed to come into life.

As elaborated in one of our earlier books (Grossmann & Scala, 1996, p. 48), we believe that:

> ... a deliberate and functional definition of the social system that is suitable for task completion is one of the essential prerequisites for a successful intervention. Before planning health promotion projects in hospitals, schools or enterprises, one must find out which organizations, departments and people are to be involved and asked to cooperate. Further, one must find out whether cooperation is to be sought with the organization as a whole or with special sectors only. If a health promotion project aims at a social context such as a city, a region or a community, one must decide which organizations will be involved.

Decisions on who to involve define the possibilities for action within the chosen setting. Such decisions require an active definition and construction of the setting and can only be made on the specific, relevant issues to be addressed.

In this book, we consider health-promotion activities just as much a collaborative effort as are organizational development and consulting with one important difference: while health promotion focuses on the content of a program or project, OD concentrates on interventions that will lead to further learning in and development of a social system.

Health in the Workplace: Concepts for Research and Implementation

In the aftermath of the Ottawa conference, iff researchers and scholars started to plan, organize, design, facilitate, document, and evaluate expert conferences on the issue of Health in the Workplace. We further developed this concept by applying the "setting approach" principles. Invitees to these conferences included union delegates, occupational-safety experts from business organizations, employed as well as self-employed teams of occupational physicians, governmental health inspectors and representatives of occupational-accident insurers.

At these conferences, people analyzed and discussed how to improve collaborative efforts in the field of employee health promotion. The conferences took place in a cooperative setting so we could "practice what we preached" and also generate a more effective outcome. Every expert represented his or her area of expertise in this setting, yet collaboration with other experts was still essential because no one individually could develop comprehensive health-promotion activities solely.

At that time, we already faced the problems of and barriers to organizational collaboration that we continue to face today, such as:

1. Agreeing on a common language shared by all represented disciplines (engineers, medical doctors, psychologists, legal experts, managers, workers, union members etc.)
2. Overcoming the difficulties that participating organizations' experts have with understanding and accepting others' specific approaches and with being willing to really cooperate across disciplines.
3. Overcoming experts' reluctance to accept the expertise of blue collar workers and their representatives as valuable, reliable resources for deeper insights into work place health issues that combine expert knowledge with practical experience of affected people.

In the 1980s, we encountered a particularly interesting example of difficulties and solutions in practical collaboration in one of our "Heart-Attack Conferences." At that conference, the greatest obstacle to direct communication in dialogues was the conference room configuration. The chairs in the room were tightly screwed to the floor and, therefore, stationary. We finally decided to have the conference room refurnished during the Department Head's vacation. As the conference keynote speaker, the CEO was quite surprised when he saw the rearranged room, yet was impressed with the dialogues' outcomes influenced by the changed setting. In the end, the CEO legitimized the new arrangement although the Head of the Department had resisted the change.

We face similar problems in many organizations today. In universities, for example, people generally don't consider arranging rooms in a way that enables lateral, cooperative communication. As illustrated by the heart-attack conference example, finding a suitable room for networking and collaborative interaction can cause difficulties.

From our point of view, three things can be learned from these experiences:

1. Accepting that workers are "experts" in certain aspects of their health as may be doctors lead to increased practical solutions for the implementation of programs and changes.
2. Bringing together different independent experts and people from expert organizations and establishing a cooperative framework is a promising way to understand, analyze, and prepare alternative actions to improve workplace health.
3. Involving and integrating affected organizations' management is essential if efforts to promote health in the workplace are to be successful. Neither could health issues be resolved by health experts alone nor could political or strategic decision-making be delegated from leaders to experts.

Subsequently, the World Health Organization (WHO) set up a network of health-promoting companies and strongly emphasized involving the networking organization's top management. They had realized that in a business-organizational context, health promotion was the management's responsibility (Adelaide Conference).

Having initiated and facilitated a number of health-promotion conferences, we have learned that managers often do not take health issues properly into account when making purchasing decisions. For instance, chemical substances are used in many industries, which might pose certain risks to the health of workers. However, management generally decides which raw materials and/or chemicals are used the production process. Consequently, the level of health risk actually involved depends strongly on the decisions management makes about the price and location of materials' purchase. The crucial question is whether or not management takes the implications of purchase decisions on workers' health into account and if so, to what extent. If managers' purchase decisions are solely based on product price and product quality, they have not sufficiently considered the potential consequences for workers' health. Although an occupational physician working for such a company probably would notice this issue, he would not be in a position to make decisions relevant to those health topics, as their voice is silent in the organizations' decision making bodies.

Besides facilitating and organizing conferences, we also developed a specific applied research approach to studying employee workload and employee health (see Grossmann, 1984 for a complete description of the project). The traditional occupational medicine research is based on a natural science-oriented research paradigm. To comprehensively understand workplace health issues, we found it necessary to also include the perception of employees with health issues as well as the surrounding environment's impact on health as relevant data, therefore applying a more social science-oriented perspective (see Chapter 3).

Scientists and experts in favor of the traditional paradigm criticized this approach, arguing that valuable knowledge can only be acquired by strictly adhering to scientific research requirements based on traditional measurement models. By applying a purely experimental scientific approach, however, one can miss the opportunity to gain empirical insight into understanding the subjective views of those actually affected and the increased risk of dividing research from practice. As our approach concentrates on bridging research and implementation of health promotion programs in and between organizations, we learned that most traditional scientific research is of limited value.

The following example illustrates our approach to applied organizational research, conducted in a group of companies. First, we invited several delegates from the staff council to conduct empirical research on workplace health and safety together with experts and scholars from the iff. The team was responsible for defining how health and safety conditions should be explored and how the data collection should be organized. Second, after the data had been collected and evaluated, we invited several groups of employees to discuss the results in a focus-group setting; 3) different experts such as occupational physicians and labor inspectors commented on the survey results on which the research team and group discussions had elaborated. In a joint effort, employees, experts, and scientists generated practical knowledge, which then served as a useful basis in their respective companies for taking further action towards decreasing health risks. Furthermore, the employees from the companies participating in the research process became experts themselves and more effectively served their companies after the project.

This approach allowed us to bridge the gap between research and practice and led not only to insights but to beneficial changes. The type of research conducted in this example is still one of our core research methods today.

Health Promotion in the Region

Based on our experiences in occupational health promotion we started to transfer our work to regional settings. What brought us to this shift was two-fold. As scholars, we wanted to gain deeper insight into how our interventions would affect different regional settings and which conclusions could be drawn from a scientific point of view. As consultants, however, we were responsible for organizing and setting successful interventions based on our OD approach. In other words, our role was to implement socially-effective interventions as well as to study the impacts of our interventions and how they differed in various regional settings. For the first time, we were deeply confronted with the problems of organizational networking and inter-organizational collaboration on a practical versus theoretical level.

A first model project focused on a rural area where we conducted a health initiative known with the catchword "back pain" (see Breitwieser, et al, 1991). The aim of this health-promotion project, implemented in the second half of the 1980s in Upper Austria, was to develop and test health-promoting services for everyday living. We initiated this project because back pain is and has been one of the most common health problems in Austria. Many people suffer constantly from back pain, among them certain population groups who cannot sufficiently access professional treatment.

We chose farmers' wives as the main target group because they significantly suffered more than the average population with chronic back pain, while handling two or more jobs (taking care of the household and looking after the farm). Sometimes, they also worked in factories because their families were only part-time farmers. Under such conditions, farmers' wives simply did not have the time to consult a doctor or physiotherapist so they often accepted taking analgesics for a very long period of time.

We encountered some cultural and social barriers that had to be considered when we launched the health-promotion program for farmers' wives. Culturally, it was uncommon that farmers' wives would be proactive in their health care. Socially, it seemed impossible that farmers' wives could spend time on physical therapy between stable work and child care.

At the organizational side of the initiative, collaboration between different professional groups and organizations was crucial in creating a helpful and participative program. In the given situation, we needed the people and organizations involved to build a close social relationship based on mutual trust with the farmer's wives. Therefore, we collaborated with the Farmer's Federation, local churches, restaurants where farmers regularly met and other groups and associations to which farmers' wives were affiliated. We sought to identify legitimate places where they could find a supportive social environment. In fact, implementing this initiative required further collaboration with professionals such as therapists who were willing and able to empathetically work with these women.

We also had to organize affordable health partners who were geographically close to where the farmers' wives lived and win over the social health-insurance providers. Our goal was to encourage them to financially support the women and the projects' activities and to encourage them to think about ways that health-promotion activities could become a regular part of their services to be permanently financed. In addition, we had to find specialist doctors who were already accepted by the local general practitioners, otherwise we would encounter too much program resistance from their side. We also had to win the Medical Association to buy in so they would not counter the campaign out of fear that people attending the program would risk major health problems. At the time, it was uncommon that physical therapists would work independently instead of being employed by a general practitioner.

In setting up a robust network of individual key players, professional groups, and organizations, we learned how to deal with networks and foster organizational collaboration. Our first conceptual understanding of trans-organizational development included the importance of developing roles for all major stakeholders and integrating them formally into steering, monitoring and implementation projects, providing them a place in the project management structure. Although individual networking and collaboration between professionals of good will seemed to be achievable through direct communication and negotiation processes, long term or sustainable effects needed to be embedded into more formal decisions from the organizations' key players.

With regard to health problems of our society, however, communication, exchange, and cooperation[1] between the mentioned organizational partners have still remained a major problem 20 years after the project. Problems have increased simultaneously with competition in the health market—organizations must compete more aggressively while working hard to cut costs and increase efficiency. The investment of time and resources in building collaborative strategies and programs are continuously scarce.

Healthy Cities: From Movement to Project

The Healthy City project was one of the first projects in which the Ottawa Charter was practiced and cities that fulfilled certain Charter criteria were awarded the title of "Healthy City." Cities striving for this title were, for example, bound to consider health in all their political decisions and had therefore to foster cooperation across organizational and sectoral borders.[2]

A remarkable aspect of the dialogue about the healthy-city project was that some key experts from WHO believed that the program was changing from a project to a movement. From our point of view, this was an amazing transition because the difficulties and efforts involved in establishing trans-sectoral collaboration had been dramatically underestimated. In our view, a "movement" brings about a change in people's awareness—of their health conditions or of broader health issues. Furthermore, a movement can represent a more weakly organized or even disorganized type of initiative. As such, an initial movement first builds a cultural ground for change and raises people's awareness before precise action can be taken or formal project groups could come into existence. Accordingly, we encouraged WHO to change their thinking by promoting the view that the healthy-city program should develop from a movement to a project.

In order for a movement to have a real impact on society, organizations that have a leading impact on people's health have to commit to increased collaboration. In the healthy-city project, this meant that the involved organizations had to cooperate and change their treatment of customers or and their problem-solving methods. This presumed setting up projects that built strong ties between the organizations involved.

One example of building connections included dermatologists who no longer just treated their patients but started to continuously collect data to find evidence of the symptoms' distribution. The dermatologists eventually discovered that it was always the same population group bearing a certain kind of skin disease. With further research, they realized that cleaning materials had made this group sick. With the established communications networks developed in the healthy-city project, this information could be directly channeled to the organizations producing the chemicals so they could change the mixture of cleaning materials.

The healthy-city project helped to establish a totally different view of health and health creation. Cities participating in the program are now better equipped to track health impacts on people living in cities as well as the possibility for change through cooperative efforts.

One of the key questions raised during the healthy cities projects was about how to help different organizations to connect, form ties and begin organizational collaboration.

A small city (60,000 inhabitants) in Austria participating in the Healthy City Project asked us to help create Healthy City partnerships. We designed a conference to foster networking among participants on a rather informal and individual basis. This can often be the first step to organizational cooperation because people just naturally start to communicate with each other. Accordingly, we scheduled speeches in which the healthy-city program, its philosophy and the concept behind the program were introduced. Although we primarily relied on workshop settings with small groups. The workshop groups met for four times throughout the conference and in those settings, figured out how to adapt the healthy-city concept to smaller cities.

Another featured conference/workshop topic included best-practice models from Denmark, Germany, Switzerland, Austria, as well as other European countries. This design allowed for simultaneous networking at various levels. Experts from different disciplines networked with colleagues from other regions or towns with differing professional experiences. As participants attended from different Austrian regions, networking was focused both locally and regionally.

As a consequence of this paradigm shift in organizing a health promotion approach with impact in a region we introduced the "change agent" role into the professional health promotion community. By promoting this role, we underlined that establishing organizational networks was a profession of its own. We introduced the change facilitator because we understood that setting up collaborations between organizations required innovative expertise.

International Training for Project Development in Health Promotion

In the early 1990s, our department developed a training program to equip health promotion experts with skills needed for becoming successful change agents. The training program was conducted three times and participants included people from different countries and cultural backgrounds such as: Austria, the Czech Republic, Slovakia, Hungary, and Slovenia. The groups consisted of people from different organizations as well as different professions and providers of health services such as public health-service providers, public administrators, education providers, health-training organizations, and hospitals. Many also worked in regional health departments.

The goal of the program was to train professional change facilitators. However, many of the participants and their organizations did not necessarily understand how to promote health on a systems level and were not aware of the importance of the change facilitator role. Accordingly, one of our major training challenges was to strengthen our participants' individual skills (see Table 1.1) as change facilitators and to help them establish this role in their home organizations.

At that time, health promotion was a relatively new concept. Key players within the organizations were not aware of trans-organizational cooperation as a prerequisite for health promotion. Therefore, the change agents first faced the "change challenge" within their organizations since they had to receive sufficient acceptance among the key players in their parent organizations. Role modeling was used to elaborate intervention strategies for helping their colleagues understand the existence of the "change agent" position and how the organization could benefit from an internal change facilitator and health promoter. In the program, we also trained them to advocate for their new role.

TABLE 1.1. Organizational Development-oriented Core Competencies for Health Promotion Experts

- Organizational behavior (specific models including role of individual and teams in the organization, and specification of organizations as systems)
- Change management (principles of organizational innovation and change, models of change, conflict management)
- OD-oriented project management (basics in project management, social life of projects, designs of structures)
- Facilitation skills (meetings, conferences, group work)

We designed the training program using theoretical lectures, exercises, and supervision that were essential because of the importance of specific environmental and cultural differences between the participants. In fact, this was another major program characteristic which provided an excellent opportunity for practicing trans-organizational communication.

Health Promoting Hospitals

In the early 1990s, WHO Europe decided to apply the health-promotion approach to hospitals since they are core institution of any health-care system. The health-promoting-hospitals (HPH) project was one of the first practice areas to which the settings approach was applied, aimed at improving the health of patients and hospital staff. Furthermore, the cooperation between the participating hospitals and external environments, such as patients, general practitioners, medical specialists, had to be improved because hospitals have many influences on patient health over the long-term, but also rely heavily on contributions made by others. Our activities as project managers, researchers, consultants, facilitators and observers of the HPH network led us to valuable and hands-on knowledge about how collaboration and organizational networking could be put into practice in a broader international context.

Piloting with the Viennese hospital "Krankenanstalt Rudolfstiftung" between 1991 and 1996 (Novak et al.1998), a European Pilot Hospital Project (EPHP) included hospitals from all areas of Europe. A transnational group of European experts invited and led by WHO Europe guided the selection process, which included the following criteria:

1. Ensure that the developmental process was followed. Each hospital was first asked to initiate a comprehensive HPH project by implementing an extensive OD process.
2. Define and implementing at least five HPH sub-projects
3. Collaborate with external advisors and consultants during implementation
4. Evaluate the overall project
5. Agree to collaborate trans-organizationally

As such, the hospitals were required to participate actively in so-called "business meetings," which were held twice a year. Apart from the member hospital delegates, representatives of the WHO and members of the coordinating institution attended these meetings. Each hospital was also asked to host one of the bi-annual business meetings so they covered meeting costs including the travelling expenses of all other invitees. Furthermore, the hospitals had to present the status of their projects once a year during international conferences. Finally, WHO required them to act as initiators and enablers of regional or national HPH networks.

In the above-mentioned business meetings, each hospital presented its internal projects and its experiences with the collaborating with other institutions. By sharing their successes and failures, they advanced the HPH concept. Although the hospitals had very different structural, financial and political backgrounds, they substantially learned from each other.

As coordinating institution, our task was to organize and facilitate the project to achieve its aims. In the beginning phase, the coordinating institution carried out most activities, which was not a desirable state for a collaboration project as authority and collaborative energy was highly centralized. Subsequently our interventions focused on encouraging the project members to gradually take on more active roles and responsibilities and to follow an "empowerment" approach, which lead to an increasingly emerging lateral distribution of commitment and responsibility.

The setting and design of the business meetings was crucial to empower the European Pilot Hospital Project (HPH), and the learning and development processes were a challenging task with 12 delegations of three to five delegates each adding up to 35 to 50 attendees per meeting. In order to make these meetings most effective and stimulating, we provided counsel on large-group design elements and involved the delegates as actively as possible in all assignments and discussions. Accordingly, each meeting design was based on our project plan as well as on the situational needs of the participating delegations.

During the initial phase of the project, the coordinating institute defined, moderated and steered the relevant discussion topics. As the process continued, we intended to promote the system's self-organization by assigning motivating, committing, and accepting project members with an active role in the meetings such as session chair, workgroup coordinator, sub-project evaluators, or presenter.

To foster learning generated by self-organization and collaboration, the member hospitals also shared their valuable experiences with the local area networks. Accordingly, meeting participants not only had lively discussions about how such local networks could best be established but also exchanged their applied approaches, experiences and results.

Another key instrument for developing the HPH network continues to be the regularly held international conferences which could best be described as a mixture of policy papers, scientific discussions, and project presentations utilizing a discussion forum and a networking medium. Between 200 and 400 people have attended each of these conferences, organized by varying local hosts throughout Europe. A scientific committee prepares the conferences in which national and international organizations and stakeholders related to the specific topics are represented. The committee determines the scope of the conference, selects the papers to be presented, steers the program, and chairs the plenary sessions. Through this committee structure and role, the conferences' ownership is widely distributed and the network increases its robustness and efficiency.

In 1998, the WHO completed and evaluated the EPHP (Pelikan et al. 1998a, 1998b) and the Assembly of National Networks of HPH (Pelikan, Krajic & Lobnig, 1998) replaced its role. In this setting, WHO discussed in great detail the HPH policies, the conceptual advancement of the HPH, and technical questions about organizational networks. Currently, about 30 national networks with approximately 400 member hospitals throughout Europe have been established and the Health Promoting Hospital is not only a visionary network but also has great impact on services and activities many hospitals are providing.

Based on our work with the HPH projects, we have drawn four main conclusions on our approach to trans-organizational development:

1. Trans-organizational development requires someone who can neutrally establish, maintain, observe, and steer the process. For the success of the trans-organizational approach, each participating partner is acknowledged and seen as equally important for overall achievement of goals. This must be an organizing principle that is clearly stated.
2. The organization of meetings and other communication opportunities is crucial. Conferences help to effectively foster organizational networking because they offer many possibilities for people to take over responsibilities and creative positions to create a common future. They may prepare contents, take session chairs, or present their projects, expertise, achievements, or thoughts.

   Conferences also influence and establish the culture of an organizational network which is of utmost importance to the perception of that network. The process of designing and holding a conference also makes a difference as it can be an example for collaborative procedures or more centralized controlled patterns. The conference itself—as well as its planning and creation—are determining factors in whether the collaboration can actually take place. Key questions in developing a conference are: Is the design process based on collaboration? Is the process borne by a group of dedicated and respected people? Has the conference been preceded by a lively discussion about the content, presentation and discussion types?
3. Projects can foster organizational networking. Since one of the purposes of the HPH initiative was to bring about innovation in the health-care sector, corresponding theories, guidelines, and policies

must be discussed. Successful projects represent the most convincing argument because they can convincingly demonstrate how the vision can be transformed into practical approaches. With these projects, the foundation of the underlying concept, the achievability of certain goals, and the potential for profitability, quickly become apparent. Our experiences support the concept that organizational networks should rely on best-practice projects and should establish channels in which findings are clearly communicated within the network but also to the relevant stakeholders and the outside world.

4. Finally, networks should capitalize on their already existing expertise and knowledge. Creating interesting and challenging roles for participating people and organizations is the basis of a vivid network community. The network becomes more valuable for its members and external observers with the introduction of additional ideas and expertise and responsibility for implementation.

MASTER OF SCIENCE IN ORGANIZATIONAL DEVELOPMENT

As researchers and consultants, we simultaneously focus on and apply comparable efforts to the organizational level as well as personal training and expertise. From the beginning of our work, one of iff's major concerns has been how to qualify professionals to promote OD in general and the development of inter-organizational collaboration in particular. As already demonstrated, we began our program to train change facilitators in the health-promotion sector. As our department and expertise developed, we adapted the training program several times. After a couple of redesigns, it evolved as a master program in OD, which we have offered since 1999.

Students in our masters program include all kinds of change facilitators such as managers, leaders, project managers, quality managers, organizational development experts, and internal and external consultants. Most recently we included the issue of trans-organizational collaboration as a major curriculum component because of its relevance to our students, who are involved with this type of work. Often they are responsible for building inter-organizational forms of cooperation between organizations, including their own. To meet the specific needs of those participants, we offer a seminar exclusively dedicated to organizational networking and inter-organizational collaboration.

To date, we have had excellent program results. During the program, our students have had to gain practical experience in a real change project and write a thesis about that project. Over the past nine years, more than

90 percent of our students have completed their program requirements and graduated.

Some of the principles that guide our master's program include:

- Designing a supportive program for students to take on assigned roles within their own organizations. In this respect, the application for the course is evaluated in the beginning of the program. It includes also the nomination of a mentor, helping the participant to transfer the learnings into his or her organizational practice. A mentor, generally from higher hierarchical level of the student's organization, can help our students practice what they have learned in a real-world setting. The mentors also are invited to attend a start-up meeting to discuss the potential consequences of the student activities in the organization as well as their support role.
- Closely linking theoretical inputs to practical experiences. Our students learn about organizational theory, project-management methods, change management, and inter-organizational collaboration. However, they must also be able to connect the theories to daily practice. For this reason, we include supervisory elements in our program to support students in this way.
- Writing a thesis to qualify for graduation with an M.S. in Organizational Development. The thesis must involve a change project in which the respective student has influence within an organization. Favoring this practice-oriented approach rather than a purely scientific or observation methodology, we often receive feedback about the positive impact of our program on people doing their job.

With regard to the relevance of our student's organizational collaboration, about 20 percent of all master's theses deal explicitly with inter-organizational collaboration. Another 60 percent of our master's theses are concerned with the development of a single organization affecting changes in the way the organization cooperates with partner organizations.

NOTES

1. The terms "collaboration" and "cooperation" are sometimes used interchangeably. We refer to the definition as presented in Dillenbourgh, et al. (1995, p. 190): "Cooperation and collaboration do not differ in terms of whether or not the task is distributed, but by virtue of the way in which it is divided; in cooperation the task is split (hierarchically) into independent subtasks; in collaboration cognitive processes may be (heterarchically) divided into inter-

twined layers. In cooperation, coordination is only required when assembling partial results, while collaboration is '...a coordinated, synchronous activity that is the result of a continued attempt to construct and maintain a shared conception of a problem' (Roschelle & Teasley, 1995)."

2. For more information on healthy-city criteria, please consult the World Health Organization (WHO) web-site at www.euro.who.int/healthy-cities.

CHAPTER 2

COLLABORATION IN THE PUBLIC SERVICE SECTOR

Ralph Grossmann and Michael Stadlober

The availability and quality of public services substantially determines the opportunity and direction of social development because they are a central requirement for the ensuring social cohesion and a sense of security. The manner in which public services are established, how citizens' are involved and how their involvement is managed effectively moulds the political culture of a society.

Public services represent an important source of economic activity and social wellbeing. For the past several years in Austria, approximately *a third of all* employees worked for organizations which generated public services. Less than half of them were employed at public administration bodies and agencies, whose share in public service-related workforce gradually dropped in the past few years (see Table 2.1).

Facilitating Collaboration in Public Management, pages 19–36

TABLE 2.1. Number of Employees in Industries that Generate Public Services

Year	1995	2000	2005
Public administration	467,852	476,441	461,071
Medical, veterinary and welfare	130,044	147,740	171,232
Educational system, research	120,965	133,368	155,821
Energy, water, telecommunications, waste removal	103,297	101,320	79,905
Civil service associations, associations, foreign institutions	56,129	67,222	70,886
Transportation	135,006	132,938	140,119
Culture, sport, and entertainment	26,066	33,981	33,931
Total	1,039,359	1,093,010	1,112,965
Total amount from employees	3,069,536	3,133,173	3,199,012
Percentage of public services	34%	35%	35%
Percentage of the administration generating public services	45%	44%	41%

Source: Statistik Austria, 2007: Employed according to ÖNACE, 165, some summaries

ORGANIZATIONAL REFORMS IN THE FIELD OF PUBLIC SERVICES

How to organize established industry and service groups in these areas is an important question for the future. Since the 1980s, a series of processes for transforming society have been visible in Austria. The functions of the state, market and organized civil society have changed dramatically in relation to the connections between and alignment of public services. In this scenario, the practical search for a new paradigm to solve public sector problems and organize public services has just begun: "Two such paradigms have dominated our thinking up to now, the market model and the public sector model. What we have learned in recent years, however, is that both of these models are bankrupt" (Salamon 2001, p. 24).

From a global perspective, the basic starting points of the new paradigm search in organizing public services seem initially different (Bahle & Pfenning 2001; Salamon, Sokolowski & List, 2003). In the "Anglo-Saxon Cluster,"[1] the state always plays a relatively modest, "hands-off" role because society relies very heavily on private providers and market mechanisms to deal with the social issues referred to as public services. The percentage of services provided directly or financed by public organizations is comparatively small.

However, in the "European style welfare partnerships,"[2] the state was and is involved more strongly in safeguarding public services. Non-profit organizations commonly provide these services, whereas the percentage of private and commercial providers is low. In the "Nordic Welfare States," the choice is traditionally strongly determined by the state, with little participation from non-profit and private providers (although with a tradition of civic-societal obligations within the framework of social movements).

Global Trends Encouraging Collaboration

Since the beginning of the 1990s, however, different global trends have led to a new common challenge: "The simple fact is that what we have learned most clearly over the past 100 years that today's problems are too complex for any one sector to handle" (Salamon, 2001, p. 24). Sector and organizational collaborations in public services designed to deliver a mixed economy of care have become the central structural objective for politicians, administrators, executives and employees. We assume that in the present and future, good quality public services can and will be created only in productive discussions and collaboration between state organizations, private sector for-profit firms and the so-called *third sector*: non-profit/non-governmental organizations (NPOs / NGOs) and other organized civic group stakeholders.

The current global trends leading towards collaboration in public services include:

1. the reality that our lives are spent within the context of organizations;
2. a range of different organizations generating public services;
3. the *third sector* of NPOs, NGOs and civic organizations gaining political and economic influence; and
4. the trend to market-oriented mindsets and frameworks ("economization") creating both challenge and threat at the same time

Trend 1: A Society of Organizations

How to design collaboration between several sectors to provide public services seems initially a political question since politics formulate the basic frameworks and rules under which public services can be rendered. For instance, it is political institutions that decide whether public institutions should provide nursing care services through commission of non-profit organizations or whether they should be bought from the free market. Additionally, political institutions decide how the different organizations should work together. The political system dictates the shape and scale of the field of public services and also applies incentives and constraints for collaboration by providing services directly, creating legal and fiscal regulations and directing funds and cash flow.

A politically oriented view on how to collaborate within the field of public services, however, maintains too narrow of a focus. In our view, the focus must be expanded to the organizational level. In order to provide interrelated public services, organizations need to adjust to each other. Organizations and networks of organizations handle and influence social and individual problems. The last decade was characterized by rapid differentiation of organizations and their establishment in all sectors of society. The multifaceted forms of the contemporary organizational landscape reflect the plethora of organizational functions that increasingly have become more specialized.

On a more personal level individuals spend the majority of time learning and working in organizations and their work and private lives are influenced by rulings, regulations and rendering of organizational services (Grossmann & Heintel, 2000; Wimmer, 1995). Organizational competence has therefore become a key ability to personal success.

The rise of organizations—both in quality and quantity - has enormously increased society's capacity to handle problems. At the same time, new issues have emerged. The increased specialization and selectivity of organizations creates an enormous demand for social integration across sectors and borders. Collaboration is one obvious solution to integration demands—but as mentioned, it needs to be enabled and sustained by organizations themselves. The capacity for social change has become dependent on the capacity of its organizations to change since all change must be examined through organizational decisions and procedures (Grossmann & Heintel, 2000, p. 49). It therefore makes sense to shift our focus from political systems to organizations.

Within this context, there appear to be three different paradigms of coordination. First, the growing demand for social coordination and integration can be accomplished through the market and on the basis of simple and largely unmanaged buyer-seller relationships (Paradigm 1). We buy every day a lot of goods and services and try to watch carefully the relationship between quality and price. Our partners on the other side are sellers and producers, who also communicate with us through offering goods and services and with certain prices.

This perspective is countered by centralized hierarchical controls that are organizationally reflected in government bureaucracies (Paradigm 2). In Europe as well as in the United States, the general public discusses the reform of public services in terms of public versus private provision. Since the mid-1980s in the United States, the market model has become ubiquitous, and the idea of federal provision is unfashionable. In Europe, public attitudes are more balanced between market model and hierarchical model, although the current political ethos suggests a return to the latter.

Strongly polarized views tend to mask alternative options and hinder the search for functional solutions to problems (Grossmann, 2003). Today, the question about public service reform needs to be worded differently in terms of which institutional structures *and* set of organizational solutions are most suitable for which public tasks and services. We believe the answers to this question must be measured on the basis of the following key success criteria: a guarantee of care, the efficiency of service provision, the predictable quality of the services offered, and the additional benefits for social development.

The political system rarely attempts to answer these questions. It is the organizations themselves that create new organizational arrangements while searching for solutions (Grossmann, 2004a). If you look at the organizational basis on which public services are generated, then reality has long outpaced the polarized political discussions and decision-making processes. Given this dynamic, at least one additional form of coordination has emerged in this bottom-up self-organizing—the horizontal collaboration across organizations (Paradigm 3).

Trend 2: Diverse Organizations Generating Public Services

As the role of the state shrinks in this arena, an increasing number of different players begin to fulfil the void. The proportion of public services that the state directly generates is continually decreasing worldwide. This has been the case in the United States since the mid-1980s and in Europe since the mid-1990s. This trend can be seen from a purely *financial* perspective, in terms of the changes to the ratio of public sector spending as a percentage of GDP which decreased or grew at a slower pace in most European countries from the middle of the 1990s to the start of the new millennium.[3] Since the early 21st Century, however, the GDP/ expenditure ratio has again stabilized or increased slightly.

More significant than the financial perspective is the way in which the state has stepped back *organizationally from the delivery of services.* The arrangements that generate public services and control their production have changed greatly since the mid-1990s, and this trend remains unbroken.[4] Many services that public organizations previously generated themselves have been outsourced to private sector or non-profit organizations. Their provision has been secured through other contractual and organizational forms such as public-private-partnerships or simply relinquished through full privatization to private competition (Schauer, 2000, p. 32).

Since the mid-1990s, outsourced organizations in German-speaking countries, which were previously part of the public sector, have expanded into in increasing areas of public service. In contrast to full privatization—for example, the deregulation in the area of telecommunications—outsourced organizations remain as corporations, institutions, foundations or as corporate bodies in the area of public rights that are predominantly state-run. These entities, however, must still assume an important part of economic and organizational independence. National or local government controls these organizations via service agreements, using laws and regulations to control them. As an example of this trend, in 2002, Austrian universities were spun off from public administration as public corporations.

As a result of various legal and organizational frameworks, these outsourced organizations differ substantially from one another by their marketability, i.e., their ability to act autonomously and successfully. In addition to the negotiation of service agreements with these public bodies, the administration can commission private companies and various non-profit organizations to provide specific services. These organizations may include charitable organizations, self-help groups, citizens' initiatives and foundations. They operate independently, but the public services that they provide under contract are state-financed, and the state therefore continues to take part in important decisions of variety, quality and quantity.

These options illustrate an extremely varied and pluralistic organizational landscape, where an organizational "welfare mix" (Evers, 1992, 2002) emerges in public services. Private companies can generate these services through public commissions, controlled by the state or state-commissioned regulators. Outsourced organizations, working at various levels of government—from a local authority construction yard to a State theatre company—fulfill duties of their government stakeholders. Within this context, civil society institutions can also fulfill public services financed through the state, while mixed business organizations and public-private partnerships finance the construction of organizations related to infrastructure (see Figure 2.1).

Within the new welfare mix, new types of organizations have emerged. Organizations of the third sector (NPOs, NGOs, Community groups), exhibit a particularly large range of organizational diversity, including: associations emerging from State initiatives that specialize in public service generation, such as a large number of societies focused on the area of labor market policy; welfare organizations such as large charities whose services are subsidised by the State; or community groups, citizens' or self-help initiatives that generate socially beneficial services with assistance from public budgets.

The examples that follow illustrate this new welfare mix.

- *Example 1*: In Linz, Austria, since 2006, outsourced companies and private organizations have generated approximately 80% of all public services through service-level agreements (Grossmann & Mayr, 2005). The general hospital and the city's retirement homes were

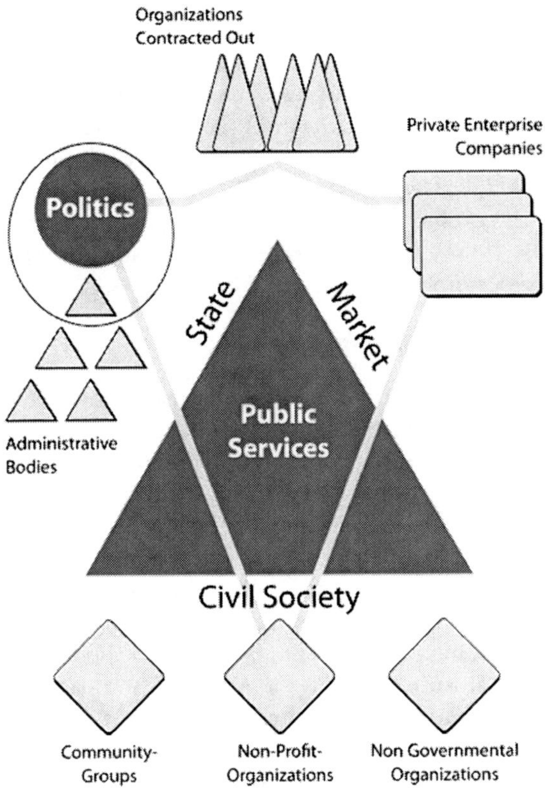

FIGURE 2.1. Different Organizational Types Providing Public Services

converted into businesses under state ownership and the performance of many other public services was handed over to associations.

- *Example 2*: The city administration in Muenster, a mid-sized German city, currently collaborates with about 500 private organizations in the social and health sectors, and an additional 270 organizations in children's and elderly services (Zimmermann, 2000).
- *Example 3*: Up to the middle of the 1990s, legal regulations almost entirely excluded private companies in Germany from the provision of long-term elderly care services. When the law was changed in 2000, private companies provided half of all long-term elderly services and a third of the respective personnel (Alber, 2000, cited in Gilbert, 2005, p. 5).
- *Example 4*: In Austria, the public sector—including public administration and state-related outsourced companies—comprises over 4,400

organizations. Since the early 1990s, almost 230 public non-profit-similar organizations and 800 market-oriented public companies were started at all levels of public administration.[5]

- *Example 5*: In Great Britain between 1979 and 1996, the amount of public expenditure for individual social benefits that was generated by the private sector contracting tripled from 11% to 34% (Burchardt, 1997, cited in Gilbert, 2005, p. 5). Similarly, in the 1970s in Sweden, the public sector provided 90% of all beds within children's homes. By 1995, however, private organizations operated 60% of all beds (Lundstrom, 2000, cited in Gilbert, 2005, p. 6).[6]

Trend 3: The Third sector as an Industry

In Europe, the "third sector" includes non-profit and non-governmental organizations that provide public services. They represent the *organized civil society* because they are not part of the public sector, nor are they intended to make a private profit.[7] In parallel with state withdrawal from directly providing public services, the importance of the third sector has grown in all respects over the past two decades. It now serves as a central pillar in the provision of public services, which is visible in a number of indicators.

Globally, the third sector is the seventh largest economy in the world. In Austria for example, many services are operated by the third sector, including one-fifth of all hospitals (in 2003), about 25% of pre-school facilities, 26 to 45% of elderly and nursing homes, 90% of outpatient social services (domestic care, home nursing, meals on wheels, and so on), 60% of all museums and theatres, 90% of fire-fighting units, 70% of adult education institutions, 100% of animal welfare organizations and over 95% of development aid organizations (Simsa, 2003, p. 135).

In the U.S., these third sector organizations operate half of the nation's hospitals, one third of its health clinics, over a quarter of its nursing homes, nearly half (46%) of its higher education institutions, four-fifths (80%) of its individual and family service agencies, 70% of its vocational rehabilitation facilities, 30 % of its day care centers and over 90% of its operas and orchestras (Salamon, 2003, p. 11f.)

The third sector also represents a large and rapidly growing employment market. In 2002, Austria's non-profit sector employed around 4.9% of the total labor force, and in the US around 9.8% (Salamon & Sokolowski, 2005, p. 22). These civil society organizations employed more workers than other sectors such as agriculture, textiles, the food industry and the transport and communications sector (see Figure 2.2).

Between 1990–1995, in Western Europe (Germany, France, the Netherlands and Britain), non-profit organizations were credited for one fifth of all newly created jobs (Simsa, 2003, p. 135). Recent data clearly shows that this trend is also taking place in the U.S. (see Salamon & Sokolowski, 2005,

p. 24). In addition, the non-profit sector assumes an increasingly important role in the mobilization of public service resources ("capital for charity") both in the form of donations as well as voluntary work, compensating for some of the state's withdrawal from the field of public services. For example, in 2000, 51% of young people over 15 years old in Austria worked as non-profit volunteers (Simsa, Schober, & Schober 2004, p. 32). In the U.S. in 1998, the share of private donations of non-profit total revenue was 13%; add in volunteering and the total would be 27% (Salamon, Sokolowski & List 2003, pp. 32, 36).

The non-profit sector is not only large, it is also *innovative.* NPOs are developing an increasing number of innovative solutions to major social problems, such as the integration of asylum-seekers and immigrants, the development of multicultural communities, the care for the elderly and the application of the vast knowledge and experience of older people in the community. Non-profits replace many of the failures of both state- and market-provision, such as the inability to provide functional solutions or foresee new problems, and thus fill the holes in the social safety nets whilst at the same time providing high-quality services (Salamon, Hems & Chinnock, 2000, p. 16).

Over 50 percent of the Austrian population no longer looks to the government, public authorities or large organizations such as health insurance companies for solutions. The population has greater confidence in individual initiatives as well as self-help groups and the services that third-sector organizations provide (Zulehner, 1999). This perceived crisis of the modern welfare state is even more pronounced in the U.S. (Salamon, 2001, p. 5). NPOs and NGOs are the organizational solution maintaining the balance

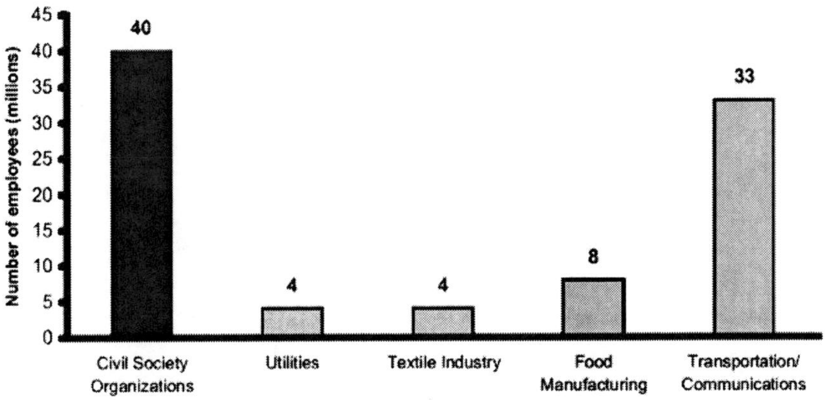

FIGURE 2.2. Civil Society Employment in Context, 35 countries. Source: Salamon, Sokolowski & List (2003, p.15).

of America's central values such as pluralism and freedom on the one hand and solidarity and social responsibility on the other (Salamon, 2003, p. 82).

On the strengthening of the third sector, the hopes rest on adequate performance as well as the development of participation and democratization. Third sector organizations provide public services in a specific way by actively striving to involve citizens and customers. In this *civil society approach*, public service is more strongly performed through pronounced self-organization rather than bureaucratic hierarchies. Third sector organizations are internally and externally oriented towards horizontal relations, enabling them to more easily pursue collaborative interorganizational relationships. By building up social capital, they make an important contribution to the establishment and development of civil society (i.e., the community building function, Salamon, 2003, p. 13), counteracting the potential for growing tension and disintegration of a society.

In addition, the *civil society approach* aspires to influence public opinion, political decisions and the behavioral patterns and attitudes of citizens and administrative staff. As mission-oriented organizations, NPOs always claim to participate in socio-political decision-making and therefore they perform an *advocacy and expressive function* (Salamon, 2003, p. 12). They exert an important, independent and often socially critical influence on the politics, which in turn causes them to be viewed as unpleasant governmental and public partners. Third sector organizations are prepared to offer

TABLE 2.2. The Civil Society Sector: Ranked as a Country

Country	GDP (trillion $)
US	7.2
Japan	5.1
China	2.8
Germany	2.2
UK	1.4
France	1.3
Civil society sector expenditures (25 countries)	1.3
Italy	1.1
Brazil	0.7
Russia	0.7
Spain	0.6
Canada	0.5

Source: Salamon, Sokolowski & List (2003, p. 14)

public contracts jointly and can supply quality, experience and efficiency, although they will often criticize the politics and the behavior of administrative units and political parties. With a primary aim to make money, private organizations tend not to bite the hand that feeds them, making them more attractive to political and administrative clients.

Both the NPOs, as well as their political and administrative clients must tolerate the rising tensions between mission and self-preservation, as well as advocacy and service function.

An example from Austria illustrates what is at stake if this is unsuccessful (Grossmann, 2004a): In 2003, the Federal Ministry of Internal Affairs transferred segments of refugee care services from confessional welfare associations (the protestant *Diakonia* and the catholic *Caritas*) and other NPOs to a private German company. This had an obvious impact on the cost and quality of these services as well as on the related job market. But additionally, this switch to the private market also paralyzed the debate in society about the appropriate care of refugees and asylum seekers and reduced civil society's influence on this delicate social problem.

In a functionally differentiated and *organized* society, where autonomous organizations deal with most of the social and individual problems, social participation is achieved through debates between the organizations (here between the Federal Ministry as the client and social service organizations), and possibly exert influence through direct and democratic political participation. This also means that the relationship between the public contracting authorities and the service providers is of great importance, because of how the form, quality and quantity of the commissioned services is negotiated, defined, controlled and supervised. For politicians, these negotiations often are exhausting, conflict-laden and full of political risks. For this reason, hiring private companies (privatization), also can be perceived as an externalization of political conflicts and a reduction of associated public discourse (Grossmann, 2004a).

A key success factor of civil society organizations is how they successfully develop networks and collaborate with other organizations. Success of networks in civil society should have multiple meanings. On one hand, networks can be used jointly to request public funds. Furthermore, organizations in the third sector cooperate politically by generating platforms where various approaches can be discussed and influenced on a local, national and international level. Finally, third sector networks are currently considered the most innovative means to provide various public services, such as care for the elderly and integration services for foreigners.

These collaborative arrangements *within the non-profit* sector can also be very challenging. Against the background of limited resources and growing competition, it can be difficult even for like-minded NPOs to find common ground. Collaboration *between non-profit and state-run organizations* runs the risk of the arrangement being trapped in a purely market-based relationship or in a reestablishment of hierarchical structures. Particularly in continental Europe, where welfare states are more paternalistic, political players find it difficult to enter into binding horizontal relations with NPOs because of their dual role: on one hand, many state and state-related organizations are continually providing public services and are therefore logical and essential collaboration partners; at the same time, however, they simultaneously provide the general framework for a particular field and define and finance its goods and services. From the political perspective, collaboration also means giving up autocratic control. It often seems less risky to delegate limited services to individual NPOs or to actively obstruct their cooperation in a certain field (divide et rule), than to encourage collaboration among the NPOs and embark on painstaking discussions with these often demanding, mission-focused, critical partners.

The proactive role that state organizations deliberately play to encourage or promote collaboration between them and NPOs can have its pitfalls, as is shown in detail later in the volume (see Chapters 3, 6 and 7). But regardless of difficulties and obstacles, this type of collaboration is evolving, mainly being driven by the growing mutual interdependence between state and NPO players, and has generated many successful examples, some of which are clearly described in this book. Some indicators show these interdependencies: Even in the U.S., where state contribution to NPO revenue is relatively low, it still amounts to 30% of grants, contracts, reimbursement payments and therefore is more than twice as high as all private donations (13%; the remaining 57% are fees and charges). In Western Europe, the state contribution to NPO revenue is about twice as high, reaching 60% (Salamon, Sokolowski & List, 2003, p. 32).

Collaboration *between private companies and non-profit organizations* seems to be on the rise as well, at least in the United States, which is reflected by leading publications focusing on the cooperation between non-profits and businesses (Austin, 2000). Likewise, in Europe, many national and international companies get involved with important areas of public or common goods with the aim of realizing social responsibility and added public value. Later in their careers, a number of successful profit-driven managers involve themselves in public service, either on a full time or voluntary basis.

Trend 4: The Trend to Market-oriented Mindsets and Frameworks

With the contracting of many public services, the hope is that outsourced organizations are being managed more economically and that funded services are performed more efficiently. Additionally, outsourced organizations should generate additional funds through the sale of other, non-publicly financed services. Against the backdrop of government funding, the growing number of outsourced service agencies and non-profit organizations has dramatically increased competition between public services providers; many service organizations must compete for the first time for publicly-funded assignments and face competition with private sector organizations. This causes increasing economic pressure from two sides, undoubtedly stimulates the organizational development of enterprises and is a key factor in the visible, increasing professionalism of outsourced and non-profit organizations that can lead to a more careful—and desirable—use of public resources.

Economization is considered a necessary prerequisite for improving services and developing new ones because available resources are used more appropriately. We have formulated the following thesis: only if the conversion achieves a more efficient and effective organizational structure of public services will many services continue to be available as public goods.

Many organizations, of course, try to cope with the pressures caused by scarce resources by putting one-sided emphasis on mere business calculations and success criteria, which eclipses the quality of services, the connection to the mission and the level of innovation. To become more efficient, many organizations must focus on core competencies and only offer better-funded or more profitable services, while cutting back or even stopping others. This often leads to greater organizational specialization and a limited portfolio.

Pronounced economization will often make the problems that should have been cured by its implementation even worse, including ineffective customer service and employee burnout. As Collins (2005, p. 5) summarizes:

> The confusion between input and output stems from one of the primary differences between business and the social sectors. In business, money is both an input (for archiving resorts greatness) and an output (a measure of greatness). In the social sectors, money is only an input and not a measure of greatness.

A key question, therefore, is how organizations in the field of public service succeed in being measured and evaluated by a broader set of success criteria than sole business indicators. It is far more challenging to generate an appropriate track record of the quality and efficiency of public services than to generate business balance sheets.

Nevertheless, NPOs have successfully dealt with economization and proven themselves to be very adaptable (Salamon, 2003). Non-profit organizations combine various organizational and market-driven logics for survival (*survival imperative*), while also having to fulfill their mission. The management and directors of such organizations face a challenging task because they must also balance the fundamentals of the business market with the fulfillment of political and humanist objectives. The latter ultimately differentiates them from the private sector ("distinctiveness imperative"; see Gray & Schlesinger, 2002).

Against the backdrop of increasing competition, stagnating governmental resources and the resulting focus on fees and charges, balance of business and social objectives is increasingly difficult for NPOs in the U.S. Many NPOs (especially those in lucrative markets, such as the university or health sector) hardly differ from the business sector. This jeopardizes the specific mission of the NPO and can potentially lead to an "identity crisis" (Salamon, 2003).

IS COLLABORATION THE ANSWER?

The trends described above have generated a highly diversified field of public services with many specialized players pursuing very different and specific goals and missions. However, what on the one hand leads to a higher level of organizational efficiency, on the other, makes a coordinated approach to a wide range of problems difficult; as evidenced in particular in US response to Hurricane Katrina.

It seems that many public services can only be realized through cooperation between the government sector, NPOs and the private sector ("inescapable interdependency"; Austin 2000). For example, when it comes to the medical, nursing and social support of the chronically ill or the elderly who are limited in lifestyle choices, the government, as the sponsor and initiator of integrated care processes, has to work with outsourced public organizations such as hospitals, social security institutions, physicians, mobile emergency services, as well as clients' relatives. Collaboration and networks can create linkages between these organizations that are stable, flexible and open to self-organization.

Collaboration is not only desirable from the perspective of the citizens affected, but it can also be considered a survival condition for individual service providers. Collaboration between organizations provides a chance for an organization to improve its regionally competitive position for public resources and customers. But with global markets competing with other global corporations, such self-organized and integrated solutions are needed for an organization to keep its market position and at the same time ensure that the needs of the people continue to be met in less profitable service sectors. The political initiatives to liberalize the services sector (G.A.T.S.—General Agreement on Trade in Services) increase this tendency.

Collaboration is an obvious answer to many trends in the field of public services and often recommended by experts. At the same time, successful multi-sector collaboration remains the exception rather than the rule.

Adopting the view of potentially collaborating organizations, the prerequisites for collaboration can be very contradictory. Contradictions must be dealt with for successful collaboration. They may include the following issues:

- Few organizations have real experience in dealing with other professional and organizational entities and have little strategic interest in such experience.
- Collaboration is only slightly supported by governmental institutions. Hardly any financial incentives are offered to such cooperative efforts.
- Government institutions as well as NPOs and businesses are bound to their own recipes for success and their specific identity. In an increasingly competitive market, they have to distinguish themselves from other service providers by focusing on core competencies and branding.

The main challenge is to consider differences between these organizations and how to manage them in relation to growing competition. The starting point for collaboration of organizations under the current conditions can therefore be described as follows: *delineation* of competition, competitors, partners, customers and contractors on very different levels, and *at the same time*, collaboration in *selected* areas.

The *successful* examples of where public services were innovatively performed through networks and close collaboration between two or more different organizations very clearly illustrate one thing: collaboration does not function by itself or because of external necessity. On the contrary, the organizations involved and the people responsible need to go through an arduous process to create this rather improbable form of organization. The people involved are especially challenged in dealing with the different traditions, working practices, cultural peculiarities, and certain restrictions of potential partners. As Drucker (2001) has eloquently argued:

> There is need for acceptance on the part of leaders in every single institution, and in every single sector, that they, as leaders, have two responsibilities. They are responsible and accountable for the performance of their institution, and this has to be concentrated, focused, and limited. They are responsible however, also, for the community as a whole. This requires commitment. It requires willingness to accept that other institutions have different values, respect for these values, and willingness to learn what these values are. It requires hard work. But above all, it requires commitment, conviction, and dedication to the Common Good. Yes, each institution is autonomous and has to do its own work the way each instrument in an orchestra plays its own part. But there is also the 'score,' the community. And only if the individual instrument contributes to the score there is music. Otherwise there is only noise.

Our Understanding of Public Services

We define public services as those services that focus on *maintaining the well-being of individuals and groups.* For instance, they might include education, health, social and cultural institutions; regardless of whether these services are provided by public or private organizations. But public services are also any services that *foster the economic, social and cultural development of a society.* These can include, for example, telecommunications, transportation, environmental protection, energy supply, and communication and legal services, such as the courts, prisons and the police.

For a long time, the economic sciences have attempted to clearly differentiate between public and non-public services and goods on the basis of their intrinsic properties. They define public services as goods of collective interest whose production and securing cannot be guaranteed by the market because their non-excludability (nobody can be excluded from their consumption, e.g. from breathing clean air) and non-rivalry (it can be consummated by diverse individuals at the same time, e.g. everybody can breathe clean air at the same time).

We assume that the boundary between private and public is decided socially: "A public good is one that the public decides to treat as a public good." (Malkin & Wildavsky, 1991, p. 372). Whether a society can leave individual decisions to its members or whether it is necessary to take collective measures depends on social change and on political decisions (Kickbusch, 2005). This becomes very clear when looking at certain changes in health, pensions, security, and lastly the role of government in the last two centuries (Pechar, 2004).

In our understanding, the term "public goods"[8] also refers to the concrete organizational form and the quality of the process in which public services are rendered. We assume that it is an important characteristic of quality medical care to involve patients in the design and generation of the service process. If the outcome is the result of a co-production process between experts and patients, then the service provided adopts characteristics of a *public service* simply through this participative process.

Given the personal and social situation of chronically sick and elderly people, improving the resources that foster an independent lifestyle can become a decisive public service quality factor. If cooperation is realized between the health insurance companies' financial services, the care services offered by non-profit organizations, the clients and their related organizations, then the term "public good" can be used to describe the quality of this cooperative process. Only through the type and way the elderly and chronically ill are supported, is the term "public good" justified. In this context, the term "common goods" should be preferred to the term "public goods" because it better emphasizes the process of collaborative production of the service via various players, whereas the term "public goods" refers more to public benefits. There is therefore not only simply a political definition of what one considers as a public or common good, but the common good is also constituted in the very process of its generation.

NOTES

1. The Anglo-Saxon cluster is comprised of the United Kingdom, the United States and Australia (Salamon, Sokolowski & List, 2003, pp. 34ff).
2. This cluster is comprised of the Western European Countries and Israel, without the Nordic welfare states (Finland, Norway, Sweden) and the UK (Salamon, et al, 2003, pp. 39ff).
3. The state expenditure ratio measures the percentage of expenses from state organizations by the gross domestic product in percentages. Thus the state expenditure quota in Austria sank from 56% (1995) to 49.6% (2005) and in Sweden from 67.1% (1995) to 58.2% (2005), whereas in Germany it remained relatively stable with 48.3% (1995) to 46.8% (2005), as in the USA (1995: 37%, 2005: 36.6%). See OECD Economic Outlook 79 Database, although there appears to be a trend between national economies toward equalization.
4. This discussion concentrates on Europe because we assume that from the more challenging European situation more can be learned about the welfare mix and collaboration issues.
5. Individual calculations are based on data from Statistik Austria, Status end 2006. The breakdown between state-related companies and market-oriented government companies refers to whether more than 50% of the revenues were derived from state financing or net sales.
6. The data from research and official statistics for organizations are illustrative and clarify the trends discussed. Conversely, this data can also be read as a symptom that the public perception of changes in the organizational landscape lags behind the dynamics of the field. Thus, the official statistics still draw the main distinction between the state and the private sector, where organizational differentiation like contracted-out organizations or non-profits are not at all observable at this level. Therefore, the new organizational realities are only accessible at a very limited extent in a quantitative sense, which is also valid for the quality of many public services. Most of the international data given here comes from the Comparative

Non-profit Sector Project of the Center for Civil Society Studies at Johns Hopkins University, Baltimore (www.jhu.edu/ccss/); since then there have been intensified attempts to reposition the statistical groundwork upon these new realities, particularly with NPOs.

7. Salamon (2001, p. 3) counts five central criteria for non-profit organizations: These include *organizations* that are *private*, hence not part of the state, do not distribute profits to their owners (non-profit-distributing), maintain a sufficient amount of *autonomy* (self-governing) and a significant participation in voluntary work.
8. In this book we prefer to use the term "service" instead of "good" because the latter is almost exclusively used in pronounced economically-oriented discussions. As our analysis focuses on an organizational level, it seems more appropriate to talk about organizations generating public services instead of producing public goods.

CHAPTER 3

ORGANIZATIONAL CONSULTING AND DEVELOPMENT

Ralph Grossmann and Klaus Scala

This chapter outlines the conceptual guidelines for our understanding of organizational development (OD)—a particular approach to bringing about change—and our function as consultants and teachers. The discussion lays out the theoretical foundation of our OD research and the connection between organizational consulting and research. The data on which the volume is based on are presented in Appendix I.

ORGANIZATIONAL DEVELOPMENT AS A CONCEPT OF SUSTAINABLE CHANGE

In the previous chapter, we suggested that productivity and the ability of organizations and networks to change determines a society's potential to handle problems. The ability for people to perform and adapt, fundamentally determines their resilience and quality of life. Coping with change has become a permanent task for organizational members as external en-

Facilitating Collaboration in Public Management, pages 37–54

vironmental conditions are always in flux. The question regarding organizational success is not whether the organization can cope with change, but how rapidly it can execute change (Schein, 1995b). The challenge is to identify and organize the necessary changes at an appropriate rate and with sustainable results.

The growing change-pressures on organizations have produced an extensive range of change concepts derived from different theoretical foundations offering principles for action and diverse effects. The concepts and methodologies of organizational change become increasingly crucial to success. Management and consultation of change processes within and between organizations also determines the likelihood that development and changes will be sustainable. Sustainability in this context is oriented towards securing an organization's long-term future

The discussions about change concepts are, on one hand, driven by the need to identify usable theoretical bases and guiding principles and, on the other hand, they are influenced by the work of consulting agencies that are driven by the dynamic of a competitive market to brand, promote and execute their own particular approach. These dual influences encourage discussion but also hinder exploration of relevant issues in any real depth.

In the fervor of branding, OD is often disparaged as a passé concept that belongs to the second half of the last century enabling people to champion other, newly (re)invented approaches. This approach neglects the more recent development of OD concepts (see Janes, et al, 2001; Königswieser & Hillebrand, 2005). From our vantage point as researchers, teachers and organizational consultants, we conceive OD as being based on three pillars:

1. a socio-psychological foundations based on group dynamics (e.g., Cummings & Worley, 1997, 2001; Schein, 1987, 1995a, b);
2. newer sociological systems theory (Luhmann, 1997; Willke, 1991, 1994, 1995, 2007; Seidl & Becker, 2006); and
3. a philosophical practice embedded in a reflective communication process with relevance to everyday life (Heintel, 2005a, 2005b).

As basic concept, we rely on "Systemic Organizational Development," a systems-based approach that is appropriate for organizations seeking to become sustainable over the long-term and implementing changes that will last.

Over many years, the Faculty for Interdisciplinary Research and Further Education of the Alpe-Adria University of Klagenfurt (IFF) established and practiced an approach to OD in association with consultants from the Austrian Association for Group Dynamics and Organizational Consulting (ÖGGO). Within the German-speaking world, this approach has assumed a prominent niche position and it differs from other concepts mainly in emphasizing the sustainability of the introduced change.

THEORETICAL GUIDING POINT: THE SYSTEM AND ENVIRONMENT AS A SURVIVAL UNIT

Organizations, just like all living systems, are interested in survival and maintaining an identity. According to new perspectives on social systems theory, systems form a survival unit with respect to their relevant environments. This theory provides OD with a framework of organizations that is oriented towards sustainability. This concept focuses on change that is built to last and ensures the systems involved to survive. Change processes should not solve one problem in an organization at the cost of another.

Organizations, with their structure of departments, teams and units, adapt and respond to internal and external environments to guarantee their own survival. Sustainable development of organizations can therefore be seen as a social process as the environment, within which an organization operates, influences its efforts to secure its long-term survival. Many organizations, however, attempt to achieve success at the expense of these environments by externalizing costs to their stakeholders, including employees, political systems, public budgets and the physical environment.

Sustainable development is characterized by aiming for success in the present which is *not* at the expense of the future. A capable sustainable organization is one that can assume and respond to the perspectives of as many relevant environments as possible in their internal operations, decisions and work programs.

Both internal and external environments need to be taken into consideration. Examples of internal environments include the knowledge embedded in an organization's processes as well employee knowledge. External environments include the prevailing markets, customers' and clients' interests, natural resources and political conditions, as well as any changes to these.

Systemic Organizational Development: Developing the Entire System

Systemic organizational development is oriented to securing an organization's long-term future. To this end, it aims to develop the system as a whole rather than implementing a specific stakeholder perspective. To be committed to systemic development implies growing the capacity for problem-solving across the whole organization and its processes instead of simply importing external solutions that may address symptoms rather than enabling change.

Giving those stakeholders who are often excluded (in other words, customers, external experts, senior managers from similar organizations) having a voice in the process is key in identifying neglected perspectives. And dealing with these (neglected) perspectives is crucial for systemic OD work and is built upon an understanding of organizations themselves: complex systems with many differences and contradictions and which are often exclusionary. An organizational structure that is able to accommodate different views and perspectives results in ambiguities that require ongoing decision-making. Organizational development (through management or consulting) also has the task of maintaining organizational paradoxes and dealing with them rather than artificially eliminating them once and for all. This commitment to encompass the relationships between system and environment as part of an organizational strategy verifies the specific criteria of the OD approach.

Critical Success Factors for Achieving Sustainable Change

There are a number of factors that form the basis for sustainable change, from the scope of the change itself, the role of leadership and member participation, and the use of pilots to test and refine new frameworks, to training and communication processes and procedures.

Decision on the Scope of Change

Organizations must continually change in order to safeguard their stability, performance and identity. The *status quo* is a dynamic state. Well-practiced routines for handling problems help maintain a balance between business-as-usual and change. Change management involves intervention in these routines. Each intervention may have a different scope and goals. Understanding these differences also has consequences for the design of the change process.

Within this context there are three kinds of change management. First, *optimizing* aims to develop the organization's existing potential for success, which, in essence, means removing obstacles that have previously hindered further development. In this scenario, we are addressing the "first-order of change" (Bateson, 1980): the basic structure of the organization; how it is managed, how it performs, and how it behaves given its surroundings. Second, *changing patterns*, which involves intervening in key aspects of the organization's identity, including its governing values and procedures. The organization basically faces up to "how things are done around here." From a systemic view a second-order change must to be carried out. When organizations fundamentally realign their core processes and systematically decentralize their management a change of patterns on how to deal with tasks and problems is introduced (see Cummings & Worley, 1997, 2001; Janes, et al, 2001; Wimmer 1999). Changes on such a scale are commonly associated with radical transformation and major cutbacks that redefine work procedures, tasks for the individuals and groups, decision making processes and so on.

Changing patterns requires a deeper examination of the organization's current ways of working through introspection. In order to mobilize organizational energy and support, it is essential that organizations identify and make the business case for this level of change management, as well as the goals of the change effort, to the executives and employees who will be affected.

Management needs to prepare for and address the emotional reactions (both expected and unexpected) of the parties concerned. The people and systems involved require time and resources to shift from their old routines and to learn new ones. Changing patterns requires broad participation while top management implements more control and support. In many cases, the scale of potential change is underestimated. On occasions, organizations adopt an *optimizing* approach to changes that really require *changing patterns.* The results can be major chaos. In such instances, optimizing is unlikely to deal with the core of the problem, which can lead to a form of immunization against more meaningful changes.

A third approach involves learning capacity. Wimmer (1999), for example, focuses on an increase in an organization's learning capacity in terms of proactive, strategically- oriented self-renewal, which is beneficial to an organization's sustainability. In this context, Grossmann and Scala (2002) address the significance of increased organizational intelligence.

Regardless of current crisis situations, attempts are being made to influence established patterns that irritate the organization to stimulate learning and increase the internal processing capacity. Examples of this include: shared learning with customers and competitors; benchmarking of results as well as processes establishing self-observation that provide new information; participating in organizational networks; and offering training within the context of the change process (Grossmann, 1995).

Executives, possibly supported by consultants, must work on the differences between organizational functionality and dysfunctionality and adopt optimization or changing patterns as appropriate. Anticipating future risk is a continuous task of organizational development, which has a retroactive effect on the ability to implement more drastic changes and to achieve improved performance routinely.

Leadership-Driven Change and Selective Participation

Leadership-driven change and selective participation require the answer to a very specific question: what knowledge will be used for the change, which groups and organizational units can be involved, and who will influence the decisions? The critical issue is the distinction between involvement and exclusion.

Organizing participation requires appropriate structures and processes and should not be dictated by personal attitudes and values. Cross-departmental team meetings, collaborative work on process chains between professional groups and organizational units, and cooperation within and between project teams can be more effective than formalized learning processes at encouraging new experiences and learning opportunities. Employee participation is important for the quality *and* acceptance of solutions to any problems if you are to create sustainable organizations. The new and demanding challenge for executives at all organizational levels is to influence and stimulate participation simultaneously. This applies to day-to-day management as well as to change processes.

Executive and employee participation must be embedded into the process architecture of a change project. It should be adjusted to the topic in hand and timed appropriately. Internal and external consultants need adequate experience with a variety of participative change models and processes if they are to suggest the most effective structure or setting for each step in the process.

Using Projects and Developing and Testing New Models of Working Together

Sustainable development that involves changing patterns of behavior requires an inclusive and participatory management style capable of supporting the development of new methods of working together. Living systems develop as new distinctions and changes to procedures for reflection, decision-making and program management are implemented. Projects can represent this form of organizational tolerance, because they bring people from different sectors and with different expertise together. Heintel and Krainz (1990) pointed out this tension between the hierarchical organization and the innovative system of the project as a development engine.

Training People and Developing Systems

As scientists, consultants and executives, we have experienced training that does not necessarily result in organizational change. The theoretical foundation for this view is grounded in sociological systems theory. Individuals and social systems have different modes of development. People learn through changing awareness by participating in programs that involve reflection, senses, emotions and action whereas social systems evolve through communication.

Training may be a necessary but insufficient condition to guarantee organizational change. The distinction between individuals and social systems and defining individuals as an "environment" of social systems has facilitated the design of social system interventions and an understanding of their impact.

The development of systems requires an appropriate combination of changes at the individual and social system level—changing people's knowledge, skills, values, attitudes, *and* changing structures, procedures, culture and rules of the game. This distinction also illustrates the limits of attempts to make scientific knowledge effective, primarily by transferring it to people. It also reflects an underlying transition from advanced training to systems consulting.

Re-introducing Communication into the Organization: "The Process Makes the Difference"

Understanding and expertise in process management are probably the biggest strengths of OD consultants who are trained in and inspired by group dynamics, as in the case of the University of Klagenfurt and the Austrian Association for Group Dynamics and Organizational Consulting. Their approach involves designing work and decision-making processes, which exploit a variety of technical and organizational perspectives and prevent hasty or one-dimensional solutions. These types of solution rarely fit the problem to be solved exactly and can generate unintended negative consequences.

Integrating the various stakeholders in a change effort is only possible through proper communication processes. Participation is realized with binding agreements and through trust between partners. New governance and management ideas only achieve credibility if they follow these principles and establish proper communication processes. The development of process designs that include the difficult task of linking topics with social settings and time in every situation can be considered the "key technology" of systemic organizational development. Process design competence is therefore a key qualification for executives and organizational developers who are interested in sustainable change.

An Over-emphasis on Rationality

New research results stress that thinking and feeling, as psychological and physiological processes, are inextricably linked. Dealing with emotions in change processes is essential in two ways. Organizations fulfill the social function of managing insecurity encouraging stability, while organizational changes can be perceived as threatening and generating fear. To manage change productively, emotions need to be considered in the process design. Emotions are a key indicator of success, and feelings within organizations have the same function as those within an individual. The OD specialist should "use emotions to think" and use the awareness of others' emotional state as an important guide to gain new insights and create new ideas.

It is also important to use emotions as indicators of conflict or agreement. Emotions are especially important in decision-making; since decisions are only necessary when the best solution cannot be found with solely rational methods; therefore emotional evaluations are particularly necessary for decision-making. An essential dimension of organizational competence is self-awareness as well as the capacity to reflect on emotion within any kind of group settings. (Ciompi, 1988, 2003; Grossmann & Heintel, 2000).

DEVELOPING PRACTICAL KNOWLEDGE ABOUT ORGANIZATIONAL DEVELOPMENT

Currently, there are a number of large and very visible discrepancies between different approaches to generating organizational knowledge. The approaches to organizational development (OD) introduced by organizational theorists and organizational psychologists differ greatly from the views and experiences of practitioners, including executives, company staff members and consultants. Although the latter often only selectively apply the findings of organizational research in their practice, an animated discussion and reflections on research can be observed among practitioners. However, the gap between the academic and practical views seems to be very unproductive. In order to overcome this gap it is necessary to examine the various approaches and the relationships between them more precisely.

Three Fieldwork Models

Taking a closer look at the community of organizational experts, we have identified three different methods of fieldwork used to collect relevant data for understanding and dealing with organizational change. On the following pages we will characterize these models and distinguish between them. One group, which follows the traditional social-scientific paradigm, is often labeled "empirical." In this *experimental model*, empirical studies are significant because they derive their findings in experimental settings.

The second method of fieldwork includes a number of methods that are characteristic of the social sciences and are frequently labeled as "qualitative research methods." This is not particularly significant and mainly serves to distinguish the qualitative versus quantitative aspects of the experimental model. With reference to Schein (1987, p. 11), the qualitative research method is called the *ethnographic model*. A distinction is drawn between the ethnographic model and the third model which is called the *practitioner's model*. The practitioner's model, as its name indicates, is the one most commonly used by managers, executives, and consultants.[1] As a form of fieldwork, the practitioner's model provides valid data for further development in OD.

The three models cited are not mutually exclusive and all three models are quoted in the scientific literature about OD. The application of each model depends on the questions to be answered and the type of information needed. However, it is important to know the difference between the three models as well as their strengths and limitations so one is aware which model is most appropriate under various circumstances.

The Experimental Model

Classical physics was based on the illusion that we could describe the world without speaking about ourselves. One of the basic and traditional principles of scientific research is the idea of the external observer; someone whose observation does not interfere with the observed object. The scientists' aim, therefore, is to determine and describe the objective reality and to exclude the individual researcher's specific view.

The experimental scientist applies the criterion of replication to gain scientifically valid results. In other words, another researcher examining the same research object should observe precisely the same things. The methods of gathering data and information are constructed so that individual perspectives do not have an impact on the results anyone repeating the research on the same basis will reach the same research results.

The ideal is captured in Nagel's (1986) notion of "the view from nowhere," an approach that relies mainly on measurement and conforms to Galileo's Principle, where the world is viewed mathematically. The goal of scientists is then to rely on the experimental model, measure the objects of their research as precisely as possible, and thus make as much as possible measurable. In order to achieve this set of goals, the observer conducts active lab experiments. Since the beginning of modern natural sciences, the basic concept of research has been predicated on the belief that intervention leads to more insight than does passive observation. This is based on the assumption that intervention in the form of an experiment does not change the object of the observation. "No machine goes red and starts stuttering when it is called 'stupid,' no chemical falls into a crisis of self-esteem when the chemist doesn't like it, and no computer can be enticed to work faster by incentive trips" (Simon F. B. & CONECTA, 2004, p. 18).

Physicists have been shocked when they discovered that the setting of a nuclear experiment had an impact on the observable processes. Within the framework of the experimental model, it is very important that the relationship between researcher and research object has no impact on the object or the results. The methodology and beliefs of natural scientists also play a role in social and psychological sciences. According to their scientific concept and basic principles, quantitative methods are applied and results that are generated can be expressed in numbers.

This methodology is very useful for defining and examining what are usually labeled as the "hard facts" of an organization such as organizational size and economic data. It can also be applied in studies (e.g. surveys) where a greater volume of data is required. The scientific standards of this type of research (reliability, validity, objectivity) are aimed at obtaining true answers which cannot be interpreted in different ways.

One issue with this model is that it still alters the very social situation for which it is intended to describe. If the experimental model is used as a tool of organizational analysis, a resulting intervention can affect the observed social system. For example, a survey dealing with employee satisfaction of working conditions will not only produce information, but will also stimulate a process of communication that can cause unplanned effects on the system. After the study, the social situation will definitely have changed. Employees might talk about the survey and its topic, exchange their views about leadership and other issues, and in this way widen their views, creating ideas what could be changed. At the very least, the employees will watch carefully whether or not the survey has any impact and this creation of expectations is a challenge to managers. The researcher's observation through the survey is already outdated by the observation itself. This is evident in the phenomenon of electoral forecasts. Organizational analysis and intervention cannot be separated in organizational research, because analyzing an organization always includes intervention.

The experimental model has limitations in other areas as well, because research projects based on this model are necessarily very selective. The researcher chooses very few variables and relationships between those variables to study in any particular research project. Inevitably, the question arises about what happens to all the unconsidered empirical material. No absolute criteria exist in science or research about what has to be included or excluded from a research project. Yet science as a system is designed to reveal the whole truth about everything. The necessity to act pragmatically in single research projects introduces strict constraints. The decision about the scope of a specific research project is based on pragmatic, rather than scientific, arguments (one exception is that research should generate new knowledge) because everything is potentially a worthwhile object of research.

As a continuous system, scientific research primarily produces the need for further research because all results lead to new questions which have to be answered in new research projects. The experimental model is based on the logic that scientific research is a self-reproducing system. The results achieved generate, in turn, new questions for future research projects.

Communication (as an object of observation) is extraordinarily complex. To be manageable, any research needs a mechanism of complexity reduction, which needs to be document and described. Therefore this form of research no longer complies with the basic tenet of the experimental model since it will not be possible to replicate the results.

As far as complex social systems, which are in a constant state of change, the goal of copying reality is so far from reality itself that the value of research results cannot be rudimentarily understood. The model leads to a paradox. By stressing the empirical aspect as a scientific criterion, the empirical database is lost due to the exclusion of all data that cannot be observed in an experimental setting. The complexity of social realities cannot be deconstructed into independent individual perspectives without serious drawbacks, because social structures are ultimately interrelated systems.

The Ethnographic Model

Users of the ethnographic model seek information that lies beyond hard facts, and that cannot be gathered by conducting surveys and studying paperwork produced in organizational operations. The various views of internal players and their formal and informal communication provide as many relevant elements as do 'hard facts' to the nature of how the organization functions. The research methods of the ethnographic approach are therefore broader than those of the experimental model and include both the observation of daily work as well as interviews. The ethnographic model, however, shares with the experimental model the idea that social facts can be obtained without affecting or disturbing the social system.

It is assumed that ethnographers do not interfere with the group observed. They are supposed to adapt to the group and avoid any attempts to change or influence the social system. Scientists usually assume that an organization exists outside the sphere of its own awareness ("Bewusstsein"), and that it can and must be understood and deciphered without being disturbed (cf. Schein, 1987, p. 30). As with the experimental model, the ethnographic model is based on the assumption that the observer is not a part of the system but that he or she remains outside of the subject of observation. It is assumed that there is a separation between thinking and being ("Sein"), and between subject and object, and that the researcher's task is to capture reality and picture or display it mentally in the "realm of the mind."

Philosophers from Parmenides to Hegel have frequently criticized this approach, claiming that if observer and observed object were thought as separate entities, it could not be explained how they should ever create mutual knowledge in a shared effort. More recently, a group of researchers from different disciplines have described the *process of observing* as an active research effort, defining this position as radical constructivism.[2]

To experience is to construct, since the observer observes by drawing a distinction. For example, if the observer is studying the subject observed and the rest of the world, then the observer uses this first distinction to draw a second distinction between himself and the subject at hand. Nothing can be observed and recognized if no distinctions are actively made. In sociology for instance research focuses on selected differences in gender, class, generation, education, wealth, profession etc. Based on this assumption, a researcher determines the research project results by choosing the distinctions that are made. The research process is seen as a process of differentiation where new and more detailed distinctions are constantly being introduced, any new difference then becomes new information (Bateson, 1973).

The Practitioner's Model

"You cannot understand a system until you try to change it" (Kurt Lewin, cited in Schein, 1995a). The experimental and ethnographic models have proven to be inadequate as a basis for observing and understanding social systems and their development for three basic reasons. First, social systems are *self-observing systems.* How they perceive themselves has a great impact on their actions and development which implies that they are learning systems. For this reason, they cannot be considered stable realities because they are in a state of permanent change. Many people have noticed that how an organization is perceived strongly depends on which people, departments, leaders, and employees are observing it. The various self-observations of the social system and the differences in individual impressions are important elements of respective social realities.

For this reason, an organizational researcher needs to avoid discovering the single, universal truth about the system. Rather, the researcher's goal should be an attempt to observe and interpret the different points of view about the system. The relation between certain points of view and the people who utter them must be examined. Different stakeholders will have different views of the same organization. It is important to identify and understand these differences as a relevant part of the social reality.

The truth lies in the complexity and a variety of views about the system and not in a single description of it. The *experimental* and the *ethnographic model* do not have the theoretical resources to appropriately fulfill the task of observing self-observing systems. As self-observing systems, social systems are learning systems that develop in ways that influence their future through the process of self-observation. In social-systems theory, these are called non-trivial systems (Simon & CONECTA Authorgroup 1992, pp. 23, in reference to Heinz von Foerster). While trivial systems (machines) react predictably and consistently to specific inputs (press the "on" button and the TV will start), non-trivial systems learn through experience and will therefore change their reactions in response to certain inputs.

Second, an OD researcher working on organizational change can only gain insight into change through active involvement. This is also called action research. In this way, the methodological flaw of the experimental and ethnographic models—where observation changes the subject observed—is constructively used, whereby the active role of the researcher is deliberately staged in the change process and is an important part of the observation. An organization undergoing a change process should have a specific image of the actual situation and the need for change associated with it. It also has hypotheses about how it might best achieve the self-assigned goals. In this way, a change process is comparable to a scientific experiment in which the researcher has a number of hypotheses and attempts to determine their validity.

In a similar way, an organization undertaking change will experience whether or not its plan for change is as effective as expected. An OD researcher has to play an active role in the OD process in order to gain experience and generate knowledge. The main difference between Organization Development and scientific experimentation is that OD takes place in a real life setting as opposed to a laboratory. The primary goals and motives of change processes are not to achieve research results but to use OD to improve and sustain organizations. Whoever wants to gain relevant insight into an OD process must become part of it and actively participate in its design.

Third, the data and information gained about OD processes are based on the actions, documents, and comments of the participants. A practitioner, such as an executive or consultant, has access to this kind of information. Yet, the amount, quality, and depth of this information depend strongly on the relationship between the practitioner and the people providing information. Practical experiences confirm the view that a social scientist interested in research will get different information than a consultant who has been hired to support the system as it changes.

Relevant information tends to be provided to a person in a helping role, for example such as an OD consultant. In the case of a research project, the people within a system may be unclear about the benefits to them of their cooperation. Indeed, it is an important part of the consultant's professional role to build a relationship with his or her client-system that promotes open communication. The consultant's ability to prove the value of his or her contribution to the client system is an important condition for success.

Internal players such as managers are often in similar situations. The information flow between a CEO and all other employees strongly depends on the relationship between the two parties. A researcher, on the other hand, who is not part of the system and does not share the ongoing goals of the change process is in a weak position because they may not have access to relevant information about current organizational events. The result is a paradox. If a researcher adheres to the principles of empirical research and attempts to examine an OD process, the very act of following these principles prevents the collection of empirical data. The researcher would have to abandon their distance from the studied object before re-establishing the necessary distance in a feedback loop. Empirical data are often based on empirical facts and not on personal judgments, views, or opinions. However, if social systems are studied on the basis of constructivism, personal views, opinions, or judgments are an extremely important and influencing part of social life. In order to study OD processes, the researcher needs to establish both a supportive relationship with the client system as well as an active role in the organizational change process.

The practitioner's model also generates a different kind of knowledge than the other two research methods. The experimental model provides quantifiable evidence of reality and how it works independently of the observer, where the ethnographic model also adds relevant non-quantifiable results. The practitioner's model and its associated research produces findings about intended change processes in social systems with the express purpose of enabling those systems to learn to grow (Scala, 2000, p. 31).

The critical researcher will argue that a practitioner is bound by the interests of the system. An organization's change process is rarely, if ever, initiated in the interest of science but is requested by internal and external stakeholders. Executives and consultants are charged to guide the process and must therefore act and intervene appropriately. An OD change project is not a research project because the topics raised and the measures implemented during the change process almost certainly serve a different purpose than to pose questions or solve scientific issues.

A relationship based on supporting the client system is a very powerful and productive channel for obtaining relevant data that could not otherwise be collected in an experimental or ethnographic research project. Because a change process is not a scientific project, the opportunities and limitations of potential experiences are determined by the specific tasks and goals to which a client and contractor have agreed. These constraints aside OD research is therefore a byproduct of the management of a change process.

Because social systems are self-observing systems, the management of a change process requires considerable observation and reflection. For this reason, OD fieldwork includes implicit research methods that permanently allow an OD researcher to switch between action and reflection modes (see Table 3.1). An organizational developer addresses the system(s) involved in a change process through careful interventions. Knowledge is translated into interventions that support the development of the social system. Such

TABLE 3.1. Three Fieldwork Models

Model	Experimental	Ethnographic	Practitioner
The Ideal	The observer does not have any impact on the observed object or subject	The observer does not have any impact on the observed object or subject; the observer tries not to interfere with the research object or subject	The practitioner is part of the system (as an executive, expert or consultant) Fieldwork serves the purpose of the (client) system Research is therefore an additional reflection on the fieldwork Fieldwork and research are based on the same empirical experience but on different products and customer situations
Collecting data through...	Experiments in a laboratory setting	Observation and qualitative interviews; observed system controls the data flow and depends on the relationship between the researcher and the social system	Interventions based on hypotheses and methods of observing the effect of interventions; observed system influences the data flow and depends on the relationship with the researcher
Initiative and goals	Set by the scientist	Set by the scientist	Customer/Client system sets initiative and goals of the fieldwork; scientist sets research initiative and goals
Validity criterion	Replication of the experiments	Data collected in a sufficiently large number of case studies	Data collected in a sufficiently large number of case studies
Type of knowledge generated	Quantitative findings of how reality is and functions, independent from the observers	Quantitative and qualitative findings of how reality is and functions, independent from the observers	Findings about how intentional change works in social systems and how social systems can learn to develop themselves
Use of quantitative results	Use of quantitative results (hard facts)	Use of quantitative results (hard facts) and qualitative results (soft facts)	Use of quantitative results (hard facts) and qualitative results (soft facts) as an opportunity for reflection

interventions strongly differ from a research report which can only provide complete results without consideration of any effects that may occur during data collection.

THE SCIENTIST AND THE PRACTITIONER: A SPIRITUAL DIALOGUE

In order to gain valuable insight into organizational change processes, the researcher should take an active role in the change process and also manage his or her relationship with the system they are observing. The researcher's role is not an alternative to the practitioner's role (see Figure 3.1). Rather, the researcher's role requires the practitioner's work in order to be able to conduct research—although any research project is likely to go beyond the tasks and responsibilities of a practitioner. Although both researchers and practitioners gather information, researchers also evaluate, document and publish the information systematically. The researcher depends on up-to-date contributions and discussions in the academic literature.

Research can foster OD as a science and be key to the practitioners' professional role. While OD as a practice is applied to organizations in need of change, consultants compete for contracts and offer advice (interventions, know-how and so on) as a product, whereas research addresses the "scientific and professional community." Their products are publications and presentations and their market place are books, journals and conferences. Research-based practical knowledge gathered and applied during organizational change processes is clearly distinguishable from the theoretical evaluation and scientific discussion of empirical data. However, a

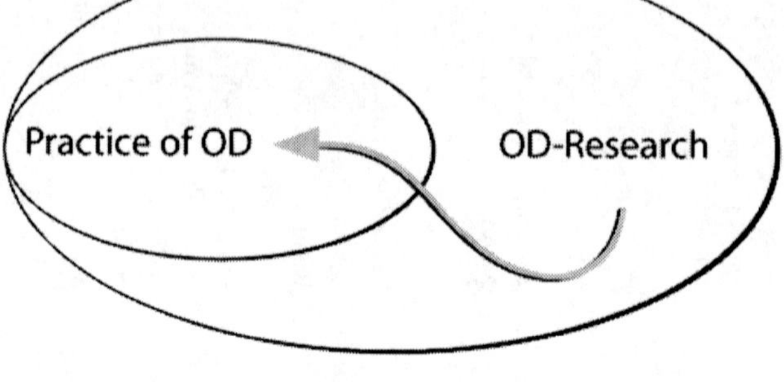

FIGURE 3.1. OD Practice as part of OD Research

scientific analysis and description of OD processes has also been helpful in the training and education of leaders and consultants. The argument we have presented supports the view that the use of case studies by both practitioners and researchers is relevant. Case studies reflect the fact that any organization and organizational change process are individual and unique. Accordingly, case studies have been the basis of many OD research projects. Their results are usually discussed in the scientific community and not used as interventions in the examined social systems since researchers have a completely different focus and interest than the client systems they study.

An OD intervention differs greatly from an intervention based on natural-scientific principles. The criteria applied to an OD intervention or to a case study serving as a feedback tool do not meet the requirements of natural-scientific experiments. In an OD process, an organizational developer's feedback is only part of the assignment. The other part is to allow the system to reflect on that feedback. For this reason, OD practitioners must create communications settings so feedback can be digested. Sometimes scientists are disappointed to learn that their work has not earned the popularity and attention they expected. From an OD perspective could the answer for increasing their impact would be to create situations that enable employees to reflect on their input.

Dealing with Theories

"There is nothing as practical as a good theory" (Lewin, 1951, p. 169). In the context of research and science, the role of theories needs examination. Theories are the result of summarized and interpreted experiences. They help people understand and explain their daily experiences and provide a systematic framework to which these experiences can be applied. As such, theories offer ways in which things can be seen and interpreted and are similar to a lens through which events can be observed. Theories shape people's consciousness about what can be expected if they act within a specific context. Theories act as guidebooks that help us to view and interpret the world. Therefore, theories are not only aimed at scientists and theorists.

Everyone's brain is full of theories. While some of us use some theories explicitly, others are implicit. All research models presented use theories to represent existing knowledge *and* to provide the basis for classifying new experiences. This makes it apparent that theory and experience are linked in a circular relationship. In order to make relevant observations, good theories are necessary. In turn, effective theories result from diverse, experiences and require thoughtful and detailed reflection.

In light of this understanding of the connection between theory and experience, applied theories serve to be confirmed or adjusted by means of new experiences. Therefore, certain social science theories, and particularly those in OD, have to be adapted to the context via constructing situation-related hypotheses. Only a set of well thought-out hypotheses will enable an observer to encounter experiences that are relevant to the task.

NOTES

1. Schein (1987) uses the term 'clinical perspective,' Lewin (1951), Argyris, Putnam & Smith (1985) talk about 'action research' or 'action science' in the general meaning of the *practitioner's model,* the term which we prefer, in order to integrate new conceptual developments since the 1980s.
2. See also Gregory Bateson (anthropology), George Spencer-Brown (mathematics), Humberto Maturana, Francisco Varela (biology), Heinz v. Foerster (cybernetics), Chris Argyris (action research), and Niklas Luhmann (sociology).

CHAPTER 4

THE CONCEPTUAL FRAMEWORK

Ralph Grossmann and Hubert Lobnig

This brief chapter focuses on a number of distinctions that are essential to understanding cooperation between organizations. We define networks and collaborations as two different forms of cooperation, and further differentiate between different forms of networking. The discussion presents the criteria for successfully organizing cooperation between organizations and discusses various scientific research approaches and contexts, drawing out the implications for those wishing to establish, manage, and create opportunities for consulting in cooperative ventures. The thrust of this work focuses on shaping cooperative systems as the basis for longer-term collaboration. A fundamental pre-requisite for systemic organization development and corporate consulting is that the change agent understands the culture and related processes for each of the constituent organizations. The chapter defines the processes for organizing collaborations, on the basis of our consulting experience.

DISTINCTIONS THAT MAKE A DIFFERENCE

Making distinctions helps us to make sense of the world around us. One way of facilitating this dynamic in an organizational setting is through the role of an "observer" who draws on personal experience of "doing" the work

Facilitating Collaboration in Public Management, pages 55–58

and/or being an observer while also applying practical theory. Depending on the theories and experiences used in reference to such observations, of course, certain aspects of inter-organizational cooperation become more or less important. Combining these different perspectives allows us to create a conceptual framework that draws in contributions from founders, managers, consultants and other relevant parties.

The conceptual distinctions explored in this chapter are essential resources for understanding and shaping cooperative efforts. They also define areas of conflict and tension and shed light on contradictions and paradoxes. These distinctions are especially helpful in avoiding an "either this or that" mentality by opening our eyes to the possibilities of "both this and that."

As researchers and consultants, we gain knowledge by observing how the various stakeholders of cooperative efforts observe and define their own systems and actions, since self-observation is another crucial part of learning. How do we perceive the system and how do we react to it? How do we process our various observations into intervention strategies? We find the 'both this and that' mentality (e.g. competition and cooperation) particularly helpful in understanding and shaping internal and external support between cooperative partners.

Cooperation in Networks and Collaborations

By combining interests and resources, people willing to work collaboratively make it possible for organizations to achieve goals and objectives that they could not achieve alone. Cooperation is based on and driven by considerations of benefit—a decisive criterion as to whether an organization is willing to participate in a cooperative relationship. Failure to realise these benefits within an acceptable period reduces the motivation for people to cooperate. This kind of self-interested motivation is an important factor for initiating cooperative efforts, but is not the only one.

Interestingly enough, there are always tensions between the motives of the different partners. What are participants willing to do without requiring immediate and short-term benefits in favour of the interests of their organizations over the long term? By understanding long-term benefits, they adopt the approach of 'enlightened egoists' (Willke, 1995, p. 130). The attractiveness of cooperating also depends on the specific resources and performance of the prospective partners, the extent to which the parties complement each other and the potential for joining forces.

A number of examples of cooperative projects can be found in the public sector or in the delivery of public services (those produced in collaboration between the public and private sectors) that have been induced, encouraged, or forced by pressure from above. Political decision-makers are able to create parameters for cooperation by providing a corresponding distribution of funds and/or communicating political intent. In such cases, the challenge lays both in generating the willingness of partners to cooperate and in creating an initial foundation of trust.

Based on our experience, we draw a distinction between networks and collaborations. Networks offer the opportunity of profiting from one another and of creating a mutual basis for productivity, which opens up the possibility for later work and more sustainable collaboration. Collaborations, on the other hand, have the capacity to realize selected and defined benefits within projects, processes, joint ventures, and so on. Thus, not all network activity leads to close cooperation, even though organizations that collaborate closely need networks between their teams. Very often the apparent options are not attractive enough for actual collaboration, or the partners involved are unable to realize them together.

Researchers or consultants, often, come together in networks. They make up a communication network that allows those involved to get to know and learn from each other and to exchange professional knowledge. Subgroups within these networks may decide to work together more intensely and join forces to dedicate themselves to collaborative projects, or even co-found companies.

Companies from the same region or branch, for example in a regional tourism area, may be invited to form networked clusters. Two or more of these companies may unite in order to work together, develop or produce products and services, introduce them to the market, or jointly use cost-saving infrastructure and support processes. This type of cooperation requires a close linked network between participants. A collaborative effort between companies, however, requires a stronger connection on the part of the participating organizations and also has a greater impact on the partners than participation in a network. In the case of a collaborative venture, the need to be organized increases as does the demand from each participating partner to invest, decide, steer, and monitor.

Both forms of cooperation—networks and collaborations—are "loosely linked systems" (Orton & Weick, 1990; Weick, 1985), formed by two or more partners who maintain their autonomy. A fundamental feature of these systems involves dispensing with hierarchy in favour of cooperative control and management—which leads to the horizontal connections characteristic of this type of working.

Networks and collaborations both work in a similar mannerwith similar designs. Yet they also show clear differences. It is important for managers and consultants to be aware of these differences and to intervene accordingly—because transitions between networks and collaborations are often continuous. Consultants who decide to collaborate are rapidly confronted with the question of how to develop appropriate legal and organizational structures and processes. Even if they decide to remain merely partners in a network, as the degree of organization and the number of regulations increase the level of autonomy decreases.

This context and its implications raise a number of critical questions: To what extent is exclusivity in the relationship to the different partners? What costs need to be covered (e.g., overhead costs, long-term development)? Are such costs considered to be individual or joint responsibilities? Is some form of joint investment required? How should the partners deal with products, processes and knowledge that have been developed as a result of the collaboration? While these questions are by no means exhaustive, they provide a general sense of the range of issues that need to be addressed.

Human networks also constitute a core foundation of inter-organizational cooperation. Researchers and consultants, who come together in special interest groups or in their own associations, might form a network that can be detached from their parent companies and institutions. Networks often begin with clusters in which the companies are members and represented (ideally) by leading employees. These representatives are chosen on the basis of what the cooperation is designed to achieve. Individuals continue to represent their companies, even when they decide to form a collaborative system that moves from an informal to a more closely linked form of cooperation. When this is the case, their role as representatives of the participating organizations becomes especially important. Underlying these interactions is the reality that the driving force is based on a network of people. An essential component of fostering cooperation is the stability of the relationships between the leading representatives. The development of these interpersonal relationships is indispensable for the success of the cooperative venture.

Cooperative Organizational Processes and Structures

A new cooperative effort also needs to establish its own basic form of organization. If it merely builds on the organizational structures of the participating partners, it jeopardizes the cooperation it seeks. It can only gain the appropriate structure via purposeful management. As our society is built by organizations, the development process of organizing systems becomes an important issue. The success of these processes is the decisive factor that determines whether solutions for complex problems will have an impact in the world. This principle can be best observed in the way cooperative efforts develop, regardless of whether they are planned or simply evolve. If networks and collaborations are to be successful and to make a difference, they need to focus their attention on the processes and the implicit and explicit principles around which they are organized.

CHAPTER 5

EIGHT CASES OF NETWORKS AND COLLABORATION[1]

Hubert Lobnig and the Research Team at iff oegd[2]

The chapter highlights the variety of options that organizations have at their disposal as they enter into collaborative arrangements, including the various conditions, nature and forms of relationships. Collaborative efforts differ according to their application, services provided, size, structure, and whether the parties involved are public institutions, non-profit organizations or commercial enterprises. The examples that follow display successful collaboration, provide instructive templates for good-practice models, and offer practical solutions for a variety of challenges and pitfalls that are likely to emerge during the process.

In some of the examples, the pitfalls had a greater impact on the development and outcome of the collaborative effort. However, we do not treat these more critical examples as unsuccessful, because it is simply not possible to meet the demands of complex social systems' with simple value judgements. Rather they provide us with a pronounced view of the difficulties that a collaborative effort may face and the opportunities to learn how to intervene to increase the chances of success.

Facilitating Collaboration in Public Management, pages 59–72

Collaborative efforts need to be managed skilfully. They do not automatically lead to success. Their outcome depends on the participating organizations and their commitment; the individuals responsible, the decisions they make and actions they take, all of which results in a unique "process of organizing" (see Weick, 1969). Each of the following case studies will illustrate different key dimensions of these organizational processes.

A COLLABORATION OF NECESSITY: TWO HOSPITALS COLLABORATING IN THEIR RADIOLOGY DEPARTMENTS

A local government authority decided to create a collaborative relationship between two neighbouring hospitals in order to avoid duplication and save resources. They implemented the collaboration in their core radiology departments, since both hospitals were required to introduce record and image digitization by developing and applying software and the use of a joint technical infrastructure.

To realize this project, an inter-hospital project organization was formed with both hospitals' board of directors as clients. A joint project committee, made up of the directors, heads of radiology and project managers of both hospitals was set up as the steering committee. One of the two hospitals already had in place a well-developed infrastructure for quality and project management—the project manager of this hospital was therefore made responsible for the focus of the project.

In course of the process, the project manager was unable to secure the requisite buy-in from the other hospital. Its staff persistently considered him as an outsider, "one of them" instead of an "agent of the common cause." Because of this lack of support and commitment, he was not able to carry out the necessary management functions, and the joint project committee could not solve core collaborative issues such as the distribution of tasks and functions.

When political decision makers attempted to pressurize the collaborative efforts in order to generate financial benefits, a number of pitfalls emerged. First, public service organizations collaborative efforts and mergers are just as much subject to competition and conflicts as those in the private business world. Policy-oriented owners often fail to take this into account. Attempting to initiate collaboration in core processes between two independent hospitals—such managing a shared service radiology system—is like suggesting to two banks that they should merge both of their risk management departments. What appears to be obviously problematic for commercial organizations can often be considered a "logical" and therefore straightforward collaboration for non-profit organizations. However, the organizational dynamics are similar—in both cases, a merger could eventually translate into the threat of job and/or career loss, disruption of existing processes and routines, as well as a reduction of revenue.

Second, the commitment and contribution of key players is essential for success. A well-conceived structure (such as a joint project committee) is important, but not enough. The decisive factor is the quality and depth of the communication and negotiation process, which takes place before decisions are reached. Project structures provide room for such negotiations, but without the heartfelt commitment of the key players, they stay mere formal arrangements without impact. In the example case, the two hospitals were in a position of "forced collaboration," resulting in limited amounts of energy and commitment required for change.

Third, core business processes such as radiology procedures are typically hard to change in isolation, for they have a lot of collateral impacts on existing routines, decision-making processes and work culture. People in charge of the hospitals had clearly underestimated the magnitude of change occurring in the digital radiology department because of its effect on routine upstream and downstream operations (such as patient documentation and operating room preparation). In a project that crosses organizational boundaries, developing core procedures requires a differentiated work setting and a clear desire for success.

Finally, the political initiators of collaborative efforts should *not* seek to avoid negotiating expectations and objectives. In this case, the political instruction "collaborate!" hung over the project without any opportunity for negotiation. In such situations, those involved in project implementation should exert pressure to demand a dialogue to clarify expectations and aspirations, for example in the form of a kick-off meeting. An adequate understanding of organizational development on both sides (the political initiators, the organizations' management) as well as an associated consulting system helps to organize this process.

Universities in Cooperation to Bring Faculties Together

Two universities (one technical) in the same geographical area agreed to collaborate in order to merge gradually their natural sciences departments in those subjects where curricula already overlapped. The aim was to generate a critical mass of students and expertise in order to achieve excellence and safeguard the continued existence of the faculties. The stakes were high: in both universities, the natural sciences departments represented the largest organizational units and more than 1,500 staff members were potentially affected.

As the supervisory bodies of the university, the university boards supported the merger as a way to create a more sharply distinguished profile in the respective scientific and education markets. The regional government, as main financier, earmarked funds to increase the chances that the project could be designed and executed.

The two deans of both universities launched the project with great conviction and mutual understanding—a favorable starting point for project implementation. In numerous one-on-one meetings, they developed trust and gradually allowed the plan to mature. Because the planned collaboration had radical consequences for both organizations, the close cooperation between them was especially important.

As a first step, the deans developed a concept and an action plan. A steering committee, including the two deans as well as two professors from the affected departments, managed the project. The faculty deans were put in charge of the operational implementation. The scientists' reactions were understandably varied: they feared competition and identity loss in the traditional departments while harbouring hopes for more dynamic development of the joint department. Such mergers, of course, do not take place merely on a structural level, and involve a series of tangible, jointly established steps. During the first phase of implementation, expert groups involving all organizations developed future curricula. Other more structural issues were postponed; for instance the integration of research fields as this was classified as complex and conflict-rich. The deans also shifted the integration of the service contracts and the financial planning and regulations (such as dealing with third-party funds) so they could first concentrate on implementing well-defined joint projects.

The deans' approach also had its drawbacks: from the outset of the project, members of the university staff accused them of a lack of communication, because of their close collaboration and decisive action. This ran counter to the existing culture of self-governance and the high level of autonomy within departments. For similar reasons, a number of university board members and policy-makers attempted to intervene in order to cancel the project.

But despite the resistance, one and a half years later, joint education is now offered in the fields of geology, chemistry and molecular biology. The merger has successfully started with a true collaboration in a limited, but important part of the universities' services, without first phasing out the existing institutes and combining them into one new unit. This has been achieved without additional financial resources.

In the future, the key development issues for two faculties are to enable greater integration of the scholarly institutional leadership and department heads, initiate a collaborative management structure, and clarify the basis for staff allocation.

DOCTORS CREATING A REGIONAL NETWORK

Resident general practitioners and medical specialists joined together in a regional network to take advantage of collective bargaining with health insurers and establish a strong position as a regional network in developing joint approaches to managed care. They chose a registered association as the legal form to describe the collaboration. Membership in the association was only open to individuals not organizations.

The value of this form of association was limited, however, as the members identified the requirement for medical business activities that were beyond the actual non-profit oriented business case. As a result, the members founded a joint stock company that served as a purchasing pool for medical and pharmaceutical commodities and acted as the owner of managed care facilities. The different organizational structures that arose enabled a differentiated range of services, but also created a need for integration because of the very different rationale of an association and a joint stock company.

To bring the two organizations together, they are joined at the level of the personnel: only association members were able to apply for shares while at the board level, the association's board included the same personnel as the joint stock company's supervisory board. A stock ratio was formulated for the joint stock company so that 55 percent of the shareholders were required to be resident general practitioners and 45 percent medical specialists.

The association initiated the implementation process of the joint stock company and the network and the founding group called several association meetings to move the project ahead. On an operational level, this meant establishing a coordinating office and a purchasing buying syndicate; expanding the already existing managed care facilities; finalizing facilities contracts; building up an interlinked computer system; and setting up quality development and research projects.

This establishment of the network "from top to bottom" and the role that the founding group played in providing structure created a good organizational and economic basis for the network. At the same time, the energy and participation from the "bottom up" member base remained limited and needed to be developed and fostered. For this reason, a number of physicians who were committed to the network participated in a strategy development process to improve the network's constitution, encourage the involvement of the network members, integrate the network into the company, and decentralize the associated activities. Ultimately, the integration was successful and both those involved and not involved considered the network as "an integrated organization." In addition, a mission statement was written which provided reference points for the integration.

Further objectives are very ambitious: the management board and committed members aim to integrate all members of the regional network, representing approximately 50% of all doctors, in a coordinated collaboration of services.

NANONET STYRIA: A NANO-TECHNOLOGY NETWORK

In a regional network of nano-technology organizations in Styria, Austria, consisting of research institutes, companies and the provincial government, the network members collaborated to pool their know-how and expertise, explore possible project partnerships and design collaborative arrangements for project proposals. The vision was to make Styria into an internationally recognized region in the field of nanotechnology.

The initiative rose from a number of well-connected researchers who managed to attract governmental and political support. Initially, a survey was funded to explore relevant players, as well as the opportunities for the success of nanotechnology in Styria. The results of this survey led to the foundation of NANONET, Styria. The provincial government of Styria provide financial support for the development of the network and its infrastructure, through a large research institute owned by the province that served as a network "host" as well as via political lobbying assistance.

The province was both a partner and co-financier of the network, while the participating organizations were put in charge of it. The research group initiating the network retained overall responsibility for the network project and carried out the preparatory work which involved set-up, support and strategy development. A project assistant acted as a "server," doing day to day organizational support. The 35-partner central platform was called the "core group." From the beginning, the project benefitted from successful collaboration of the participating partners' top executives who represented research, business, politics and administration, as well as from a jointly worked out strategy. The network allowed the core group members to:

- scan cooperation potential;
- generate knowledge about relevant legal and financial options, projects and priorities of the partners in the field;
- quickly recognize where to set the research course and the political infrastructure; and
- build necessary human resources (through a university program).

Entry barriers for membership were relatively low; the network membership was deliberately kept open to all potentially relevant institutions and enterprises.

The network subsequently proved its worth by winning huge subsidies from federal calls to tender. The preliminary work of setting up a highly connected network increased the partners' capacity to put the required collaborative projects into action efficiently. These projects ("applications") were carried out with different configurations of partners. As concrete and exclusive collaborative efforts between two to four partners, they were not part of the Nano-Net Styria, which acted as supportive and facilitating platform ("operating system").

Both the projects and the network also received additional funding for further development. It founded "subsidiary networks" which are specialized in content and have become increasingly independent. The achievement of these subsidiary networks increases the centrifugal pressure on the network, encouraging it to split apart—in the future, the challenge will be to keep the network together as a whole.

THE INTERNATIONAL NETWORK OF HEALTH PROMOTING HOSPITALS (HPH): A MODEL FOR THE IMPLEMENTATION OF HEALTH POLICY INNOVATIONS

The WHO/Europe founded the International Network of Health Promoting Hospitals (HPH) in 1990 to promote health in as many European health systems and hospitals as possible. Started by a small group of "visionaries," this network is now probably one of the most interesting and robust in Europe.

In the first phase of network development, an international group of experts developed the "Budapest Declaration on Health Promoting Hospitals," which provides the substantive, conceptual basis for the network and formulates the basic strategies for health promotion activities of hospitals including:

- improving the health of patients (in contrast to treatment of illness and injury);
- health promotion for staff members; and
- making the hospital a key player for regional health promotion

The network pursued several approaches. It was necessary to connect experts from healthcare professions, healthcare policy-making, hospital management and health promotion into a professional discussion to gain the support of hospitals for implementing relevant projects. These connections were also critical in building alliances with politicians in order to facilitate public health projects. Two overall coordination centers in Vienna[3] and Copenhagen support the network.

During the last 15 years, the HPH network has experienced a number of favorable developments as an innovative and experimental network in the health sector. It has been successful in carrying out substantive projects, learning from experiences, and simultaneously expanding and consolidating the network of organizations. As a result of considerable interest from hospitals seeking network memberships, the WHO established national and regional coordination centers.

The coordination centers act as "servers," which on a national and regional level push ahead the implementation of the Health Promoting Hospital in the hospitals as well as in healthcare policy. But the coordination centers also have responsibility to participate and engage in the overall international network. Together with WHO, the network delegates form the "General Assembly" and then select an "Executive Committee" that acts as an operational steering committee. In 2007, more than 700 hospitals in 41 national and regional networks belonged to the HPH network. The membership rules include some of the interesting design aspects of the HPH network. The membership criteria were more openly defined in the early years, where, in principle, only a memorandum of understanding was necessary for the plan or project implementation corresponding to the "Budapest Declaration." At that early stage, the primary goal was to develop membership interest and to increase the number of participating hospitals to a level that would generate appropriate attention from public health and professional sources.

The interest of hospitals in membership grew rapidly, largely because membership provides WHO accreditation and thus could bring benefits in regional competition. This intensified the discussion about membership schemes, which is as old as the network itself, and raised the following questions about network development: how open or closed, discriminating or welcoming, and prescriptive/evolutionary should the network be? The more demanding the criteria, the more exclusive is the participants' club, which, in turn, narrows the scope of effects. On the other hand, the fear exists that excessively loose conditions for membership would devaluate the approach and bring disrepute to a hospital bearing the "WHO" seal.

As time passed, a differentiated approach emerged that makes defining membership criteria a national and regional responsibility with decision-making requirements. However, these requirements are based on "minimum standards," which meet the internationally valid accreditation conditions of the WHO as well as those of the overall network.

If one compares the membership policies between individual countries, considerable variations become apparent: the forms range from those that are deliberately kept open and are limited by the recognition of shared mindset along with the formal rules of the international network, to demanding membership conditions that include quality strategies for optimizing projects and project evaluations.[4]

The differentiated access as a result of the various internationally applicable conditions along with nationally and regionally adjusted structures creates a very robust network. One that can deal with changes in public health policy objectives, in the state of the art of the hospital world and with the different national cultures—the membership regulations co-evolve with developments in the relevant external environments. The membership criteria are reflected in the meetings of national and regional coordinators where the comparison of different approaches can be helpful in critically examining personal and collective suggestions for change.

A QUALIFICATION NETWORK DISPLAYING THE OPPORTUNITIES AND DIFFICULTIES OF A COOPERATIVE SOLUTION

In 2001, "Lebenshilfe Salzburg" (Life Support Salzburg), a non-profit organization with approximately 500 employees which is involved in taking care of people with disabilities—as well as other organizations active in this field—decided to organize a collaborative staff training system.

The organizations jointly found a qualification network in the social sector, called "Qualibu." For such alliances, the regional labor market service sponsor two-thirds of the course and training fees with funds from the European Social Fund (ESF). This allows the partners to use the same level of budget to educate and train three times the number of staff. Besides the benefit of financial support, the joint training sessions are also intended to encourage transorganizational learning. The initial successful launch of the initiative with five organizations was followed by a growth period during which nine organizations from the social work field joined the qualification network.

The "Network Management Team," composed of delegates from the participating organizations, is responsible for network development and the collaborative activities. A steering committee also exists to which the executives of the participating organizations belong. At the start, this steering committee awards the joint assignment of developing and implementing training programs to the network management and thereafter takes a backseat role. From the outset, the human resources manager of Lebenshilfe Salzburg assumed the coordination and management of the qualification network.

After three rather successful years, four new organizations had now joined it. This expansion was attractive for the training program because the number of participants significantly expanded and the range of offerings was broadened. Staff members of the organizations in the network enjoyed the training, which then lead to its expansion and gained greater significance for the participating organizations. The trainers described the cross-border composition as beneficial because it motivated the participants to learn from each other.

At the same time, some of the participating organizations may have found it difficult to build the necessary confidence for collaboration amongst otherwise competing partners. Because of the membership's expansion, the network management team faced new challenges: the group expanded, the personnel composition changed, the individuals' affiliation were no longer grounded with the initial pioneering spirit, and the need for organization and structure increased. During this phase of expansion, the network management team experienced only limited success in attempting to reflect the social, structural and organizational changes in network management.

In reality, various elements of the network remained unchanged, including the performance systems and the management's roles and tasks, particularly those of the network management team's delegates. This resulted in a strengthening of the operational bias and a reduction in interest in innovative and forward-looking issues. The subsidies granted by the regional labor market service have held the collaboration together, whereas the network's sources of creative momentum had fallen by the wayside.

After the first round of funding ends, the control group decided to continue the collaboration in order to exchange information regularly. Half a year later, when new funding was received, all the organizations remained involved and jointly set up a new qualification network—with increased commitment and balanced involvement amongst the individual organizations in network management.

BRINGING ECOLOGY AND ECONOMICS TOGETHER: A NETWORK APPROACH

In order to strengthen ecologically-oriented economic activities in an Austrian province, the provincial government set up a project to develop and implement a model that awarded environmentally friendly businesses with appropriate publicity for their regional ecological activities.

To establish a project base in the sophisticated world of the environmental and economic institutions—and with expert environmental organizations and leading regional companies—a collaborative model was introduced as a network.

During a network strategy meeting in which representatives from 13 institutions participated, the work program for the coming year was finalized. After the head of the Environmental Management Office introduced the strategic plan, work groups were formed which developed strategic guidelines and suggestions that were both pragmatic and bold.

As the responsible administrative body, the Environmental Management Office accepted the work results, but weren't able to reach decision about the next steps. The representatives of the participating organizations were disappointed by this noncommittal attitude and the unwillingness of the Environmental Management Office to express its intentions and they clearly communicated their frustration.

An observation made two years later (by an external observer) was that the originally intended network had ceased to exist. General meetings about the initiative's development were cancelled, and activities such as the creation of project documentation had been assigned to individual expert organizations. Instead of joint decision making and development with other involved organizations, the Environmental Management Office was now making key decisions and deals with strategic issues on its own. This proven approach of focused decision making along the lines of the formal political power structures has certainly made the program easier to implement and has also avoided some conflicts, but the bold thrust toward a new collaborative management model has been abandoned. The political administration has switched from a broader network approach to the common top-down model of awarding projects.

ITS (INTELLIGENT TRANSPORT SYSTEMS) VIENNA REGION: COOPERATIVE TRAFFIC CONTROL MANAGEMENT ACROSS SYSTEM BORDERS

Three provinces jointly launched a comprehensive traffic management system within a major city's conurbation. The intention was to include both public and private transport, which represented both a technically and socially quite innovative and bold approach. Traffic problems are pressing—mobility demands are expanding, but also do the negative ecologically and economically impacts of the growing traffic load. In the area concerned the infrastructure capacities, including roads and railroad lines, were exhausted and could no longer be extended. Therefore, improvements could only be accomplished by implementing a unified traffic management system throughout the entire region. To change the day to day behavior of the people and the organizations, an *integrated* and comfortably accessible information system was needed, which provided reliable information about both the actual traffic situation and alternative routes and transport possibilities.

The responsibilities were divided between political entities (cities, counties and municipalities), each with its own administrative institutions and traditions, as well as between national, regional and local transportation companies with different customers, promoters of public transport and lobbies for private transport. Traffic management systems required complicated technology and needed to integrate the expertise of technology companies and scientific institutions.

To deal with those challenges, the project was able to build on some significant resources. The political representatives and administrative bodies that initiated the project managed to reach consensus to avoid day to day political conflicts and discussions, which consequently created a stable and supportive environment and allowed for the independent work of experts.

Among the experts involved many important players from the "transport management community" were already known to each other, shared similar technical interests, professional identities and collaborative experiences. At the outset, a stable project team was formed drawing from multiple organizations and representing a significant number of skills including: technical knowledge, insider expertise of the administrative apparatus, as well as important contacts with policy-makers. In addition, several members were able to build on long-established collaborative relationships that have withstood the test of time.

In the first attempt to organize the collaborative effort, the public institutions attempted to establish a joint limited company with the transportation companies. The attempt failed because the decision-makers were unsuccessful in formulating a viable common business case. Their interests, cultures and approaches were too varied, the fear of losing control was too great, and there was insufficient confidence in the participants' professional and negotiation skills. The conflict mainly arose between the reluctant national transport operators (the federal railways and the highway commission) and the other players. By extensively discussing organizational issues at the beginning, any content-related work was relegated to a lower priority which hindered bottom-up progress driven by the experts.

After two years in this unproductive circle, the political players started a new attempt to set up collaboration. This time, they applied a more process-oriented approach using gradual steps instead of one sudden move. A federally funded research project acted as a trigger, providing the financial incentive and impetus to establish a collaborative system around the existing core project team which comprised about 15 different organizations. The reluctant (if not intransigent) national transport operators, whose data was technically indispensable, were more loosely integrated through individual contracts around data exchange. Players who wanted to cooperate to a limited or lesser extent were therefore still involved in order to keep the options open.

The work and professional interest of the specialists moved the process forward. They were then able to phase in the successful implementation of sophisticated data collection and networking among the organizations. What seemed difficult or even impossible to implement was now seen as a reality to be addressed through viable technical solutions within the context of changing interests. This, in turn, puts pressure on the organizations' decision-makers, particularly among the national transport operators, to participate with more commitment.

In order to connect the various participants and to manage conflicts, the core project team used the political arena, a professional approach to project management and both formal and informal channels. In this collaborative system, very different interests needed to be served, including:

- The technology experts who were entering new territory and revealed the capacity for innovation and experimentation;

- Companies who were seeking to establish a platform for follow-up assignments;
- Research institutions who were interested in pursuing a lucrative project which could enhance their reputation;
- Policy-makers who wanted traffic information that was citizen-oriented and easy to access. In the process of obtaining traffic information, administrative institutions involved also wanted to preserve their routines; and
- Finally, it was important to address the contradiction between treating traffic management and information as a public accessible service or as a special service only offered to paying customers.

Timing in this politically and technically highly volatile area was critical. To maintain momentum throughout tough times and to profit from windows of opportunity, a step by step approach has proven successful.

The question now at stake is how to institutionalize the collaborative system and provide a stable organizational platform for operating and further developing the traffic management system over time, without losing its collaborative character.

SUMMARY

The cases presented in this chapter illustrate the great variety of collaborative efforts and processes. They highlight, that collaborative systems do not convincingly "function out of necessity," and may not generate growth in energy and commitment solely by their sheer existence. It is not the "collaboration" itself that necessarily sparks success or failure, but rather the very elements that develop and shape a collaborative relationship. In this regard, our case studies examine the *management* of collaborations and networks, illustrating the different dimensions and success factors of these organizational processes.

NOTES

1. Some of the examples in this chapter are portrayed anonymously because projects may still be in progress, are in critical phases, or interview partners have requested anonymity. The cases are based on a series of interviews with key actors and stakeholders, observations, organizational documents and archival records, and field notes gathered during consulting interventions.
2. The research team is composed of Hubert Lobnig, Ralph Grossmann, Klaus Scala, Michael Stadlober, and Marlies Garbsch.

3. Additional background information on this case—associated documents, archival records and materials, conceptual papers, and so forth—is available at http://www.hph-hc.cc.
4. The Austrian Network of Health Promoting Hospitals (ÖNGK) is based upon a more selective membership policy; see http://www.oengk.net.

CHAPTER 6

THE KEY CRITERIA FOR SUCCESS

Ralph Grossmann and Hubert Lobnig

Organizing a cooperative venture involves agreeing on a set of rules that distinguish new activities from previous ones. It also demands commitment, beginning with designing shared and reciprocal activities in order to define an independent system. According to Weick (1995, 2001), organizing is based on the diverse meanings of joint activity. Organizations create these meanings in the course of their work and later formulate them together. As Giddens (1984) argues, the resulting duality of structure and action is the basis for organizing in organizations.

WHAT DOES IT MEAN TO ORGANIZE A COOPERATIVE VENTURE?

Participants create cooperative structures through their interactive efforts and reproduce them actively and constantly, resulting in further activity. However, a paradox also exists that limits the *initial options* for action happening at the same time. As activity progresses, structures are reproduced, differentiated and changed. To some extent, this can even occur "behind

Facilitating Collaboration in Public Management, pages 73–95

the backs of those involved," with limited or even no intention or a planned approach.

Nevertheless, those involved in cooperative efforts have the ability to control the conditions and results of their actions and to modify these actions through conscious informed interventions based on reflection, feedback and evaluation (Sydow, 2004). In this sense, the organization encountered is both the product and medium and this recursive process of structure and actions and ranks among the most effective cooperative ventures. Appropriate forms of organizations have to reflect the specific external and internal requirements and may change and develop over time (Chisholm, 1998). It is especially impressive to observe this phenomenon in the development of cooperative efforts.

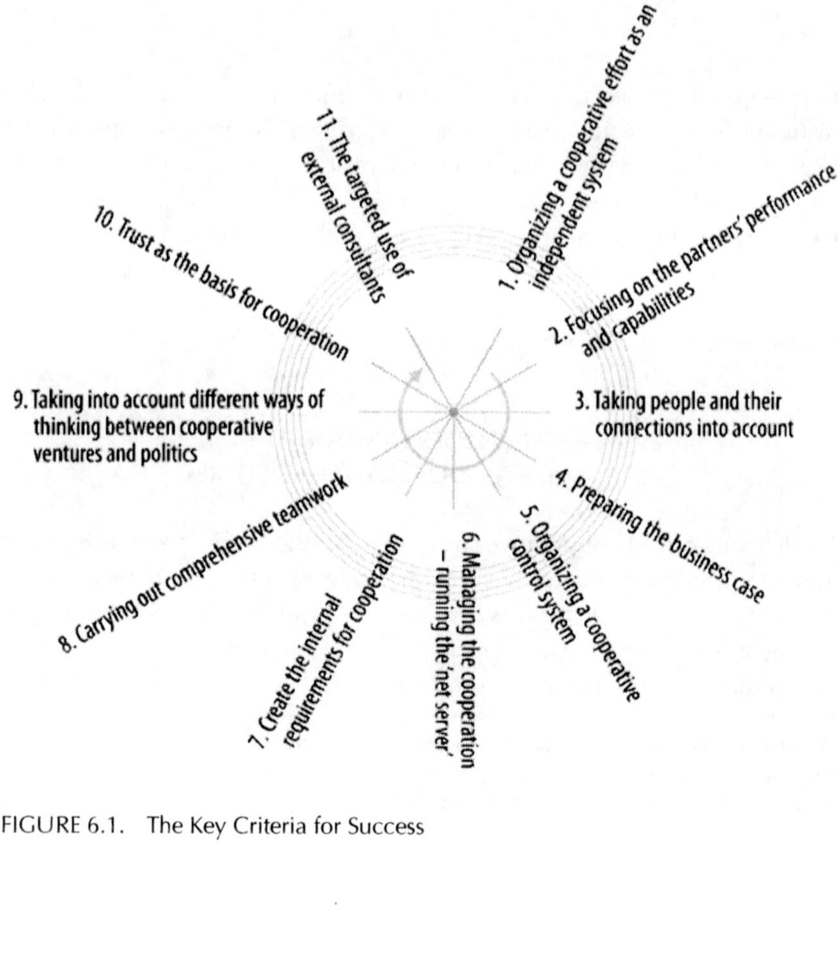

FIGURE 6.1. The Key Criteria for Success

Organizing Cooperation as an Independent Social System

One of the most important concepts that has resulted from our research and consulting experience is that cooperation between systems should be processed as a social system—defined as a system between systems, run by the participants so they can realize their mutual expectations, and involving the process of joint development.

The way in which a cooperative arrangement is organized is a decisive factor in its potential for success. Partners must decide the functionality of this intermediary system and design the joint processes around the benefits they seek to achieve. This process provides the participants with experiences that either encourage them to continue cooperating or make the relationship more distant, disinterested, or competitive.

In addition, organizations do not merely cooperate. They create their own social systems with goals, rules, and structures that distinguish them from other organizations. These sorts of "collaboration systems," as Gray (1989) calls them, come into being when organizations start tackling and solving problems together. Collaborative systems are not created externally; rather, they are emergent and fragile ones *developed* within a process. They require constant maintenance and methods for constructively dealing with differences (Gray & Wood, 1991).

From the point of view of group dynamics and systems theory, the most important components of system formation are the definition of boundaries and the creation of identity. What is very special about forming cooperative ventures is the paradox that only highly differentiated organizations can effectively cooperate, while those systems also must be invented and organized from scratch. Pooled routines, organizational solutions and management concepts must form the basis of the shared system be used and, at the same time, need to be put aside. It is a process that requires the evolution and opening up of mental frames and organizational preferences by those involved and creating new ones with potential partners.

Both the processes and agreements about structure result from the formation of cooperative systems that comply with the logic of management and the prerequisites of successful relationships. Collaborating partners follow the principle of equality between partners, while building trust and implementing consensus-based decision-making. This is why hierarchical structures of the participating organizations have a paradoxical effect on cooperative systems: on the one hand they are obstructive, yet they also are an indispensable condition for real cooperation.

The participants in any cooperative venture have to balance double memberships of their organization of origin and the emerging identity of the partnership with divided loyalties. In their own interest, cooperative systems need to distance themselves from the partnering organizations and make decisions to build and maintain their own identity. At the same time, they also must open up and remain closely related to their home organizations and take into account their expected benefits and associated decisions.

Cooperative systems also require stability in order to work properly while remaining flexible and open to the participants' interests and decisions. These differences between distancing and restarting, independence and connectivity, structure formation and fluctuation need to be continuously managed. The fluctuating organizational structures that necessarily come along with this way of working, as well as the various mediums of communication and management, can be particularly irritating for observers who are used to defined structure. For example, these cooperative processes can oscillate between establishing and penetrating structures. For that reason, Littmann and Jansen (2000) characterize networks as "oscillodoxes"—something that continually changes its definition—a force that allows them to adapt to and learn from changing conditions particularly well.

Cooperative systems are completed by reverting to forms of social and management control structures that either follow the principles of hierarchy, by market-oriented types of relations between the partners (selling/buying principle), or by creating new organizations. In our opinion, cooperative systems are organized as connected social systems, not as independent organizations. New organizations might be the result of a cooperative system; for instance, a joint partnerships creating a new ventures or a company with a shared ownership. Cooperative systems may also run a joint service organization quite well, provided that a sufficient distinction is made between the organization itself and the cooperative system.

Cooperative system formation is an unalterable part of both networks and collaborations. Networks also have to follow up distinctions between internal and external matters, members and non-members, expectations of benefits and reasons for disassociation. Not only are the ground rules for networks different from those of collaborations, they even differ from network to network. Yet many collaborations and networks lack a creative and efficient answer to the question of organizational formation. Instead, they often follow the patterns applied in individual organizational formation and not those of a transorganizational approach.

A network is a forum of options that serve to realize common benefits. As such, its efficiency is manifested in drawing intra-system distinctions concerning joint decisions and other commitments. For instance, just because the founders of the network of health-promoting hospitals decide to attach conditions to their membership does not mean that the network becomes a collaboration or an organization. The opportunity for all hospitals (whether regionally, nationally or globally) to participate in a network is restricted so specific expected benefits can be realized. Therefore, when hospitals arrange to work on running joint management systems, benchmarking quality, or investing in health promotion programs, the cooperation experiences a character change. The systematic dependency on the decisions and budget planning of all participants becomes vital. The tasks and the room for manoeuvre that have been allotted to the project managers must be clarified. Good relationships among top managerial staff give the cooperation support and make it easier to resolve conflicts.

Focusing on the Performance and Capabilities of Cooperation Partners

A thriving network depends on the commitment of many people and on working hard for differentiated products and results. These factors have the retroactive effect of strengthening the feedback loops in networks. The more creative and benefit-oriented the work within networks is, the more attractive the network becomes both for members and the relevant external environment. Ultimately, the tangible results (usually the product of sharing work responsibilities) advance a network rather than the decisions and resolutions of various boards of decision-makers. That is why it is especially important to consider how groups of people at the operative level can perform as productively as possible.

A thriving network depends on the commitment of its participants. Experience has shown that, for the most part, successful networks are generated by commitment that goes above and beyond agreed-upon expectations. It is our observation that such a heightened sense of motivation correlates to the following conditions within a network: professionally attractive task setting, participation in relevant decision-making, responsible and accountable roles and responsibilities topics and results, the opportunity to develop one's career, positive work relationships, responsiveness to and appreciation of contributions made, and a working culture that does not only take care of business but is also fun and enjoyable.

When it comes to the decision of what types of working principles should be introduced, cooperative rather than hierarchical principles ought to be taken into consideration. Weick and colleagues (Orton & Weick, 1990; Weick, 2001) developed the concept of "loosely coupled systems" in which organizational elements are not tightly connected with each other. The degree of independence between the elements of a loosely coupled system is rather high as is the autonomy of the organizational entities. Wherein "strictly coupled systems" commissions, contracts, hierarchical orders are feasible strategies for steering, loosely coupled organizations require different approaches: suitable practices include those that have a participative influence on the selection and differentiation of subjects, rely on voluntary participation, and require personal commitment from all parties. Clarification of methods to provide results-oriented feedback must also be made. Such operating systems are referred to as working groups, experience groups, quality circles, knowledge communities, practice groups, task forces, and so on.

The principles of community building are helpful if one of the purposes of work forms is to broaden the network's activity base. Community Building is an approach developed and widely applied in neighborhood and community work, in regional development and in developing coalitions for social issues. Applying the principles of community building help cooperative ventures and especially networks to systematically combine increasing activities with growing participation.[1]

The starting point of community building is the recognition that identification of stakeholders and potential network partners. It also requires the willingness to make active contributions that are notably increased by consciously involving people in key activities and decision making-processes. Community building gradually promotes the social penetration of the entire network by shaping roles and forums (in line with performance) and by creating rooms for step-by-step participation in the process. Within this context, central questions include the following: How can the largest possible number of activities be introduced with as much breadth as possible? Which people should and can be involved with which issues, and which work forms should be employed so that their commitment brings about increased value for the cooperative venture?

Early on in this community building process, it is advisable to rely on teams. They should be established on the operational level so that cross-organizational teams engender new networking opportunities that lead to cross-organizational perspectives and assessments. These do not necessarily have to be assessments that are shouldered by all participants, but the mental models and notions of the network partners become part of the shared dialogue. In this manner, a "cooperation experience" emerges, building trust and introducing development opportunities.

An important prerequisite to teamwork, however, is that the common practice and work relationships are perceived as productive and personally valuable which requires the right working culture in groups and teams. This culture should deal respectfully with group member contributions, organize meetings with clear goals, be able to handle differences and conflicts, and deliberately establish decision-making models. In short, the culture should represent a form of work that involves the content of the operating system as well as the social network.

In our experience, many networks pay too little attention to teamwork methods, instruments for problem analysis, and facilitation techniques, so working groups are left to operate within an autonomy that is partly misunderstood or undermined.

Taking People and Their Relationships into Account

Less distinct formal structures such as procedures, areas of competence, hierarchies, and the instability of organizational structures lead to a higher level of people orientation within networks and collaborative efforts. Attractive and successful networks are largely based on the activity of individuals, the trustworthiness and role model function of 'flag bearers', and the willingness of people to get involved in tasks, committees, and projects. The communication between people in general and the ability of those who occupy influential positions to communicate is vital to the success of networks.

Strong, people-oriented dependence does not mean that questions of system or process are not relevant to the success of network control and management. It is rather a question of developing an adequate understanding of network management practice. This understanding should integrate the concepts of organizational development, the approaches of social psychology and group dynamics, as well as topics like influence, power, trust, and teamwork.

A relatively high level of people orientation applies to all types of cooperative ventures, including: informal networks such as a circle of colleagues or fellow students, more formalized networks such as sports clubs, professional associations, and self-help groups and ventures in which organizations join together to collaborate (see also the importance of trust in organizational partnerships presented by Lewis, 1999).

In addition, participants in member organizations' networks should continually remain on track with the interests and terms of their home organizations. This is precisely the reason why—when it comes to questions of weighing benefits, forms of membership, and cooperation and competition—that no one person should dictate decisions or actions. Rather, attention should be paid to proper arrangements in discussion and decision-making procedures to represent the organizations appropriately. This "delegate dilemma" is not a one-way street since organizational networks imply independent decisions. Representatives must have sufficient freedom to creatively and effectively act within the network.

Preparing the Business Case

Collaborating organizations expect positive results from their networking with others. A main prerequisite for network membership consists of a clear understanding of organizational benefits. Foreseeable benefits compensate for the investments, hassles, fears and risks that come along with cooperation and partnerships. The binding force in networks is largely due to the opportunity they offer of meeting personal and organizational goals. Network participants or partnering organizations can remain more or less autonomous, retaining the ownership of the basic strategies that affect their organization of origin. Therefore, their decision to take part in a network is theoretically reversible and/or renewable.

The benefit for participating organizations is the starting point for involvement in a network or partnership. Ultimately it is the members' self-interest that constitutes a cooperative effort and is the motivation for successful participation. A broad understanding of interests allowing for respectful variety of participants increases the probability that member organizations will provide essential inputs. On the one hand, it is imperative to represent the interests of one's organization of origin and to set a course that serves those particular interests. On the other hand, it is also a matter of acting 'in the spirit of collaboration' and of 'nurturing, embracing, empowering, involving, mobilizing' it (Huxham, 2003). In this way, cooperation and competition, obstinacy and solidarity (in the context of civilized selfishness) have to be balanced anew. As the researchers on collaboration Huxham and Vangen (2002, p. 22) note "partnership means going behind peoples backs in a trustworthy way."

Individual benefits and the opportunities opened up by participation form the 'cement' that holds a network and associated partnerships together. Network members have the expectation of a speedy return on investment, even if some good-natured participants are willing to wait longer for positive effects, such as pre-financing for the network. Such initial investments may be financial contributions to personnel costs, additionally allocated working time, investment of specific knowledge, or developing rules and regulations for the network. However if the desired results are not produced, or if they 'get lost on the way', it can be expected that the network will sooner or later have 'investment problems' and the lack of incentive that comes with them. Such networks become unattractive, and can appear hollowed out, even if they still function as social systems. Their continued existence usually indicates that no one has been authorized or has the motivation to end to it.

Although the basic conditions for benefits may be given, the actual and energizing sense of working together can, at best, only partially be made by assessing and planning the details of the cooperative venture in advance—out of the perspective of each individual organization. According to Weick's concept of sense-making, the purpose is not achieved by simply absorbing goals and interests, but rather by collaboratively creating the purpose using an intensive communication process. The main concern is to establish clear communication processes between the network participants so the undertaking itself can be clarified, weighed, criticized, and differentiated. Through this process, a clear purpose can emerge, shaping the direction for future activities and allowing for the possibility of cooperative action.

Cooperation between network partners focuses only on limited services and activities and not on the whole of the organization. For that reason, the business case and the commitment to networking with others must be distinguished from other forms of services and performance that exist independently or competition with the other partners. In addition, cooperation only makes sense between entities if it is mutually beneficial. The formulation of common goals and the organizing force behind the cooperation also requires respect for those goals of potential partners who are in conflict with each another. After all, cooperation must function within the context of both competition and common ground, as is described with the word "co-opetition" (Brandenburger & Nalebuff, 1996).

Ultimately, participants in networks and collaborations must be convinced that the cooperation is important to everyone involved. Key players in the cooperative effort need to recognize the importance the network can have for their future and be able to arrive at a commitment without knowing all the details in advance. The more intense the cooperative agreement is, the more important the approval of top management and the relationships between top managers are, since they are the ones best able to engender commitment.

The social system of the cooperation can only be brought to life when the goals and business case have been jointly developed and carried out. Yet it is difficult to set precise goals on which all participants totally agree. Individual organizational interests often conflict with each other or are influenced from the outside. Instead of trying to focus on the differences in the goal-setting process, it is sometimes better to proceed with "functional ambiguity" (Huxham & Vangen 2005)—seeking a common ground rather than exploring conflicting and diverting issues (Weisbord & Janoff, 2000). Although this tactic can create friction, it has proved to be successful and promising as people involved experience a cohesive collaborative effort. Some useful questions to use during this process include: What number of common goals should be set before embarking on a cooperative effort? What issues can remain open? What can be left to the course of development?

Another important step in goal setting involves agreeing on an understanding of how material and intellectual investments, earnings, costs, and losses are distributed and handled. Managers should be convinced that the cooperation yields long-term benefits and results. Short-term profit orientation is detrimental to the basis of cooperation, especially when it puts any one of its partners at a disadvantage.

Organizing a Cooperative Control System

Cooperative ventures need a control system that the partners create and shoulder together. The tasks of this group, consisting of at least one party from each group, are clearly outlined: defining common goals and agreeing on ground rules, making necessary decisions, monitoring the process, and ensuring strategic reflection. The efficiency of this system is reliant on open and trustworthy communication. It is also of the utmost importance that both the potential and the limitations of all participants are taken into account, and that objective arguments as well as emotions have their place in problem solving processes and negotiations. Participating organizations' upper management normally takes advantage of these steering systems, which have great symbolic and cultural value for the entire cooperative undertaking.

Collaborations, as the more binding form of cooperation, additionally require a direct "line" or communication with the key players of the parent organizations who are responsible for monitoring and decision-making. At the same time, it is not advisable to place all those steering and monitoring processes—including the communication and decision-making—in the hands of the top players whose time and technical resources are limited. From the start, a more broadly conceived control system offers the possibility of including other management levels in shaping the cooperative system so that the agreed course of action is safeguarded, obstacles can be removed, and decisions can be made on time.

The control systems of cooperative efforts and networks are clearly different from those of conventional organizations. For instance:

- Leadership and control are distributed more horizontally across the organizational structure
- Commitment to the system remains tenuous
- Participating organizations aspire to more autonomy and can be more obstinate, often creating a riskier basis for negotiations

Decisions should always in the physical presence of all key players. Cummings (1984) describes such control systems as *trans-organizational systems.* These systems are basically "sub-organized social structures" characterized by difficulty in making decisions from the start since they have not yet established a common premise. We agree that is why the formation of steering processes should be the basis for cooperative development.

Managing the Cooperation: Running the "Net Server"

Kotter's (1996) distinction between leadership and management is also very useful in thinking about the challenges inherent in managing cooperative efforts. According to Kotter´s concept, leadership should plan and build organizations and later adjust them to changing conditions. The leaders' main concern should be to: define visions and goals, coordinate future-oriented programs, organize the necessary cooperative efforts and participative interests, and motivate participants.

It is the job of management, on the other hand, to plan and budget, as well as to carry out projects and activities by applying various methods and tools, to facilitate implementation, and to process results and problems.

In our experience, we realize the special need for professional management in networks and collaborations in comparison with individual organizations because of the fragility of leadership and the particular combination of steering systems:

- Networks or collaborative ventures are often organized in boards/committees with divided responsibilities, requiring the need for voting in decision-making processes.
- Responsible positions are often occupied only temporarily or are organized according to rotating principles; new decision-makers need to familiarize themselves with the subject matter and the culture of the decision making processes continuously, creating difficulties in establishing continuity.
- The decision-makers often work in an honorary capacity or receive only a limited financial compensation for network activities.

The impact of these factors on network management—in comparison to individual organizations—is a highly increased need for cooperative performance that fosters continuity and stability. Networks need a manage-

TABLE 6.1. The Core Competencies of Coordination Systems in Networks

- Project management: time and resource planning, multi-project management, support to individual project managers
- Competence in organization development: an understanding of the logic behind the development of social systems, adequate understanding of performance management in network organizations, basic management skills
- Communication skills to connect the decision-makers in the network and 'ordinary' network partners (as opposed to external clients and interest groups)
- An understanding of community building: competence in shaping roles; designing meetings, projects and activities to increase the community's participation
- The productive shaping of communication-related activities: the preparation of, documentation for, and follow up to meetings, work sessions, and other large events
- Competence in building and maintaining virtual forms of communication: homepages, e-tools for work groups; skills in combining virtual and face-to-face forms of communication
- Controlling network activities; survey implementation and evaluation
- Professional connectivity skills: to prove valuable informed expertise in network-related fields to achieve credibility for key players

ment headquarters, a hub that does not represent partial interests but takes over coordinating functions for the entire undertaking. The job of this unit is to coordinate the maintenance of any organizing structures and various network functions, and to provide services, support, and evaluation or performance systems. The operations content, organization, and strategy that are integrated in such a hub provide an overall view of the situation as well as the complexity of the network, and should recognize the need for requisite action or control.

Network management provides the stability within the social system in order to support the entire organization and provide its members with the resources necessary for promoting productive communication and decision-making processes. Network management also should coordinate and help the teams at different operational levels with various programs, projects, tasks, and tools without falling into the trap of doing the things themselves. Although those demarcations are often unclear, the role of network managers is to offer support and not to carry out individual network tasks. Table 6.1 illustrates the critical competencies of a network hub.

Create the Internal Requirements for a Cooperative Effort

A prerequisite for stimulating cooperative efforts are certain processes that have to take place within the participating systems. The more the cooperative ventures are focusing core business processes of the parent organizations, the riskier it becomes to develop some 'creative or spontaneous planning approaches." Instead such cooperation requires additional support from top management, which should view the undertaking more critically and with necessary caution. In collaborations, the participants have to consider sound procedures even more closely, as the mutual commitments and investments of each partnering organization are notably higher.

In less binding forms of cooperation—like networks—it is sufficient for top management to act as an initiator or network mentor. Because participating in a network normally does not have as severe implications for the business or the processes of the participating organization or collaborations, the intention to create internal changes is rather limited so it isn't necessary for top management to be as involved.

For a collaboration to work properly, it is of utmost importance to anchor the undertaking within the partnering organization in a way to secure the capability to act effectively in a collaborative system—together with delegates from other organizations. This requires a solid internal basis for decision-making, actively involved key players, and a clear strategy to represent the organization in the collaborative system. The necessary functions, roles, and committees in the collaborative system have to be defined as well as the working structures and processes in each participating organization. To find feasible and attractive solutions which the partners also accept is one of the first tasks for the cooperative work. However, it already requires a cooperative structure beforehand to define the cooperative system—a paradox each collaborative venture faces in the beginning.

Ways out this paradox in launching a collaboration include kick-off events and preparatory meetings where systemic questions can be addressed through consensus based decision-making, since rash decisions can often lead to dysfunctional structures. The system itself motivates organizations to meet in-house requirements, but because these internal processes affect the entire cooperative venture, concrete details have to be defined within the cooperative structure. Organizations that are clearly internally geared toward supporting the cooperation form a solid prerequisite for the emergence of trust between partners.

Strategy is an important aspect of participating in a cooperative venture, and requires that the players skillfully balance the challenge of cooperation and competition. A collaborative effort can only be successful when strategic decisions include setting expectations, organizing priorities, and partially suspending competition. The purpose of and strategies behind cooperative projects should openly be revealed to colleagues who are not directly involved so efforts are transparent.

An organization also must be open to the effects the cooperative effort can have on its routine business. The more successful and convincing the cooperation, the more influence it will later have on other areas of business. For instance, work experiences and results are usually shared with other parts of the same organization. Newly created processes can either serve as examples or deterrents. In addition, support areas must adapt to the demands of the cooperating system, and personnel managers should prepare for double assignments and personnel transfers. The blurred borderline between cooperative ventures and start-ups can become particularly apparent in the way people and managerial assignments are handled.

In order to process these retroactive effects, companies are urged to connect in-house communication systems with the cooperative processes. Experiences and results must be observed and evaluated, possible implications for the whole organization should be anticipated, and the affected areas should be prepared for the consequences. The balance between expenses and benefits should constantly be evaluated and communicated.

Successfully participating in a cooperative effort means that organizations should be flexible and willing to learn and experiment internally. At the same time, they should be open to externally induced learning possibilities derived from work with others. One can see those impacts as advantageous in terms of business outcomes.

Participation in such intermediary systems is common, and as a result, the cooperative venture in which businesses take part requires a 'portfolio management' structure (Odenthal, et al., 2002) for partnering organizations. Who has an overview? Who is responsible in the company? How are the different activities related to each other? These questions and their solutions require specialized tasks that must be expressed and realized in professional roles. While with enterprises, such roles assume names like business development, investment management, or alliance management, they are hardly differentiated in public organizations and other establishments that provide public services. The capability of organizations to participate in cooperative arrangements has become increasingly advantageous and even necessary in the case of public institutions.

The Individual Organization as Network Part and Counterpart

Experience has shown that individuals drive the initial stages of network development, while pioneers and experts can often be visionary and want to reach beyond organizational boundaries. Yet when organizations—and not individuals—unite to form a cooperative venture, they are both inspired by and uncertain of the potential. Questions that often arise in these early stages include: What happens to us if we join? How much harm can the network and our commitment to it do to us? What will change? What will we have to give up? Are we strong enough to enter partnerships, especially when other organizations in the network are larger? Are we equipped to survive competitive situations that might arise?

Cooperative efforts can quickly become a nuisance to partnering organizations. When involving "others" in one's own company, areas of tension often develop between the groups working together and those that remain uninvolved, which can create grounds for possible conflict. It also can result in the intrusion of rules and internal procedures. The need for decisions may arise when no one is yet responsible for making them and people may begin asking inconvenient questions like "what should be my stance?" or leave meetings without understanding their purpose or knowing the results.

Management has a central task to prepare companies for the participation in networks (see Table 6.2). An in-house contract is necessary so key players can determine the opportunities, risks, and requirements of participation. In addition, it is imperative to develop and foster decision-making that will guide the network participants to intended results.

One of the key reasons for the failure of networks is lack of internal preparation by involved organizations. Very often, companies rely too much on visionary and highly motivated individuals to realize cooperative projects while neglecting to secure their position through internal procedures and regulations. An over-personalized approach may lead to uncomplicated communication procedures on the one hand but also to a greater dependency on individual performance, capacities, and morale-generating risks for sustained action and impact.

TABLE 6.2. Characteristics of Organizational Capacity to Participate in Networks

- The question of why to participate in the network and the 'case for action' is clearly formulated and communicated.
- Key players are capable of cooperation.
- Organizational representatives in the network are adequately organized and selected for particular skill sets.
- Internal decisions and strategies are incorporated into the network's agenda.
- The organization is sensitive to the network's influences and is open to feedback.
- In strategy work, experience and composure are an advantage.
- External contacts are internally acceptable when people act as "ambassadors" for the organization
- A survey of existing cooperative efforts and network involvement and/or a strategic control helps to organize commitments.

A company's participation in a network largely depends on established in-house governance and work structures. Several factors influence the way an organization realizes and "lives" through the network—both internally and externally. Factors can include the company's internal preparation by management, decision-making processes and, in particular, the network's importance as communicated by managements' words and actions.

Odenthal, et al (2002) recommend a series of methods to plan and monitor partnerships in cooperative ventures and networks from the participants' point of view. Some important questions that organizations might ask include:

- How much sense does a cooperative venture make for our organization?
- How do I find the right partners?
- How can I observe the cooperative efforts that we already are part of?
- How can I create the required capacities and roles within our organization?
- How can the cooperation play its due role in the management of our organization?
- How can I protect my interests?

Many organizations often must deal with their cooperative partners in one area of business while they are competitors in others. The ability to switch quickly between these modes of cooperation and competition can determine the effectiveness of an organization's ability to participate in networks.

Carrying out Comprehensive Teamwork

Early in their development, cooperative ventures should utilize teams and invest in teamwork since it is easier for individuals to escape patterns of their company's organizational culture and learn from others. New social environments also enable the participants to better identify with the goals and tasks of the effort.

The productivity of a cooperative effort is primarily dependent on work quality, productive work relationships, and congruent experiences of how decisions and results correspond. Because the work of cooperative relationships and networks takes place both during and after hours, meaningful relationship experiences are of the utmost importance and an enormous factor in individual involvement and organizational investment. In this manner, networks can achieve success more readily than members could do individually.

Teamwork can pull together loosely coupled systems (Weick, 1985) since it provides the individual with intense interaction as well as meaning and relation to the overall undertaking. The current efforts of many organizations to decentralize also result in an increased need for teamwork. It also allows the experience of a highly differentiated organization as an entity without dismissing the unique approaches and work environments encountered. The strength of teams in particular can help to express and revise these differences.

Teams can be especially helpful in working on networks and their differences. Precisely because networks are seldom equipped with the same detailed guidelines and roles as institutions, they must continually define their goals and capabilities. The patterns that result from these reflective processes create the 'spirit of collaboration' and 'culture' that are required for innovation (Huxham & Vangen, 2003a). That being said, the general principles of how to implement teamwork in cooperative ventures are as follows: organize as many important functions as possible through cross-organizational teams; control management and work teams in performance processes; and design teams for event preparation.

Different Ways of Thinking

Cooperative ventures and networks in the public service sector are unthinkable without the involvement of public administration and/or political decision-makers. Public policy and innovative networks are especially interesting to public administration since public goods and services are widely connected with and provided by them. For that reason, public administration representatives are more intensely and directly involved by providing resources, participating in management decisions, as well as boards, committees and event involvement.

Direct involvement of public administration in performance and support processes can be counterproductive as collaborations or networks may consider them an interfering intervention. In such situations, appropriate steering mechanisms should stimulate desirable networking by providing seed money or grants. Guidelines for monitoring resources can be very motivating with tools like financial bases (allocating project funds to cooperative efforts) and performance contracts (allocating services to collaborations). Financial contributions, however, also bear the risk—when the money is spent and the financial support ends, the cooperative ventures may fall apart.

In addition more sustaining strategies may intervene in a variety of ways, including: allocating projects geared toward network coordination, funding cooperative efforts as well as activities that promote them (such as conferences and communications platforms), support for facilitation, and training for those involved in networks and cooperative ventures.

The roles traditionally attributed to service providers and public institutions can be jeopardized when decision-makers from public administration get involved in cooperative and networking efforts. Although these institutions often can function as clients or financers, they get involves as partners and network players through input and intervention with other participants, meaning that two different role models are set in place.

As players from administration and politics get involved in networks, their roles become more complex in comparison to traditional divisions of labour, requiring quality role management and streamlined communication processes: for instance, decision-makers from public institutions and politics simultaneously have to assume the roles of financer with access to funds and the ability to jointly develop something new, or as principal contractor for projects and as an equal who shows a willingness to move towards sustainable partnership models. They also must justify and secure their network participation within their own organizations. These roles pose certain risks since people from administration may back cooperative efforts and networks that often lack the internal support required for network activity. Other stumbling blocks to successful role formation also can include the resistance of in-house departments and interest groups who regard cooperative efforts as a rival to their own strategies.

This situation also can be frustrating to the representatives of service providers and businesses who may lose an important external client previously regarded as a 'counterpart', with whom they have to negotiate and confront. Representatives from the administration could easily be seen as part of external institutions, while this internal/external relationship begins to convert when cooperative ventures commence. When common strategic considerations, negotiation and decision-making processes take place in a network, the former counterpart models shift to an approach of greater interdependence.

In spite of (or perhaps even precisely because of) these challenges, the integration of players from administration and politics in networks, as well as the efficacy of decision-making processes, are important factors for long-term success. Integration offers two opportunities: politicians and administration can monitor relationships among service providers and decision-makers with an emphasis on negotiation and communication processes between the partners; and service providers can partake in political decision-making processes and actively shape negotiation processes.

Political and administrative representatives involved with the cooperative efforts should work to resolve disputes through negotiation and must remain open to the service providers' needs and realities, while continuing to protect political and administrative interests.

Trust as the Basis for Cooperation

Because a central aspect of cooperation includes foregoing one's own interests in return for future benefit, it can only work with mutually trusting partners who adhere to that condition and invest in the joint venture. Trust is constantly renewed between action and expectation (see Table 6-3).

The trusting person determines future action without limiting the partner's capacity to act. This is somewhat risky because the other partner may not cooperate. A breach of trust can heavily impact cooperation partners in the beginning of the effort, since there are few safeguarding measures and lack of regulations. Efforts to build trust are especially important in the initial phases of cooperative ventures. When trust is not initially developed, fall-back positions and negotiation techniques begin to control the venture which in turn reduces trust.

Long-term Cooperative Ventures and Trust

Trust has many functions and advantages. It reduces insecurity and complexity and absorbs risks. Instead of formal rules, trust makes cooperation less rigid and more creative. It replaces legal regulations—and can even

TABLE 6.3. Trust Expectation and Action

Trust is ...	
Act of trust	... is the rendering of a risky advance performance without explicit measures of safeguarding or control in order to forego opportunistic behaviour...
Trust expectation	... is the expectation that the interaction partner is reliable and will refrain from acting opportunistically.

Source: Ripperger (1998, p. 45)

bring them to life—while facilitating communication and the ability to deal with difficult situations.

Trust has a wide-ranging impact by changing people, situations, priorities, and cultures. We do not often do not realize how important it is until it is missing—a loss of trust can quickly leads to a crisis in every cooperative effort. However, trust is neither fate nor a natural phenomenon but a communicative experience that can be re-established.

Trust is the result of acts that create it and is the foundation for work in cooperative ventures and networks. Lewis (1999) has helped a number of large businesses in forming alliances and joint ventures through a series of methods to build foundations for trust, which are addressed below.

Winning Trust

A few basic conditions for building trust are necessary, including the *right choice of partners for a mutually beneficial relationship*. The cooperative venture must make sense for all participating organizations that are willing to pursue their own interests and contribute their energy to the joint project. Partners must debate and formulate common goals, while rooting and maintaining those goals in their individual organizations. Everyone must respect their partners' competitive goals while simultaneously balancing cooperation and competition.

Another important prerequisite for winning trust is the establishment of a system that secures and maintains it, requiring the distribution of existing investments such as know-how, expected losses and benefits, and balancing transparency between the cooperation or network partners. Trust is also built inside of the organization, when those involved perceive the internal performance and behaviour of key players: Does top management do all it can to secure long-term commitment to the collaborative venture? Are the key players of the organizations prepared to follow through with the undertaking? Are resources being allocated and respective roles identified? Those participating in the cooperative effort should have the ability to perform required duties and build the cooperative relationships to foster trust. These ventures live through people and are backed by interpersonal relationships on all levels, from decision-making to performance processes. The management staff, in particular, should function as role models.

Work and decision-making processes stimulate, verify, and help to develop trust and are key to successful cooperative efforts. Quality depends on an open and transparent style of communication, especially in the transition between solution-oriented work and reflective processes. "Enlightened egoism" (Willke, 1995) in a cooperative effort requires an understanding of the situation and the facts behind the underlying issues, as well as the partners' motives, even if they have differing points of view. Contrary to the liberal market-oriented relationship-model, where the individual motives of the counterpart are out of individual concern and interests, understanding and sympathy for the cooperative partners' situation is necessary for building trusting relationships in a network and in lasting collaborative efforts.

To fully consider the partners conditions of action also requires balancing the objective dimensions of work with the emotions involved. Finding this balance is the fulcrum of trust-building communication between participants. Emotions also should be considered in decision-making processes, as well as in teams involved in performance processes (Grossmann, 2002). Transparent communication is especially important in steering systems, during negotiations concerning the strategic significance and conceptual framework of the cooperative effort, the venture's progress, as well as the potential for conflict, success and failure.

The conscious promotion of communication processes is relevant for interpersonal relationships as well as for the work's content with an emphasis on 'using feelings for thought', a phrase encountered in the work of Ciompi (2003), a Swiss psychiatrist. He emphasizes that emotions influence our thoughts as they add motivational notions to our perceived information and are also infectious in social life. For situations requiring clear communication, this means that listening to one's feelings and those of others and having the ability to express them—especially in "emotional situations" (negotiations, decision-making processes) that provide a realistic picture on the underlying layers of interactions.

In addition, when dealing with emotionally charged situations that are content-related (especially when personal interests are at stake), a communication style that includes openness to emotions can relieve work pressure. This is especially helpful in distinguishing which conflicts can be seen as a result of individual emotional situations and those that are part of the problem to be solved.

Emotional issues are significant in developing and managing collaborative efforts, especially when the subject of the effort concerns the participants' key businesses. Management staff represented in the cooperation can experience heavy pressure when it comes to questions like: How can our organization pursue the intended goal(s)? Which fears are raised? Which organizational changes are involved? Who will profit and who will be at a disadvantage? A win-win situation for the organization does not necessarily represent the same outcome for all the members. Substantive cooperative efforts are almost always subject to pattern reversals, such as drastic changes that may affect the normal routine and identity of the participating systems.

Open and transparent communication occurs when it is introduced as a matter of course. In this respect, the first meetings between participants have a decisive influence in the rest of the cooperative process. Communication also plays a key role in managing conflicts. How the first serious conflicts are managed allows them to become the subject of discussion without allowing them to escalate and may also shape the future conflict culture.

The first conflicts usually break out over ground rules intended to stabilize cooperative partnerships. Differences of interest, culture, and approach become apparent in the following situations: dealing with the presence of people in meetings and in working groups, defining necessary commitments and decision-making processes, and dealing with the knowledge base and transparency of information. That is why consciously forming these self-organization processes is so crucial to continued and effective work. This phase of initial conflict resolution provides the opportunity to develop appropriate forms of communication that will constructively address later serious conflicts.

Developing a foundation for trust becomes credible when communication is a defining part of collaboration's official work organization. The common practice of adjusting the level of transparency to formal or informal settings is counterproductive to good personal relationships (e.g. between top managers) that need a certain protected framework and only prove fruitful to the system when systemic trust can be established between all participants and organizations.

Repairing Breaches of Trust

Larger cooperative projects will encounter some crises of trust as they develop. Cooperative relationships only become sustainable when breaches of trust can be overcome by being rebuilt according to original conditions. Partners within the system have to re-examine the basis for the cooperation and whether mutual benefits and expectations can still be realized, whether the partners' strategic goals have changed, and if ground rules are still consistent or need revision. Finally, they must examine whether the internal organizational requirements for participating in the cooperative effort are still effective and what internal or external conditions have negatively affected the joint venture.

In practice, at least one authoritative person from each party should be willing to take the initiative to rebuild trust. Established structures should not be abandoned too hastily; organized communication processes are necessary tools for repairing the breach.

In the case of a breach of trust, it is imperative to maintain open communication between the partners involved. Care should be taken to consider participants' feelings and honour secret agreements while simultaneously examining the reasons for the breach. To prevent further breaches of trust, understanding and dealing with the core issues will help prevent future problems. Those with the greatest advantage in managing trust issues are the external consultants or functionaries who operate within each aspect of the system. They are not motivated by individual interests or serve as a member of conflicting partners. Rather, they normally give equal voice to each perspective.

The Targeted Use of External Consultants

External organizational consultants are key to the establishment and facilitation of cooperative systems. Support from the outside can be very effective in the consulting phase because cooperative projects often require a "third person" who can act as a committed advocate for all parties involved. Those who promote the cooperative engagement should be able to abandon their structuring function for the whole system and to fully assume the role of potential partner. At the same time the initial phase of a collaborative venture requires an authority responsible for shaping processes, which is capable of facilitating open and targeted reflection and negotiation processes with appropriate design and presentation skills.

Consultants can selflessly offer networks particularly effective support in initial and developmental phases with options for organizational processes linked to the overall system. They can also conduct surveys and preliminary talks with the prospective participants during the due diligence phase so the selection of partners is made easier. Since consultants do not represent individual network interests, they can more easily function as advocates for the new system and forge meaningful links between the participating organizations.

Organizational development professionals can also be hired to adopt both proven and tailored structures and methods to the cooperative system. Although the work should be carried out continuously, it is often undervalued, especially with regard to the demand for quality and need for complexity. Table 6.4 illustrates how consultants can be used in networks and collaborations.

TABLE 6.4. Where Consultants are Typically Engaged

Phase/Subject of the Cooperation	Consultancy Support (exemplary)
• Start/Constituting	Due diligence for the cooperation, division of duties, structuring of the network formation, development of ground rules, establishment of control systems, development of community partners
• Defining the goal	Development of strategy and future plans
• Transitions, difficulties, and conflicts	Dealing with demands for re-structuring, taking critical inventory, providing conflict management and mediation
• Re-dimensioning/ Re-structuring	Providing evaluations and change management processes
• Starting up work teams	Consulting to teams (also team development and coaching), providing project management

Consultants who work with cooperative efforts and networks provide more than ideas and solutions—they must also support clear communication and decision-making processes; remain impartial throughout the process; provide help for structuring and introducing the right work models, including team-work, decision-making processes, and problem solving; and offer professional help in overcoming conflicts. In order to offer answers to the special demands of 'trans-organizational development' processes (Cummings, 1984), they should be familiar with the intervention repertoire that offers loosely coupled systems the best chances for success. Examples of how OD professionals can positively impact these systems are mentioned in the following chapters.

NOTE

1. Practitioners interested in exploring these points may find helpful resources at The Community Toolbox webpage: http://ctb.ku.edu.

CHAPTER 7

ORGANIZING COOPERATIVE EFFORTS

Being Successful in Practice

Ralph Grossmann and Hubert Lobnig

In the following two chapters the discussion turns to ways in which the criteria for successful cooperative efforts can be put into practice, drawing on case studies of corporate consulting in various social fields. We have consulted and evaluated approximately twenty cooperative projects, networks, and collaborations between two or more organizations over the last ten years. We have chosen six of them for our purposes here. Chapter 7 is devoted to the detailed description of and reflection on the campaign "*Neue Medien in der Lehre*" (New Media in Teaching—NML) based on its success factors. Chapter 8 includes a more in-depth discussion of selected factors with case studies which generally reflect eleven decisive dimensions of controlling, managing and advising inter-organizational cooperative efforts.

THE CAMPAIGN: TEACHING IN NEW MEDIA (NML)

The Austrian Federal Ministry for Education, Science and Culture (bm:bwk) launched the campaign "*Neue Medien in der Lehre*" (New Media in Teach-

Facilitating Collaboration in Public Management, pages 97–124

ing—NML) in 2002 in order to give tertiary educational establishments an incentive to improve the quality of teaching methods and organizational processes in teaching with the help of new media.[1] Working with area universities and colleges,[2] the Ministry worked out a conceptual framework for the period between 2000 and 2003. Two key goals were set:

1. Improve the quality of teaching and internationalize the palette of courses offered through new multimedia and interactive possibilities.
2. Unite existing attempts at innovation and establishing forums of exchange for interdisciplinary cooperative ventures.

The Socio-political and Economic Context

When financing public services, Austrian universities and Colleges are subject to a higher level of competition due to development of the European and international education markets and growing budget pressures (Grossmann & Lobnig, 2003). To be successful in Europe and the international market, these organizations have to concentrate on cooperative efforts with the tertiary education sector and specialize in creating complimentary profiles in programs. As in other social sectors, the coexistence of competition and cooperation generally characterize these situations (Auth, 2003, p. 35).

One of the major goals of the NML campaign was to establish cooperative efforts between universities and Colleges. Ever since the Colleges were founded in Austria, they have competed with the already existing universities in the education market. This competition is intensified by different methods of student financing and recruiting (e.g. selective admission at College and open admission at universities).

Financial Incentives

Institutions were invited in two rounds to participate in 25 syndicate projects, and were financed with eleven million Euros. An additional three million Euros were invested to strategically incorporate new media in universities and colleges.

Starting Position for Cooperation

The NML campaign was launched during intense disputes between the Ministry and the universities. The source of the conflict was a legislative initiative designed to make the universities independent legal and economic corporations that resulted in compulsory radical restructuring. The project coordinators' explicit goal was to introduce a networking initiative that would build relationships and control structures between the educational institutions and the Ministry.

Creating Structures for the Campaign

To formulate goals, including two elements for organizational implementation, the department responsible for the campaign (VII/D *Studierende, Studienrecht und Förderungen)* worked together with researchers and media experts. These elements served as the network structure and included a monitoring group and a "new media panel" supported by a server project (see Figure 7.1).

It All Starts with the Network

The campaign guidelines, how the campaign works (how to participate, how funds are spent etc.) were published in a brochure in the spring of 2000 (Ecker, et al., 2000). Although a promotional brochure was developed to help launch the campaign, plans also included a gradual development of highly self-organized vital and cooperative systems. The first decision—of presumably far-reaching importance—was "where should we start?"

The monitoring group that oversaw the whole project was designed to develop strategies concerning the specification of and decisions about subsidies. One of its duties also was to encourage reflection of and impetus to the campaign's development. From an organizational development perspective it was obvious that the monitoring group should start the process of systems formation, although the Minister—as the monitoring group promoter and the subsidy allocations arbitrator—could and should have also taken the first step.

Nevertheless the NML campaign's declared goals were to mobilize the expertise of lecturers at universities and colleges and to network interested parties within the e-learning community and also relevant stakeholders on a broad scale. The campaign's success was ultimately dependent on the experts' professional dedication and the decisions made within the univer-

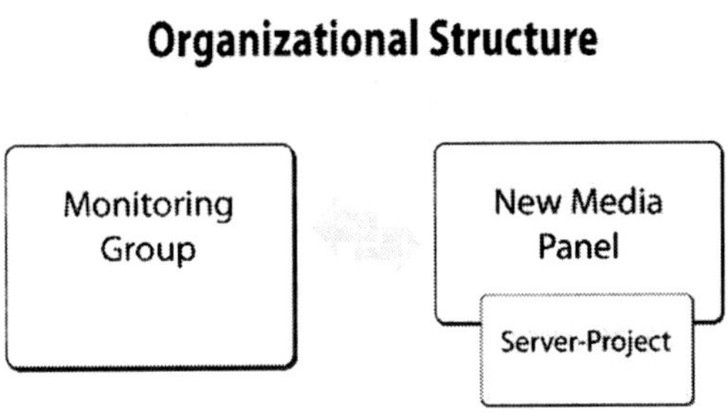

FIGURE 7.1. Organizational Form of the NML Campaign
Source: Transparency from the project management's presentation at the panel kick-off meeting.

sities and Colleges. It was expected that the experts would have problems with Ministry's hierarchical control authority (from the top down), as well as with accepting colleagues' project decisions. The "*Forum Neue Medien*" (New Medium Panel"—FNM) was to serve as the starting point for forming necessary systems as well as a sign for those involved to participate. At the same time, project coordinators and consultants intended to leverage the interests and professional expertise people committed to the project—the potential of expert businesses.

The Kick-Off Meeting as Starting Point

In mid June 2000, the Ministry invited the Austrian universities and Colleges (rectors, vice-rectors, deans etc.) to nominate representatives for a networking project. Forty-one of those active in NML joined together to form the "*Forum Neue Medien*" (New Medium Panel"—FNM) and met in June 2000 at the kick-off meeting in Vienna (Auth, 2003, p. 37; see Table 7.1). Those present had been provided with little information in advance and attended under very different circumstances. Although some attendees were sceptical, others were interested; in any case, the room was filled with energy. The agenda consisted of the *FNM* kick-off and illustrated how joint cooperative efforts can be a positive experience.

As was the case in this founding meeting, it is always exciting for researchers to experience a clearly structured and dialogue-oriented discussion since decision-making represents the core operations of organized social systems—a process that can be both satisfying and powerful. The authority to make decisions also defines social boundaries in these systems, while developing ground rules stirs participants into action and strengthens collaboration. Experiencing the acceptance of rules and decisions leads to trust-building and increase productivity within the social system.

TABLE 7.1. The Kick-off Meeting Agenda

- Introduction of the overall concept (goals and content)
- Organizational form (the relationship between FNM, monitoring group and the server project)
- Concrete routine of the day (election, candidates, server project)
- Lunchtime tasks (candidates + substitute; server project).
- Rules of the election
- Invitation for participating in the server project
- Planning the next FNM meeting (when and who will organize)
- Next steps for the campaign (monitoring group, first calls for application

The forty-one delegates present at the FNM panel were invited to nominate "their" six members to the monitoring group. Questions such as "What procedures should be followed in the process?" were few and far between. Those that were asked were quickly answered by the suggestion to develop universally accepted ground rules for the network's foundation. The consultant, who was a lawyer and a university professor in Organizational Development, helped develop and apply a simple procedure with the objective of guaranteeing the greatest amount of transparency possible:

- Participants could make recommendations for members of the monitoring group
- Those who had been recommended received the opportunity to introduce themselves and to comment on their chances as members (possibilities of filling the role)
- After a short intermediate discussion, people were allowed to recommend others not present under the condition that their approval could be obtained. Mobile phones were put to use; the people making recommendations could function in others' function. and could be questioned
- Six participants were selected by secret ballot
- A second round of nominating offered the chance to nominate three additional representatives if any of the existing representatives withdrew during the three year period of the monitoring group's work

Those chosen to participate in the panel were all highly professional and distinguished in their respective institutions. Their most important task over the next three years was to ensure the consistency between their own strategic actions as a group and the dynamic development of the Panel that would include critique, initiative, conflicts, and disputes. The kick-off meeting ended with an invitation to the first FNM business meeting in the autumn of 2000.

Defining the Organizational Principles of the Network

Due to the hard work of the key players, the campaign was up and running within six months. It was important to establish social structures and agreements that provide resolutions for a couple of reasons: it served to demonstrate the seriousness of the campaign and helped participants experience a cooperative effort that allowed the system to function seamlessly.

Although there is no "right" way to organize networks because they always have different subjects, goals and partners, successful networks usually do follow a few basic organizational principles (see Table 7.2).

TABLE 7.2. Basic Principles in Organizing Networks

- Control and work systems are differentiated and consistent with network goals. Interests of all partners are taken into account.
- Responsibilities and monitoring functions are distributed evenly among participants: no single partner should have too much influence (e.g. those with less important responsibilities or temporary functions).
- Teams whose responsibilities and processes are regulated by guidelines to carry out and manage work tasks.
- Project roles and terms of reference are attractive and to be filled with the appropriate people
- The development of a clear and transparent relationship between management and network utilizing appropriate communication and decision-making systems.
- Sensible and transparent membership rules with the possibility of differentiating rights and duties.
- Promotion of feedback and self-observation channels to provide incentive for change.

ESTABLISHING A COOPERATIVE CONTROL SYSTEM: THE MONITORING GROUP

By July 2000, the monitoring group was officially complete (see Figure 7.2). One of its main tasks was to discover the relevant aspects of developing the cooperation with the educational institutions. Beginning in 2001, the monitoring group (MG), an active task force, acted as an advisory council to the minister and was subsequently integrated into the Ministry's rules of procedure. It was also responsible for realizing the system's conceptual framework and guaranteeing the sensible distribution of funds. The responsible department within the ministry (VII/D) took charge of the group and its administration executed its recommendations.[3]

The MG and its members demonstrated to both the Ministry of Science and Culture (bm: bwk) and the educational institutions the importance of working together. Its fifteen experts for new educational media were from Austrian universities and colleges, as well as international establishments, the economic sector and the Ministry. The Panel elected six members in July 2000 (five rectors and a representative of the colleges). In addition, the Ministry nominated six outside experts including two professors from Germany, two Austrians, an economic sector representative, three associates, the project coordinator and two experts from the bm:bwk. The MG met for twelve meetings recorded by video between July 2000 and November 2003. Table 7.3 describes MG's tasks.

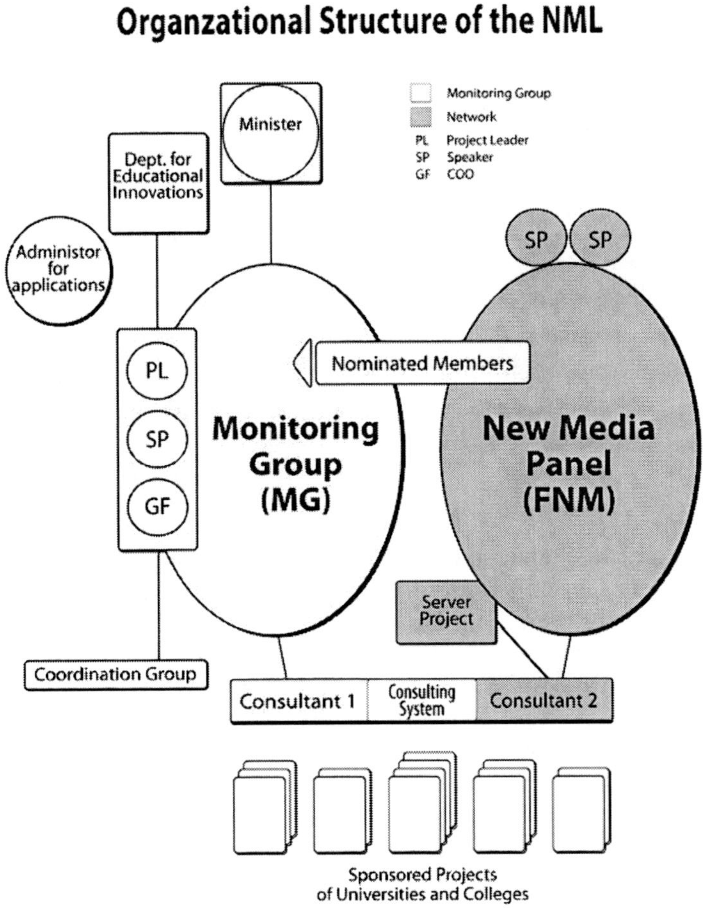

FIGURE 7.2. The Structure of the NML Campaign

Monitoring Networks

Loose coupling can have a large impact on who controls and influences networks. Because traditional forms of control—such as top-down guidelines or target agreements—are hierarchical and unproductive, they can lead to more irritation and alienation than acceptance in networked systems.

The question of responsibility, or the "personalization of control," is also problematic. Networks and collaborations usually do not have the same set of differentiated roles as do traditional organizations (e.g. supervisory

TABLE 7.3. Tasks of the Monitoring Group

- Decide on minimum standards for the development program
- Provide suggestions on task forces responsible for applications etc. within the development program
- Provide suggestions on project fund distribution with in the development program
- Begin the networking process
- Initiate cooperative efforts with partners from the provinces, municipalities, and the economic sector
- Set up an international pool of experts to develop evaluations for the program
- Publish the distribution and evaluation results
- Solve questions about network expansion
- Settle copyright questions in accordance with European standards
- Develop an activity report after three years

boards, executive management, department management) so "the network executive" is often difficult to identify. Networks also cannot be governed from the top but require monitoring from several different centres. Committees or groups commonly replace individuals, and temporary positions replace executive ones. This is why partnership must be the management concept driving networks. Network members should participate in strategic and structural processes—requiring the utmost possible dedication of all participants. Along with transparency, these conditions are absolutely indispensable for the decision-making process in networks.

In addition to the challenges mentioned above, partners' involvement in the monitoring process should never mean sacrificing clear or new incentives. Proactive individuals or groups must also lead the way, without necessarily knowing distinct areas of responsibility. In our experience, this ambiguity is often an important component in networks and other forms of cooperation, since it is often the absence of external influence that contributes to the efficiency of networks.

Because networks are highly emergent systems, they do not receive orders from any owner, promoter, or market. It is important for the leading players and committees in cooperative efforts to deal with this uncertainty in a productive and responsible manner. Dedicated trailblazers are just as important as intelligent group formation and participative decision-making. Finding the right communication process is crucial to success.

The Founding Meetings of the Monitoring Group

Although the consultant in charge went to the founding meeting of the NML monitoring group (MG) with a positive attitude, he was somewhat

TABLE 7.4. Positive and negative aspects of the MG's initial meeting:

Positive aspects

- The consultant's familiarity with the university system
- The FNM panel kick-off meeting had been very encouraging because of its results
- The monitoring groups' six members and the project coordinator from the Ministry formed an active core group that was both familiar with the goals and procedures of the campaign and willing to establish the panel.
- Trust developed between the promoter, project coordinator, and consultants as a result of these successful first steps.

Critical aspects

- Consideration of the effect of the tensions between the Ministry and the universities' cooperative effort to automate and restructure the universities.
- Consideration of how the large group of 14 people could create an appropriate social framework and handle diverse tasks in a limited timeframe.
- Concern about the limited time spent on consulting (only 3 days), contracting further consultation dependent upon success in the beginning—a procedure, which was proposed by the consultant.

critical about certain components of the meeting, which are captured in Table 7.4.

Agenda and Design

One of challenges of founding a cooperative system starts with the agenda because it presupposes certain organizational and procedural conditions—such as a quorum—which do not yet exist. As an example, the agenda of the first meeting is summarized in Table 7.5. This type of agenda also gives the "promoters" (in this case the project coordinator and her

TABLE 7.5. Agenda of the First MG Meeting

1. Welcome and campaign introduction
2. Call for quorum
3. Review and adoption of agenda
4. Constituting the monitoring group
5. Call for applications
6. Discussion of the FNM server project
7. Develop the approach to project proposals
8. Call for applications /program
9. Other business

TABLE 7.6. Rough Draft/Plan for the First MG meeting

4. The project coordinator personally introduces the goals and operating principles of the NML campaign.
1. The consultant takes over the presentation.
2. The consultant introduces himself and...
3. ... how the joint work is to be approached.
4. All members have the opportunity to familiarize themselves with their tasks and roles in the MG.
5. The members discuss possible downfalls of the monitoring group as well as any open questions concerning roles and committee identity.
6. The members establish a system of organization necessary for their large-scale program, schedule and conduct a meeting evaluation.

assistants) a sense of safety, because it uses familiar types of structures. It also was very helpful to discuss and communicate what the conditions of a successful campaign launch.

After the initial meeting, the Minister in charge formally commissioned the MG members with tasks so they understood the work parameters. In collaboration with her team the minister came up with a rough draft of the first MG meeting (see Table 7.6).

The Consultant's Position

There were a number of critical concerns that guided the consultant's role. First, it was necessary for the consultant to remain impartial in his role and to consider all participants' perspectives. This was difficult, as his support of the project would be the basis for future commissions, and the Ministry paid his consulting fees.

Second, he was obliged to facilitate result-oriented work as well as professional and strategic reflection, including the self-reflection of the monitoring group. Furthermore, he had to provide structure to the group's cooperative efforts and promote its development to ensure lasting performance.

Third, it was important to promote the group as a management system for the whole project and not the sum of individual interests. Another aspect of his work was to facilitate the development of basic rules necessary for cooperation in the MG.

The Personal Position of the Members

The consultant asked the members to share any personal feelings, hopes, fears, or experiences during the meetings. He carefully but persistently insisted on personal statements of the project in this first round and took care to limit hasty discussions on content. As a result, the group addressed many dimensions of cooperation that later proved to be vital to the joint work over the next three years. The MG members especially emphasized with the following:

- Learning and working together cooperatively and without patronization.
- Gaining experience with organizational development that may serve as an effective example of university work.
- Focusing on decision-making in order to speed up the discussion of new media in teaching.
- Abandoning particular interests and integrating periodic reflection processes into daily operation.
- Taking advantage of the initial positive experience by having the universities and Colleges first work separately and later intensify communication
- The consultants for similar German and Swiss projects are not accustomed to the main terms characterizing the Austrian campaign and were pleasantly surprised that these were based on quality improvement.
- The campaign was realized in an interesting way: the monitoring group facilitated the processes, rather than drawing on expert knowledge on which organizations base their decisions.
- Further develop new concepts on how the Ministry, universities, and Colleges can work together.

Advisory Board or Monitoring Group

The next step in the process was to have the members (divided into three subgroups) discuss what might lead to the monitoring group's failure and address any open questions concerning its role or identity. The topic that seemed most interesting to the subgroups and that was later the object of group discussion was the question of identity: Is this an advisory board or a deciding committee?

First, the group asked the project coordinator for answers: are we an advisory body with decision-making authority? Who ultimately makes the decisions? Who has influence and decision-making authority are matters to be settled before a process can be facilitated. The project coordinator explained that the MG is officially an advisory committee working with the Minister of Education since she was the one ultimately responsible for taking action. The scope of the group's influence would be largely dependent on how actively it defined its role in the preparation of decisions. She also added that: "there has not been any indication until now that the campaign's 'decisions' would not be confirmed and backed. That is also greatly dependent on how the MG members act, whether they are susceptible to external intervention, from colleagues for example."[4]

The discussion is summarized as follows:

- Although it is officially an advisory committee, the monitoring group's goal is to make suggestions that are binding both internally and externally.
- For this purpose, it will commit itself to appropriate procedures in order to be able to back up these decisions.
- The MG assumes that its recommendations will be followed when it does its job properly.
- Decisions should be backed by all members, even by those who are affected. Members who sense a conflict of interest on their part should participate in general discussions on criteria but not in the decision-making process.
- The MG may nominate a chairperson in order to have a greater outward effect.

It is important for consultants to produce summaries that reflect the group's main ideas and tenor in order to facilitate the joint decision-making process. These summaries ought to expand on positive contributions and address remaining crucial questions, such as the question of a chairperson for the MG.

Dual Leadership of the MG

It was clear that the group preferred a role-oriented chairmanship to a hierarchical one. Several models were discussed. One possibility would have been that the group select a spokesperson instead of an official chairperson to help the project coordinator and executive management prepare meetings. The settlement of this question was deferred to the next meeting.

In our experience, establishing a management committee for cooperative efforts requires a balance between certain tasks, including defining functions and roles quickly, selecting the most important topics, and avoiding rash decisions. Working together is the only way to discover necessary structures and the practicality of regulations.

Defining the Ground Rules

The question of what functions are necessary for self-organization leads directly to the question of task organization: "How should we organize our work? What burdens await us? What are the ground rules for the work and decision-making?" The time had come for the group to devote itself to the actual content of its agenda. Prior to this, it was not easy to get the group to work on questions of identity. All the members were under pressure to get their jobs done and, while some of them found this approach of investing in identity-building and self-organization useful, many were not accustomed to it.

When launching cooperative efforts, it is very common to go to one of two extremes. Many participants begin working on actual work content before the questions of identity and self-organization are settled, while others begin defining just formal structures without taking the content of their joint venture into consideration. Time management plays an especially important role here. The participants, including the project coordinator, can become nervous and lose track of what is going on. Yet a social system that wants to organize its task on a stable and accepted basis requires confidence. (The process of founding a cooperative venture spans at least two or more meetings.) That does not mean that consultants have to hide their doubts, but they should support processes—which are always weak in the beginning—with confidence and experience and try to contain implicit fears and expressed doubts.

In coordination with the consultant, the project coordinator made suggestions on possible forms of task organization, including:

- Convene the MG for day-long meetings four to six times a year.
- Coordinate the meeting dates since there are no representatives in the case of members' absence.
- Make participation by via video conference possible (although it was actually only used once).
- Prepare the orders of business by the executive board together with the chairperson.
- Send participants manuals before every meeting.
- Form subgroups to discuss and prepare suggestions about certain issues outside the monitoring group.

Order of Business: Rules of Procedure and Application

In order for the MG to be integrated into the Ministry's framework (to increase its importance), the decision was made to codify its ground rules in a concrete agenda.

Drawing on earlier experience with similar processes, some useful basic rules had been addressed in the introduction (see Table 7.7). The second MG meeting took place later in September 2000. It was arranged for the executive board to send an agenda draft to all the members and for any feedback to be given seven days before the next meeting.

Order of Business: Current Project Proposals

Toward the end of the meeting, the MG had to cover a delicate topic The project coordinator informed the committee that three projects had been submitted to the competent department between March (when the

TABLE 7.7. Ground Rules and Initial Steps

GROUND RULES

- Membership defined by commitment to NML instead of self-interest
- Garner as much attendance as possible
- Make decisions through consensus
- Maintain a high degree of transparency in members' campaign activities
- Use a high degree of confidentiality concerning cooperation
- Shared representation to the external environment

INITIAL STEPS

- The project coordinator introduces the conceptual framework necessary for rules of applications.
- The MG defines the criteria for quality and success in the distribution of funds.
- A task force made up of six members is established and commissioned to lay out the funding guidelines.
- The task force coordinator sets up a BSCW server* in order to start a discussion using multi-media support.
- The MG sets the date for when a report on preliminary results is sent to all the members.
- Members' suggestions are sent to each other one week before the next MG meeting.

*BSCW stands for "Basic Support of Cooperative Work" and is a widely-used internet forum which allows participants to share files and discuss topics.

campaign concept had been published) and June of 2000 (when the panel was founded): The discussion on this issue was intense and critical, because certain group members were affected. "If these projects are to be financed through the development program, requiring a decision by the MG, the applicants have to tender; if not, the decision should be left up to the competent department. It would be advisable to return the project proposals to the applicants and encourage them to tender according to the established criteria for this process." Even those affected showed understanding for this approach. The project coordinator also understood this reasoning and agreed to inform the applicants about the decision. As a result, the MG did not have to deal further with this order of business. The prepared proposals were not even handed out to the members in order to avoid any sort of prejudice in the tendering process later on.

That was an important step for the group's self-organization versus the Ministry because it demonstrated the group's ability to apply its own ground rules.

Consultancy Tender

At this point, the project coordinator informed the group that the author's consulting work had ended. All further consultancy services as well as the server project would have final say in decision-making. In such cases, it is important that the future consultants working with the MG and panel would not become dependent on their clients' majority decisions. It was the Ministry's responsibility to take this step in the interest of the entire campaign.

THE MONITORING GROUP: EVOLUTION TO A WORK SYSTEM

The process of organizing the MG was completed at the second meeting two months later. The MG was informed of the decision to use the consultancy on the campaign, and in spite of the summer holidays, the task forces completed their intensive preparatory work.

The first test was the debate on applications. The criteria for the quality and success of the project—as well as its organizational parameters—were discussed from various professional points of view. Finally, the necessary quorum was defined (see the following section on "Focusing on the Partners' Performance and Efficiency").

A competent task force was assigned to formulate the conclusions of the meeting. The project coordinator and consultant provided input on the basic campaign structure which was then discussed and accepted as the appropriate framework. The basic rules regulating the MG's participation in the FNM panel were agreed on.

Efforts to define the group's structure continued with a suggestion to give the head of the competent department in charge to be the monitoring group chair. A spokesperson for MG was chosen from the ranks of the MG whose job it was to prepare the group's tasks in coordination with the chairwoman and the executive board and to represent the MG externally in certain cases.

What distinguished formal legal guidelines from a real social contract in this situation are the basic rules for decision making. The quorum is defined as a simple majority with ten to fifteen members. The subgroup, in collaboration with the Minister, installed the server project. The process of structuring the campaign was now complete for the time.

Focusing on the Partners' Performance and Efficiency

In our experience, a lot of change projects can underestimate the work of decision-makers and monitors. Making decisions is work. Organizations develop based on the quality of strategic and operative control measures and the quality of decisions and decision making processes is crucial for any organization´s performance (Tichy & Bennis, 2007). According to Luhmann (1992, p. 166), organizations are social systems that are comprised of acts that "produce the decisions of which they consist." In these few words, he summarizes the central role of decision making in social systems. The best illustration of decision-making is through networks and multi-organizational cooperative efforts:

1. Both owe their existence to participatory decision-making
2. Decisions are often constructed under difficult circumstances:
   - Partners must provide consent in order to give these decisions the necessary binding character as well as a sense of security. The size of partner organizations should affect the decision-making process which both presupposes and creates trust (the paradox of trust).
   - Partners cannot revert to any established forms of decision-making (e.g. hierarchy) or well-rehearsed decision-making procedures. These first have to be developed and distinguished. That means that the partners have to have to decide on procedures before decision making can begin.
3. This paradox can only be solved in the decision-making process itself. That can be achieved:
   - by designing the decision-making process like a chain made up of many links (such as individual decision-making tasks), which result in organizing the cooperation/network step-by-step;
   - by experimenting with what would happen if various decisions were made (e.g., using a common IT tool); and
   - by working impartial external consultants who are can be helpful in introducing, recommending, and moderating the appropriate steps and procedures.
4. The chain of decisions constitutes the new social system and also cultivates its formal and strategic identity which is why the decisions also have to be tied into identity-related questions, such as: "who are we? What are we doing together? What are we not doing?"
5. Decisions are also an important part of defining organizational culture since social systems are shaped by how decisions are made as well as the results of those decisions.

The decisions made by the campaign's management (MG) are an excellent example of how important these vital operations are.

The most important part of the MG's decision-making process concerned the decisions about projects which happened in six steps and included decisions about:

- The quality of application criteria
- First screening of applications
- Which projects should be sponsored (based on two expert opinions per project)
- Further funding based on an initial status report
- Whether the tendered assignments have been fulfilled (based on a final report)
- Whether the expected results could be achieved three years after the project (sustainability check).

The MG's decisions on funding were also an important step in building the campaign's management system since they helped define its role with respect to the Ministry. The MG decided to position themselves as a group of decision-makers, rather than as an advisory board for the Ministry. They also decided to rely on external expert opinions without giving up the capacity to make final decisions as a committee. Viewed in this light, these decisions were a critical factor in developing the cooperative venture's identity and performance system (see Figure 7.3). This example illustrates why the organizational consultant had a difficult task presenting the right approach to coping with this process of setting up the rules of decision making. This stage of the effort was also crucial to maintaining the trust between the Minister, the group, and the consultant.

The group overcame these hurdles of decision making well. The reaction to the wave of community criticism following several declined projects was very differentiated, both within the group itself and toward the panel. The group had enough confidence to get involved in this process which helped to strengthen the foundation of group trust and self-confidence.

This decision-making process is described below:

- The MG was divided into four evaluation teams consisting of three people. The chairwoman (project coordinator), spokesperson, and executive manager formed their own separate team (coordinating group). Their job was to gain an overall insight into the qualities of the project applications: e.g. the top priorities and participation of the universities and Colleges as well as its financial limits.
- The coordinating group assigned each team a set of applications. Concurrently, the teams also received the appraisals of external experts in preparation for the final MG meetings where crucial decisions would be made.
- A two-stage procedure was selected according to international standards.

The four evaluation teams formed their opinions. Those applications were discussed that had not received a unanimous opinion about being

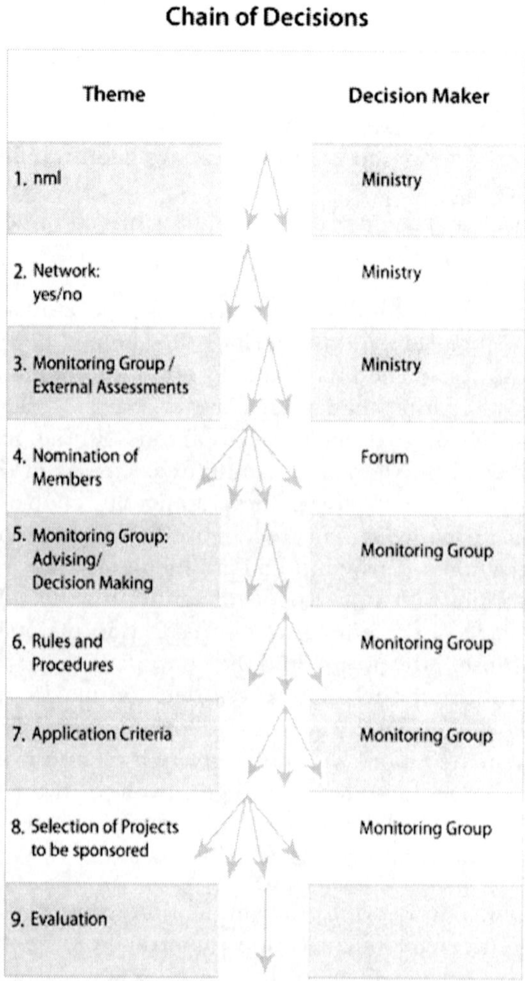

FIGURE 7.3. The Chain of Decisions in the NML Campaign

selected. The team made a decision and placed the application in one of three categories according to quality of the application. The teams then presented and substantiated their results to the entire group.

The project coordinator and spokesperson conveyed their overall impression of the various applications to the entire group. They also provided information about the requested project funding that had been positively assessed. A discussion followed concerning any possible/necessary cuts to the requested funding amount and availability of remaining funds.

The evaluation teams formed opinions about the necessary reduction of projects or how to distribute the funds. New suggestions were announced to the entire group and the content and financial aspects of the results were discussed. Official decisions about the applications were then made. Finally, the teams deliberated on various comments made about any applications in order to answer the applicants.

As part of the process, the MG presented an overview of the external assessments. They also agreed on how to incorporate them into their own decision-making process? The external experts divided the projects into three categories according to quality. The MG agreed that projects with two negative external assessments could not be accepted; while projects with two top evaluations also could not be declined.

The only exception to this process was when the MG unanimously voted against the project because the external rating did not take the circumstances specific to Austria into account, such as the sustainability of the project in Austria (all external experts were not from Austria). The assessment teams deliberated and screened formal issues, examined cost reports more closely, and ensured that the conditions made in the first step were respected. Any discrepancies between the teams and the external assessments were worked out. The teams presented and substantiate ranking results to the entire monitoring group. The MG then settled which projects had been accepted or declined.

The assessment teams were reorganized into three new ones. They made their suggestions to the entire MG about ranking and monetary distributions. After their presentations, the MG settled the question of which applications had not yet received a unanimous opinion. The monitoring group "voted" on these applications according to the predominate opinions about the applications and again discussed the results. The entire MG unanimously decided on the positive applications. The assessment teams also came to an agreement concerning the comments about the applications, especially concerning the negative votes.

Preparing the Business Case

The monitoring group and a separate panel first worked on the business case and goals and then collectively discussed them. As was already mentioned, the MG's efforts to clarify its own role as a decision-making body within the cooperative effort were a decisive step in defining its business case. The business case of the FNM stimulated the professional exchange between experts and projects and also incorporated the campaign into the organizational structures of the universities and colleges.

At the start of a cooperative effort, defining goals and the business case is an indispensable step; however, this process must also be constantly renewed during the course of the engagement.

Managing the Cooperative Effort: Running the "Net Server"

Although organizations develop through communication, organizing a cooperative venture requires an especially high level of communication as many different subgroups as members, affiliated experts and relevant stakeholders have to be regularly informed and involved in conferences, meetings, working groups e.g. In the NML campaign, this task was coordinated by the executive manager, a staff member from the project sponsoring department at the Ministry. The members of the server-project were responsible for setting up the different communication platforms and to actively carry out extensive communication work. On the executive management level, many different forms of operational and organizational logic were implemented which included the various logics of administration, of project and network management.

The coordinating group evolved in response to the campaign's development. Depending on the topics of interest, the standard line-up was later enhanced by including the spokesperson from the FNM and representatives from research teams (see Figure 7.2 for the structure of the NML Campaign).

Networks and cooperative ventures require structured and efficient management that is capable of seizing on appropriate impulses and intervening accordingly compatible with the network's structure, culture—and most importantly—its personnel. A coordination system based on these principles is an "intermediary" capable of bringing life to and motivating a network.

The Server Project as coordination centre was created as a project within the FNM. It tasks included the following:

- To structure and monitor the FNM
- To promote exchange between panel participants about relevant questions concerning the universities and Colleges
- To follow the principle of self-organization (with financial support from the Ministry)
- To ensure the panel's continuation (as a networking tool) after the end of the campaign

The project was finally entrusted by the Monitoring Group to a syndicate primarily consisting of members from research institutions in Graz (e.g., *Joanneum*, the Medical University and the University of Graz). These partners had to take their various situations and interests into account particularly when drafting cooperation contracts and creating work packages. Although not all of the partners were as closely linked with the overall project, those with a strong IT background believed their duties consisted of processing orders and expected necessary guidelines for doing so. Finally, the consultant supported the server project and the associated coordination team.

Organizational Workshops for the Server Project

Consultation began with a one-day workshop to help the Server Project team make its interests and expectations clear so it could be appropriately organized. The process began with the consultant asking the managers about their ambitions, interests, and fears concerning the project as well as what contribution they planned to make. In this way, the group was clear about their team's interests and could build a sufficient foundation to draft work packages and various subprojects.

The next step for the team was to assign tasks per contractual obligation and to nominate people and/or organizations to accomplish the tasks. In an initial workshop the consultant provided the server project with a holistic dose of advice and consultation necessary for further work.

In a workshop several weeks later, the team reflected on its progress. It also defined the project's basic rules for communication and the decision-making process. Work would be shared functionally, rather than on the previously preferred equal ranking of all members. An internal management group of three people was formed by the whole team to manage the server project. An external group that mostly operated on demand performed other functions—such as IT applications, web programming, and facilitating functions.

Tasks of the Server Project: Incorporating Management into the Technological Perspective

The server project ensured community building in the network and included the following main activities:

- Organizing the bi-annual business and delegate meetings;
- Publishing a monthly newsletter and organizing conferences on current topics; and
- Developing and running the website and project data bank.

It became evident that the members of the server project had a one-sided technical understanding of networking. Although this was useful in finding solutions to technical problems, a personal or team-related approach to communication and coordination was missing. The network was not being "lived." The various tasks involved included:

- preparing and structuring meetings;
- designing meetings as places for learning and reflection processes;
- structuring and supporting task forces; and
- developing tasks and functions within the network (e.g., conference chairpersons, workshop facilitators and commentators, team leaders)

The consultant also helped the project participants follow up on building the networked community which included introducing approaches to involve people in key activities and decision-making processes (see Table 7.8). These efforts led to a higher level of participation and provided a solid basis for commitment and responsibility in the entire network.

Over time, the server project became an important engine for the entire network. It provided the necessary organizational and technical conditions for successful inter-personal and virtual communication. It also ensured that the task forces and business meeting stayed on track, simultaneously motivating them and challenging them with results. In this manner, the network managed to keep the organizational process intact and secured the necessary level of coordination. After three years, the server project was so convincing to the network participants that it was later financed through membership fees of the new organization that followed, FNM Austria (www.fnm-austria.at).

Ensuring Comprehensive Teamwork

The introduction of teamwork in and between teams helped to promote one of the campaign's most central goals: personal, professional, and organizational cooperation. The teams were centered on certain tasks in order to set goals using various perspectives, approaches, and interests. Not only did teamwork yield results, it also led to understanding other points of view, strengthened relationships, built trust, and efficiently organized the cooperative effort.

TABLE 7.8. Central Questions in Community Building

- Which projects or activities are most suitable for fully engaging the various network groupings?
- What roles can be created for planning and execution in meetings and projects?
- How could as many people as possible be involved in decision-making (even if that meant slowing down and/or complicating the process)?
- How could project management be helpful in solving these questions? How useful is new technology?

The Development Team

The initiators, the project coordinator (including three staff members), and an external consultant collaborated to develop a basic structure, work process, and the first concrete steps for the campaign. The development team had to deal with differences such as the work and relationship between management and staff, Minister and consultant, staff and consultant, etc. The team proved itself and worked until the end of 2006 to organize and develop the campaign. This team prepared and organized all the important events under the Ministry's auspices.

Assessment Teams, Supervisory Teams and Evaluation Teams

The groups of three mentioned above, originally established for project funding, helped to form teams and managed various tasks. To date, they continue to review the sustainability of all the funded projects. The basic tasks of these three teams included:

- pre-assessing project applications for the entire monitoring group;
- explaining decisions on to project applications, especially those that had been declined;
- supervising each group of funded projects, nominating contacts from the group for the group and the project coordinator;
- evaluating preliminary and final reports, including on-site visits; and
- providing the project coordinators and other team representatives with feedback.

Projects with a Collaborative Layout

According to one of the monitoring group's decision, only collaborative projects could apply for funding from the NML. These included projects that several organizations jointly conducted. This decision contributed to motivating interdisciplinary and inter-organizational task forces and initiating cooperation between academic institutions. In particular, funding regulations resulted in a novel cooperation between universities and colleges.

External Consultants and Other Experts

Two organizational consultants supported the NML campaign over the course of three years. Both were responsible for and specialized in different areas and were independent; yet at the same time, they were aware of the others' activities. A number of other expert teams also supported the campaign. They included the applications office (responsible for all online application processing and selection), the evaluation team (responsible for the organizational development of the campaign), and research teams (responsible for special questions including a sustainability review of certain curricular programs).

The cooperation between internal and external teams was yet another aspect crucial to the campaign's development. An important financial decision (5–10% of the total budget) at the beginning of the campaign helped make possible the valuable introduction of additional knowledge and impartial perspectives.

PEOPLE AND RELATIONSHIPS

Are people and organizations a factor in preparing organizations for cooperation? From the very beginning, the initiative's promoters dedicated themselves to both promoting development in the participating organizations as well as on the project level. This contributed to sustainable results and stimulated the academic organizations to become increasingly proactive. The notion of developing both ideas and policies was even the source of tension within the initiative. Nevertheless, efforts were made to work with both sides (project vs. organization) and continuously keep in mind the link between discipline, person, and organization (Auth, 2003, p.22).

Switching back and forth between person and organization was one of the most interesting dimensions of the NML process. Because of the MG's degree of self-organization and its status, it reached a high level of organizational stability that was passed onto other systems. The MG's autonomy was strengthened because its members were selected *ad personam* by both the FNM and the Ministry, and it was not directly tied to the interests of the universities and colleges. That the universities were rather casual in the choice of their delegates created a greater amount of diversity, thereby facilitating professional peer relationships.

It is noteworthy that in many organizations, professional interest and influential positions did not necessarily go hand-in-hand. The panel continually discussed this topic which was often handled well due to the lack of centralized structures. In retrospect, the fast process of creating the project had many advantages; for instance, if the delegation's policies had been questioned too frequently in the beginning, there would have been delays and the organizations—due to their organizational culture—would have exhibited a more defensive attitude.

The fourth meeting was split between a delegate conference and a business symposium. Thanks to their position in inter-organizational networks, the delegates embodied all the tension existing between person and organization. These syndicate projects played an important role in stimulating the development and transfer of knowledge between the researchers and teachers from the participating organizations. In some cases, lasting cooperative efforts also developed between institutions (especially between universities and colleges). The repercussions of the content projects on the partner organizations varied greatly according to subject and the players' involvement. These ranged from interesting local solutions to the transformation of entire branches of study. Although precise results have not yet been determined, the combination of an open network and close cooperation proved to be efficient.

The next steps of development entail the formation of collaborations between the independent organizations (universities, colleges, and Ministry of Education) in order to jointly develop parameters and resources and could lead to further strategic projects geared toward the domestic and international educational markets.

Shaping Communication Processes

Networks and cooperative efforts usually consist of independent partners who rely on a high degree of trust to work together and accomplish goals. This form of organization is only advantageous when all partners continually work together on communication, decision-making, and reflection processes. Because networks lack the formal rules and regulations characteristic of hierarchical organizations, the communication process is a particularly important activity in networks.

To streamline communication, the monitoring group and server project implemented many different communications approaches strongly rooted in information technology and which established a prerequisite for communication. Various types of media were developed and were constantly improved through evaluative and reflective processes.

E-media

Modern technology has impacted communication for network initiatives so those networks can communicate regardless of time and place. To a certain degree, it also simplifies the transfer of comprehensive information and even interaction within and between networks. However, technical support also must be employed realistically. One of the greatest downfalls within networks is when information is exchanged without being processed by all participants, potentially leading to serious misunderstandings.

In this server project, a website was developed with a homepage that provided an overview of the various research and development projects on e-learning, provides, as well as information about workshops and conferences, and the structure, organization, and history of the NM initiative. A monthly e-newsletter was also distributed which provided an individual and institutional account of the initiative's activities. More people are being invited to help author newsletter, which increases its content and stimulates more lively discussion.

Processing Communication

During the founding stages of the initiative, business meetings were held twice a year. They offered the university and *Colleges* delegates an opportunity to work on e-learning questions of e-learning and the use of new media in teaching.

Design Teams for Conference Planning

Following the real time strategic change (RTSC) model, a method that employs large groups in situations of strategic change (see Jacobs & McKeown, 2007), the consultants developed creative ideas on the composition of design teams, described as a microcosm representing all the different network members. Their job has been to plan events thematically, and to design and organize conferences with a high level of participation and involvement.

The design teams consisted of a couple of representatives from the server project (project management), the Ministry of Education (financer), the local host, panel delegates, and of further experts. A consultant supported the teams during the first few conferences.[5]

CONCLUDING THOUGHTS

The campaign New Media in Higher Education (NML) succeeded in establishing the collaboration as a new social system with own identity, creating benefits for all partners involved. Many of the outcomes associated with the project were deemed to be significant. The network, for examples, continues to successfully function. At the end of the Ministry's initiative in 2003, the NML Network was renamed the Forum New Media (FNM) and re-launched as an independent organization run by the members of the network and supporting universities. Members include 250 researchers and teaching staff representing all Austrian universities. FNM also offers conferences (business meetings), a content pool, newsletters, Internet forums, and public relations. Another successful outcome is that the steering committee continued to function, both in subgroups for the evaluation process and as a whole, in a consultative role with the Ministry and partner universities, focusing on strategic issues.

In terms of specific results, 24 of the 25 projects were fully completed. The evaluation process included open dialogue and feedback between the steering committee (also jury members), project leaders, and contractors. The sustainability check for the projects was prepared and implemented 3 years after the contract was completed.

Reflecting back on the project, there are a number of learnings for consultants. The ideal of "co-opetition" holds significant promise. Within this context, transorganizational development can be stimulating and innovative—it appears to be the foundation for the business and market of the future, enabling companies and consultants to more effectively deal with new organizational forms.

In terms of the consulting process itself, it is critical that client organizations put aside money for the development of the collaborating system. As a rule of thumb, if such resources are not dedicated to the project, it is better to walk away from the contract. Such financial commitment is a crucial reflection of commitment. At the same time, it is important not to "over consult," even if the client is willing to pay for it. In essence, "over consulting" translates into avoidance of collaboration—and this balance is even more relevant in transorganizational consulting (for example, our consulting for the entire NML project over more than three years included two consultants and 75 paid days).

We also need a clear theoretical and experience-based concept of the dynamics and success criteria in collaboration, especially when more than two partners are involved. Consultants are faced with the daunting task of facilitating a balance between collaboration and competition, raising awareness and assisting managers in handling the underlying paradox. It is important to identify with the idea of a collaborative system, especially in the beginning, consultants generally represent the collaboration, and it is important to resist partner attempts potential to corrupt these roles. An underlying goal of transorganizational development is to capture an appropriate balance between the speed of the process, level of focus on concrete collaborative work, and reflection—even more than in internal OD work.

Finally, the reflective process itself plays an important role, getting participants to draw on their experiences and think deeply about their actions. We have found that top management, steering committees, and teams in the business process need much more time for reflection than they typically envision. The collaborative system plays out on a relatively virtual level and its long-term success is shaped by and the result of ongoing reflective processes.

NOTES

1. The authors were involved in this venture as subject matter experts (researchers and consultants) for three and a half years.
2. In Austria, each college *(Fachhochschule)* specializes in a particular field (e.g., economics, technology or arts).
3. The team from the Ministry of Education was made up of Mag. Andrea Ecker, (department head and project coordinator), Mag. Andrea Weilguny (manager), Dr. Felicitas Pflichter (expert) and Alexandra Auth (administrative assistant).
4. All quotations are based on the author's notes, which have been compared with the record of proceedings.

5. For further detail on the combination of personal and electronic communication in the initiative, see Ecker & Grossman (2001, pp. 14–16).

CHAPTER 8

INSIGHTS FROM THE CONSULTING EXPERIENCE

Reflecting on Other Case Work

Hubert Lobnig and Ralph Grossmann

The chapter draws on case studies drawn from our consulting practice as a way to further illustrate the dynamics underlying the creation, implementation, and institutionalization of networks and collaborative initiatives. These cases were selected to highlight specific and diverse challenges involved in facilitating and organizing networks and collaborations. This broad array of network organizations include workplace health promotion, improving cross-organizational processes in the provision of health care services, increasing personal capabilities to network across organizational boundaries in financial industries, strategy making in a facility management network, and steering a collaborative venture in patient oriented quality measurement in a group of regional hospitals. The case studies offer insights into very practical aspects of facilitating and steering collaborative processes, involving interorganizational groups and teamwork, decision making in interorganizational settings, elaborating designs for workshops, defining rules for the cooperation, and altering individual's capabilities to collabo-

Facilitating Collaboration in Public Management, pages 125–155

rate. The cases were selected because each of them has an interesting story to tell and—even after a relatively long period of time—still has a sustainable impact on the organizations and the individuals involved.

THE CONSTITUTION OF A NETWORK AS AN INDEPENDENT SOCIAL SYSTEM: THE VIENNESE NETWORK FOR WORKPLACE HEALTH PROMOTION

Workplace health promotion is a topic that has received increasing attention in Austria since the 1990s. This heightened interest is reflected in laws that oblige insurance companies to finance health promotion activities in companies. Although health promotion was only tested in sporadically in the 1990s, a variety of large businesses support such projects today. Because subsidization has become increasingly differentiated (e.g., EU programs), individual organizations and social insurance agencies have found it increasingly difficult to recognize and take advantage of the potential for workplace health promotion.

The most important regional financer of workplace health promotions—the Health Insurance Vienna Region (*Wiener Gebietskrankenkasse*, WGKK)—decided to set up a network involving all the insurance agencies and regional social partners in Vienna. In order to be successful, the WGKK decided that the network would have to assume the form of a collaborative effort. The most effective way for the partners to identify with and support the network would be to involve them in the process of defining goals and structures. WGKK decided to ask an OD consultant with experience in the field of health care and collaboration to support the network's set up.

Invitation to Participate (July–August)

In a letter to eleven leaders of health care insurances and social partners in Vienna, the WGKK informed them about the project and invited them to participate in its launch. The first step was to have these organizations nominate their delegates to represent each institution in the network so it could grow and prosper. Some of the invited organizations' nominated delegates were skilled decision-makers from upper-management with little involvement in operative details, while others were specialists in health promotion or administrative officers who required a strong reference to their home organizations to make decisions.

Interviews with Representatives (September–October)

After nomination procedures were finished, the consultant walked out and visited decision makers, key persons and the nominated delegates from each participating organization. The visits included advice on how to internally organize their delegation in the network and to prepare for the coming collaborative work. They further included interviews to identify the institutions' internal aims, targets, potentials and resources upon entering the network. And, thirdly, the delegates' roles were discussed and they were prepared to properly represent their organization. The interviews made it possible for the consultant to:

- understand the players' interests;
- optimize their representation in the network;
- familiarize the delegates with the network organizing plan;
- prepare a diagnose on preconditions and specific challenges the collaborative ventures faces at the start as feedback for the partners; and
- properly develop a workshop design for the kick-off workshop.

The First Workshop (October)

Approximately 20 delegates from all eleven organizations took part in the first workshop in October, 2006 acting as the core group for the network. Their task was to develop the basic strategic guidelines for building the network. The agenda for the workshop is summarized in Table 8.1.

As the delegates came together for the first time, the workshop aimed at focusing the strategies and motives for workplace health promotion of each of the participating organizations as well as for the collaborative venture as a network. The guiding principle for the agenda and the design of the kick-off workshop focused on the individualism of the invited organizations and the need to produce something innovative as an attractive business case for the start of the network.

Reporting Results

In the next phase of the network development, the delegates reported back to their home organizations while the two task forces more deeply elaborated a paper on visions and goals and a concept for the organizational design of the network to be discussed at the second workshop. Both task forces agreed that the results would be circulated before the end of the year so that first reflections and feedbacks of the home-organizations could be brought into the second workshop.

At this stage, the project coordinator was involved in both task forces and helped them to draw up a "position paper" which outlined both the network's topic and the organizational design.

The Second Workshop (January)

The partner organizations provided feedback on the concepts in the second workshop and collaboratively completed the position paper. As main elements of the organizational design a steering group ("cooperative

TABLE 8-1. The First Workshop of the Viennese Network for Workplace Health Promotion: Agenda

Time	Contents
9:00	Welcome and opening I. Presentation of interests and concerns The coordinator divided the delegates into groups of four and asked them to describe their primary interests concerning the network and to formulate questions and comments for the workshop
10:00	II. Introductions of the participating organizations Each organization was asked to prepare a flip chart with the following contents: • Name of the organization • The importance of participating in the Viennese network • Which abilities, resources, and contributions should be offered to the network? • Who will represent the network (and a short introduction including profession, function, experience)
11:00	Break
11:20	III. Consultant's presentation: "Results of the interviews and their evaluation based on the criteria for successful networks" Three groups formed according to the "maximum mix principle". Their task was to diagnose the context for starting the network based on the following questions: • What is surprising about what was reported by the organizations? • What strengths and resources have become available to the network? • What obstacles can be expected? Results were documented on flip charts by each group and then presented and discussed.
12:30	Lunch
13:30	IV. Consultant's input: the critical points of starting cooperative ventures and networks. The following questions were discussed in two mixed groups: • What is the name of the network? • What exactly was meant by "workplace health promotion"? • What would be the network's main goals? • In two years, how could we measure the network's success?
14:45	Break
15:00	Presentation of the flip charts and discussion
15:30	V. Consultant's input: what are the criteria by which the partners could effectively work together in the network? • The management level (monitoring group, core group, etc.) • The coordination level (network server) • Commitment to the network's development (task forces) • Professional expertise (expert groups) • Observers
16:00	VI. Outlook for the next phase "Homework" on further requirements and agenda for the second workshop included two task forces that would include: • The definition of visions and goals • Ideas for network structure and work methods • Closing discussion of results and examples of the network
16:45	End of the workshop

conference") and a more operative management committee ("operative panel") were set up and their members were nominated and elected. Finally this workshop ended with a draft outline of the action plan for 2007, drafted by the management committee and approved by the steering group on-line at the end of the workshop. The agenda is summarized in Table 8.2.

This project utilized processes that seriously considered the individual partners' perspectives on the involvement in a collaborative venture. All parties involved recognized that the initial phase of interviews and feedback to the home organizations was invaluable because they focused on both, the well of the network and at the same time on each organization's specific interests. Following this principle, the initial phase helped the participating organizations to balance their own interests and the requirements for a successful network development as the transorganizational system. In further development, the network performed a high level of joint activities. These included setting up the core groups in the initial phase which robustly fostered the network's capability to successfully proceed.

TABLE 8.2. Agenda for the 2nd Workshop of the Viennese Network for Workplace Health Promotion

Time	Contents
9:00	Welcome
	I. Organizational reports (recorded on a flip chart) • Participating organizations receive the first workshop's results • Discussion of what transpired between the first and second sessions • The criteria/results necessary for a satisfaction • If appropriate, the introduction of new delegates
10:00	II. Completion of the position paper The delegates were divided into four groups made up of two to three organizations. The groups read and evaluated the position paper. People color-coded their responses as: • Red: not admissible, changes were necessary. • Orange: attention to potential problems and need for discussion • Green: explicit agreement Following the exercises, the facilitator asked the groups to post their evaluations on an enlarged copy of the position paper that hung on the wall. This visual aid clearly illustrated the need for improvement. The consultant reviewed each of the chapters with the delegates and immediately made changes on the computer.
13:00	Lunch
14:00	III. Filling key positions and nominating delegates for the committees Based on the suggestions made in the position paper, the entire group of delegates selected members for the "cooperative conference" as the partners' strategic panel. The following procedure was adopted: • Each organization could nominate a total of two members • The members could provide a short explanation for their motivations • The entire group of delegates selected the candidates

(continued)

TABLE 8.2. Continued

Time	Contents
	The delegates wrote in and voted on their nominations. Since the results were similar to the ones made by the preparatory group, there were few surprises. The next phase of committee selection was for "cooperative conference" members to select the "operative panel" – the group responsible for running the network. They adopted more selective procedures for this committee: the five organizations were selected that had dealt with the topic most thoroughly. In order to guarantee a continuing working process no deputies were nominated as personal commitment and continuity was seen essential. Break
15:30	IV. Determining internal projects and responsible teams At this point, The partners defined the next steps according to a simple task-organization mode based on: 1) tasks to be completed, 2) who should be responsible for the work, and 3) the timeframe for the work to be completed. They defined the most important topics which were carried out uniformly, including: • Drawing up procedural rules for the cooperative conference and the operative panel • Developing a public relations strategy and campaign • Developing a logo and design used to implement as part of the PR campaign • Adopting and formalizing the position paper. • Drawing up a work schedule through May/June of 2008.
16:15	V. Concluding round of discussions Questions answered during the closing round of discussions included: What have we learned from the process to date? What is important to us for further development?

FOCUSING ON PARTNER PERFORMANCE AND EFFICIENCY: THE MEDTOGETHER PROJECT

The goal of the project MedTogether was to optimize the cooperative effort between hospitals and regional health services in Austria in a pilot project. In order to be able to launch concrete cooperative projects, ten groups of diagnoses were selected (e.g., heart attack, implantation of hip joint protheses, psychiatric diseases), which seemed to represent relevant cases where cross-organizational cooperation is essential for treatment and /or recovery.

By means of calls for applications and the project coordinator's "on the road" presentations, hospitals and their regional cooperative partners were informed and invited to participate. Ultimately, sixteen hospitals and regional partners with different foci from all parts of Austria participated and formed cross-organizational teams (regional task forces) to improve trans-organizational patient treatment processes. Prior participation in regional cooperative ventures between hospitals and other health services was a prerequisite of project admission.

Project Structure

Regional task forces who were closely linked to participating hospitals' departments were the centers of on-site project activity. The groups consisted of hospital's staff members and representatives of their partner institutions involved in the admission and dismissal of patients. The project managers, department heads, and the decision-makers of hospital-external partners developed the mission to be implemented. They also had to nominate regional project coordinators.

The structure of the regional task forces is presented in Figure 8.1. The responsibilities of these task forces included:

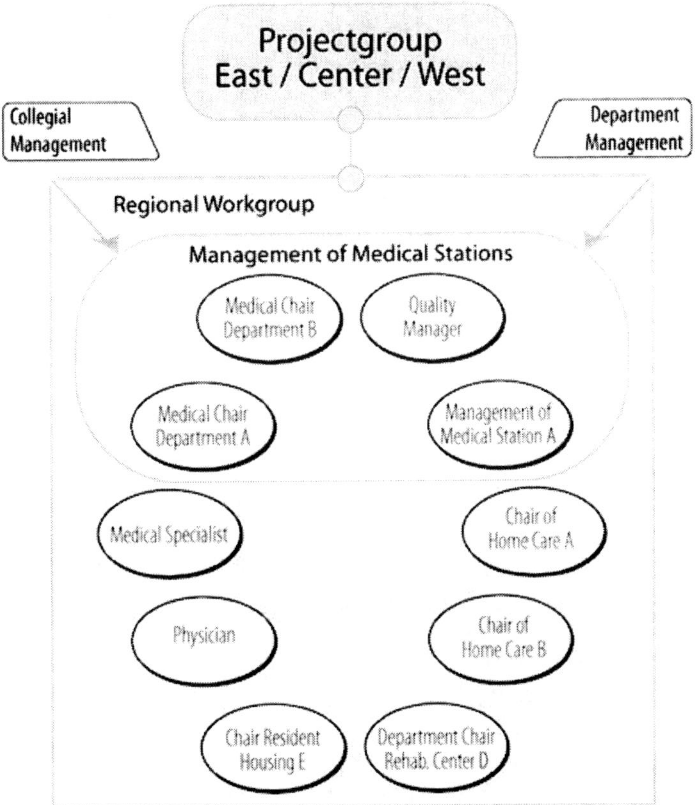

Figure 8.1. Structure of the Regional Task Forces
Source: The diagram is from a presentation on "Interface Management between Ambulatory and Inpatient Care" by Eva Maria Baumer, Heinz Ebner, Michael Haas, and Hubert Lobnig (November 2002).

- evaluating previous cooperative efforts;
- analyzing processes and procedures (within the organizations and particularly between them);
- comparing the data from benchmarking surveys (and other studies) with the on-site results;
- innovating and optimizing processes within and between organizations as well as evaluating them; and
- introducing the questions and results of the regional project to the cluster workshops and to conferences where all participants and experts were invited.

The sixteen regional task forces planned and implemented the project on the regional level. Given the fact that they addressed different diagnostic groups, they were not uniquely set up as they needed different institutions and professional services to partner with.

The participating regional task forces were assembled into three cluster groups according to geographical criteria (west, middle/south, north/east). Each regional task force sent the project coordinator and additional two to three members to participate in the cluster groups. During the course of the project, the cluster groups met for a total of six two-day workshops. Each meeting was hosted by one of the regional task forces that offered on-site project reviews.

In the workshops of the cluster groups, the delegates received technical assistance, as well as counselling and training to optimize the work of the regional cooperation projects. As the delegates represented the regional projects, they had to transfer their learnings and the advice from consultants and peers in their own regional task force activities and to implement enhancement measures on site.

For this reason, the workshops were largely devoted to training, adapting tools and models, and coaching the project coordinators on implementation strategies. Two consultants assisted at the workshops, where the following priorities characterized the agenda:

- The consultants provided input and training on issues like process management, change management and collaboration between organizations
- The consultant's team presented the data from conducted surveys in order to carry out benchmarking processes,
- The delegates from the regional task forces received coaching to steer and improve onsite project activities
- The delegates together provided mutual support, learning, and feedback in specific settings dedicated to peer group exchange.

Setting up Regional Task Forces and the Creation of Work Units

Although the regional task forces proved to be a good basis for participation of the major partners in the regional health care provision, in retrospect, the groups seemed to function very differently and with different success. With this dynamic, the project initially provided the regional task forces with various models and tools so they could properly function. The tools included checklists for teamwork, role modelling, and planning tools for project management. The cluster group workshops then became the forum for the development of regional projects.

In the first workshop of the cluster groups, participants provided a structural outline of their regional task forces and received a set of questions to assess their current state of development (see Table 8.3).

The participants' presented the answers to these questions to the entire group. Feedback was requested after every presentation, and included the following questions:

- What has been done well?
- What difficulties have been noticed?
- How could the project group solve problems and overcome the challenges? Who could do what?

TABLE 8.3. Assessing the State of Development: Key Questions

1. To date, what has been accomplished in our region?
2. Describe the current project structure of the regional task force (and it´s environment) by drawing an organizational chart. Are all the important players involved? Who is missing?
3. What is your own role in this project? (e.g., project coordinator, facilitator, promotion representative, task force member, etc.) What difficulties have you experienced in your role so far?
4. Describe the communication processes in the initial stage. Have you held discussions about purpose and goals? Have you openly addressed questions or problems the project is facing? Have there been information or communication deficits, and if so, do they continue to exist? How has discussion evolved?
5. What are the driving and the restraining forces in order to reach a good outcome? (Please draw a diagram)
6. Who will be most important in backing the project? Which external factors and parameters of the context have had positive effects?
7. Has there been resistance or opposition? How did resistance or conflicts be manifested, examined or resolved?
8. In conclusion, what is the most serious unanswered challenge or unsolved problem concerning the project's future success?

The ensuing discussion helped the representatives of the regional task forces to better organize and stabilize task structures and as well as to define areas of responsibility within regional working processes. The regional projects that profited most, however, were those whose main delegates already had some experience in project and quality management. Where experiences in these fields were lacking, participants tried to muddle through the complex world of inter-organizational projects. Consequently, some delegates were unable to apply the advice and knowledge they received in coaching settings to regional communication and decision-making procedures.

Optimizing Processes Beyond the Single Organization

Soon after the working structures were established on regional levels, the project elaborated inter-organizational processes applying a conceptual model where the client (customer) is seen as the central focus for the process design. The project consequently took a patient-oriented perspective instead of focusing the given operations of the institutions involved. For instance, depending on illness and diagnosis, patients have different histories which include aspects such as a first treatment (doctor, ambulance), admission to a hospital, diagnosis and treatment of the inpatient, dismissal, etc. The job of the regional task forces, therefore, was to carry out inter-organizational process analyses and to enhance these processes based on the methods introduced in the workshops. The basic concepts and of the inter-organizational processes in each region were developed with the first few workshops.

The First Workshop

In the first workshop, the consultants provided the delegates with input on the "basics of process management" (see Table 8.4) and a generic flowchart (Figure 8.2) that were discussed within the group.

Participants processed the conceptual models in parallel working groups. In order to apply those models on a case, the participants were first asked to choose one of the regional task forces as a practice case and to develop a rough normative process model:

- What organizations are involved? Who is taking part in the process?
- How can the basic elements of the flowchart be described?

The results of each working group were shared and reflected with the entire cluster group. With that experience in mind, through peer coaching, delegates reflected how to implement the process management approach in their own regional working settings. At the end of the meeting, delegates

TABLE 8.4. The Basics of Process Management: Steps in Process Analysis

1. Define the problem (or defining what needs to be optimized)
2. Identify the most important processes
3. Define the beginning and end of the process
4. Identify the most important steps
5. Provide a rough depiction of the 6–10 most important steps in the processes
6. Identifying and weighting problem areas based on their effects
7. Continue to work on the most important problem areas.
    - Depict the process more in detail
    - Depict the sub process and doing steps 1–6
8. Developing the normative process

Source: The table was drawn up by Heinz Ebner and was used by the participants in the cluster group workshops.

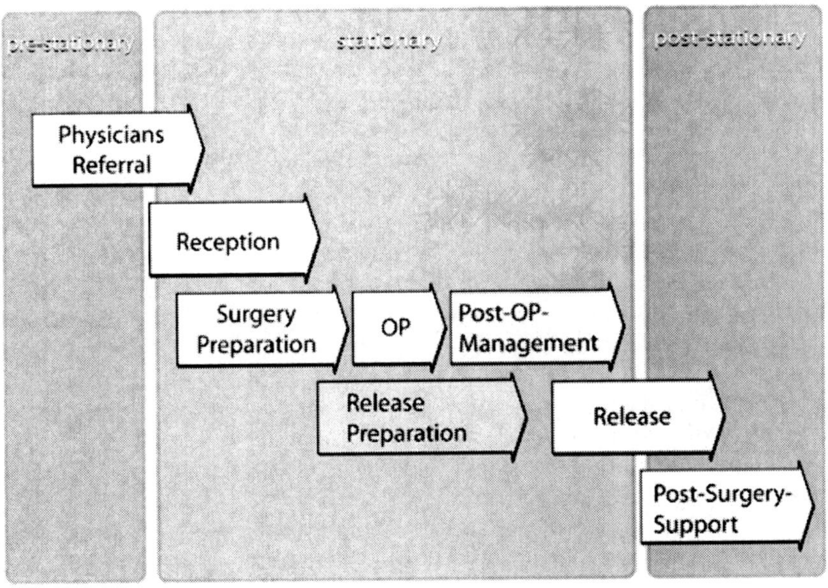

FIGURE 8.2. Generic Flow Chart Depicting the Processes of Patient Care and Treatment

were asked to create flowcharts and by the next workshop, develop a first normative process model in the regional groups.

The Second Workshop

In the second workshop (two months later), the participants finished their flowcharts (and diagrams of the project structure) and posted them on a wall termed the "gallery." After a quick survey of the gallery, each regional group was assigned the task of analyzing another flowchart and providing feedback to the other participants. Further methods were introduced—such as the difference between normative and actual processes and the process map—so participants could practice these methods and later implement them regionally.

The Third Workshop

Three months later, the third workshop of the cluster groups took place. The delegates of the regional task forces presented various detailed processes in the "gallery," including normative processes, actual processes, and the process map. As the quality and the completion of the work varied considerably between the groups, the consultants' team decided to provide beforehand detailed feedback and individualized instructions for improving the local normative inter-organizational processes. This allowed the regional task forces the opportunity to adapt their work and to integrate the consultant's instructions prior to attending the workshop.

This workshop began with mutual coaching on the draft normative process concepts which took place in groups of two regional task forces and were based on the following questions:

- Had we carried out the instructions well and did we make use of the feedback?
- How were they reflected in the results?
- Did the group have any other suggestions, indications, or criticisms to the normative process models?
- Has the normative process been sufficiently defined in order to start the actual improvement process?

If the assessment indicated that less than 80 percent of those involved were favorable, discussion focused on necessary actions and steps that should be taken before the actual process improvement or implementation would start.

With the normative inter-organizational processes defined, the regional task forces completed the first job. The next task was to implement the normative processes in the context of the given inter-organizational environments. To do this, the task forces identified a concrete need for change which varied between the regional task forces. As change management skills were indispensable, at this point the consultant's team provided inputs on instruments for change and set the stage for widely applied peer coaching in the cluster groups' workshops.

What was learned from this project? Drawing on our consultancy experience, discussions and interviews with project coordinators and promoters a number of lessons emerge. Besides professional process management (diagnosis, developing the normative process, planning of concrete measures), specific management functions had to be set. The local project coordinator acted as a mentor for the new normative processes within his or her home organization as well as the partnering organizations.

The integration of the normative process models into the existing organizational structure in and between the organizations was crucial to success. However, lack of buy-in from leading management can lead to meagre results. With this project, the coordinators often lacked the necessary energy for overcoming hierarchical conflicts. At the end of the project, the consultants were criticized for not having offered enough support on local level—specifically working with the management of the partnering organizations.

Ultimately, local project coordinators were under much pressure to clear obstacles, including competition between organizations for the home treatment of patients and attempts to convince family practitioners and other "small or one person units" in the regional health care environment to participate in regional task forces.

Numerous communication efforts became necessary to be addressed repeatedly for all partner organizations involved:

- The case for action: why can't we continue with the existing processes?
- What is the benefit (economic, work-load, quality...) of the new process to patients, staff, and the partner institutions?

In all cases, "upward communication" was extremely important so decision-makers could empathize with the problems and obstacles on the project level. This sort of communication was also the basis for open talks with superiors and other important key players who had "obstructed" certain matters.

Finally, as the project also focused on learning and qualification to improve local inter-organizational projects, some people were not always willing to participate in learning settings. Learning from results ("learning loops") can help develop one's personal skills and contribute to a higher level of quality in the cooperative effort, when there is openness to feedback. One of the best ways to strengthen new processes has been to invest in the coaching settings and in further training of those key players who are on the forefront of change (project coordinators, head nurses and heads of medical working teams).

THE IMPORTANCE OF RELATIONSHIPS ON THE ROAD TO NETWORKING: THE CASE OF BANK AUSTRIA UNICREDITGROUP

We assume that members of organizations face new challenges and disagreements when their organizations are interested in external cooperative ventures or want to optimize their internal cooperation structures between different units. In this case, it is important to be especially mindful of network-building skills (versus communication or leadership skills) when existing structures are ineffective, become volatile or serve as the basis for new cooperative efforts.

This case presents a qualification project of a large Austrian bank whose goal was to equip sales personnel and internal specialists (those involved with risk management, law) with the appropriate interpersonal skills for cooperation and networking. The training's conceptual framework reflects current trends in the financial service sector as well as the company's organizational structure and culture. When we started, current trends in the financial service sector provided a driving force for setting up and improving networks in the sales force (see Table 8.5). However recent financial crisis may have added some challenges, especially the need for cross-departmental collaboration as peer principles and second opinion models.

For the reasons mentioned above the company members were able to build, foster, and benefit from the internal and external cooperative efforts and networks necessary for success. Although successful networking is generally based on an individual's communication skills, attitude and behaviour, it also requires the ability to plan strategically, detect collaboration possibilities and the ability to use these skills in many ways (see Table 8.6)

People who want to increase their social capital through networking must understand that building successful relations does not happen au-

TABLE 8.5. Current Trends in the Financial Service Sector

- Product portfolios have become increasingly complex and short-lived.
- Counseling has become more intensive in the case of large and complex funding or assessment.
- A strategic classification of customers has led to organizational specialization in sales and marketing.
- Though necessary internal processes may be defined, efficiency is largely dependent on the partners' knowledge and connections.
- New interfaces with external partners and even competitors are developing.
- Comprehensive changes in organizations cause instability in existing networks so new ones have to be established.

TABLE 8.6. The Social Skills Necessary for Networkers

- Strategically planning one's activities
- Supporting the project and taking responsibility for results
- Being open and sensitive in communication with "distant" partners
- Managing cooperation and competition in relationships
- Accepting disagreements, uncertainties and ambiguities
- Finding and bridging undefined positions and "wholes" in responsibilities
- Negotiation and conflict management skills

tomatically. One should make a personal investment that is based on the following four steps:

- planning strategically and assessing the existing network;
- building new relationships;
- cultivating existing relationships; and
- analyzing and reassessing the network.

As the qualification project was thematically innovative, the HR management and the sales management team of the bank asked for a detailed concept to be presented beforehand as well as a pilot program. The consultant helped to develop a seminar design where the thematic models and inputs were given in two workshop days. A one day follow up workshop focused on practical help for implementation using hands on advice and peer coaching (see Table 8.7).

The first day began with a general presentation of the network concept and the importance of interpersonal relations in collaborative ventures. After introducing the concept of networking in the sale process, participants drew up a network chart that illustrated existing partners, their contribu-

TABLE 8.7. Seminar Topics

Day 1	Day 2	Follow-Up
Introduction: What are networks? How do they work? What role do they play in sales and customer services	How do network relationships work? Assess the relations of participant's networks.	Reports from practice; resolving difficulties in everyday networking.
Strategically examine the network and its structure; first assessment of participants networks.	Personal networking behaviors; developing custom-made measures for enhancing existing networks.	Increasing network efficiency; approaches on securing sustainable networking efforts.

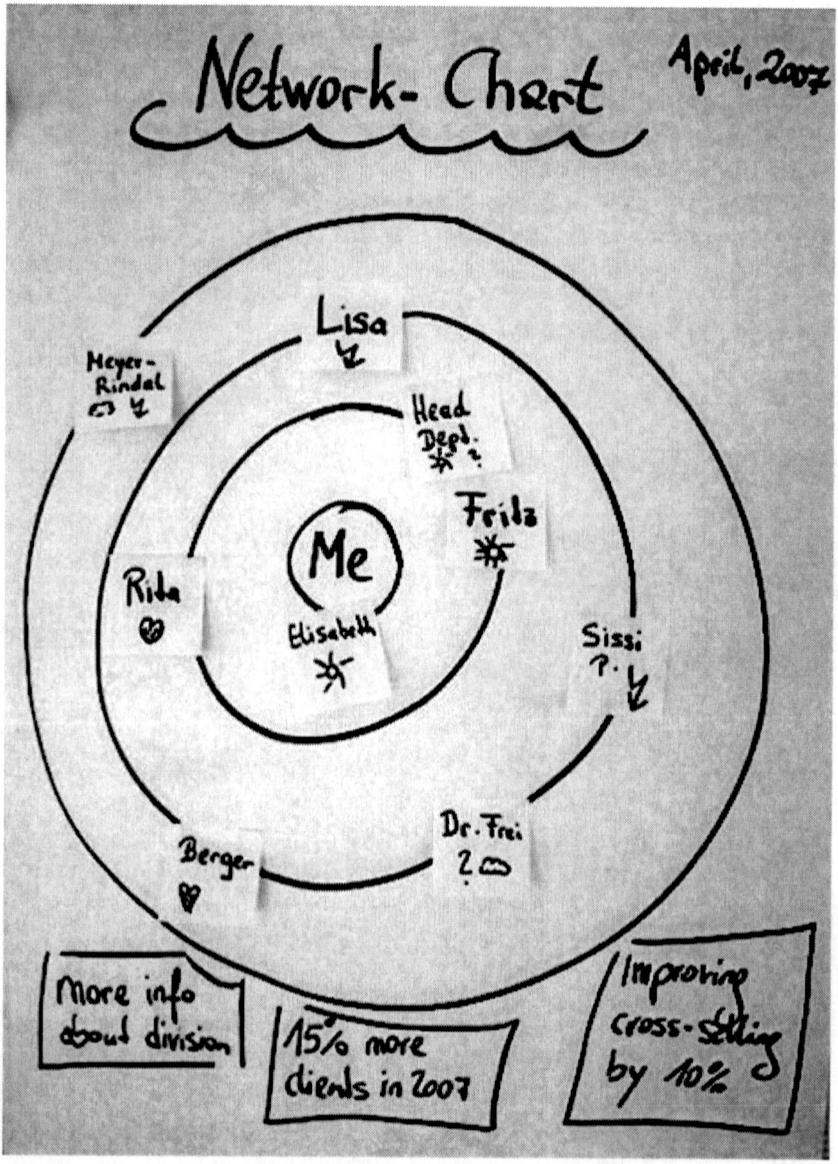

FIGURE 8.3. Example of a Network Chart
Key: In the center of the figure is the individual (my network), whereas the outer circles are in ordered in declining order. The greater the distance from the center, the less important that particular person is seen in potential for business success. Partners on the Post-It Notes are also assessed in their relationship to me (using symbols for critical, neutral, very positive). On the bottom of the chart, the strategic aims of "my network" are posted.

tions to business success, an evaluation of the relationships, and the need for further development.

Over the next sessions participants elaborated on the networks charts (see Figure 8.3), applying thoughts and instruments on the following issues: assessing business values of interpersonal relations, diagnosis of strengths and weaknesses of those relations, behavioral elements of networking, examination of one's own networking behavior, building a networking strategy, and planning action steps.

The follow-up session took place after seven to eight weeks where the participants discussed the implementation stage and worked with the trainers and peers on concrete improvement measures. Methods included peer coaching settings, counseling by trainers and ad hoc lectures when necessary. During these sessions, it became evident that the networks functioned very differently from the specific reason for which they were developed. However, individuals faced similar tasks in strategic planning and building relationships where networks had to set up or to be restructured. For the participants it was interesting to more intensively, with other networks as

FIGURE 8-4. Self-reflection on Networking

	–3	–2	–1	0	1	2	3	
I prefer clear guidelines (roles, tasks, rules).								I am flexible as far as guidelines go.
I can live with changing coalitions.								I tend to be jealous.
It makes me happy and inspires me when others are successful.								I am motivated by my own success.
I am geared to my own ideas.								I prefer to build on the ideas of others.
I like to approach people actively.								I find it difficult to approach people.
I gain trust quickly.								I am somewhat reserved when it comes to trust.
I am flexible when it comes to organizing.								I prefer to hold on to traditional organizing methods.
I am open to the cultures and terms of others.								The particularities of my cooperation partners bother me.
I have a strategic, long-term approach to collaboration.								I am geared to short-term benefits in collaboration.

Source: Developed by Ralph Grossmann and Hubert Lobnig for the elective seminar on "Cooperation between Organizations: Developing and Monitoring Organizational Networks." The course is offered in the iff Master of Science in Organization Development program.

it led to critical self-reflection of personal approaches and preferences. In many cases, however, more operational advice was provided in sharing networks. Suggestions were made such as: "I know someone who can help you. Mention my name if you contact him."

A number of challenges also arose during the course of the seminar. Network analysis offered deeper insights to the change processes the company was in as it became obvious that the networks were eroded and existing relations were captured through massive reorganizations. In the seminar, those insights also impacted participants' emotions in relation to those change processes. Some improved when they received a model on how to rebuild their relations and set up networks, while others remained angry and defensive as they viewed themselves as victims of influences over which they had no control.

Seminar benefits have been evident only if the participants really want to enhance their networks by openly examining and improving them. For the purpose of deepening the individual learning, we applied a set of questions (the networking test) for self-reflection, which has been particularly helpful when trying to clarify what the essentials of a collaborative mindset (see Figure 8-4).

DEVELOPING THE BUSINESS CASE: FACILITY MANAGEMENT AUSTRIA

Facility Management Austria (FMA) is a non-profit organization that is dedicated to spreading and developing the approach of facility management (FM) in Austria. Its members include business organizations, associations and educational institutions, as well as participants in FM education. The FMA was founded in 1995 and has since developed a concrete structure which includes: a managing board that combines the different members' interests; the founding of syndicates, headed by one person, which include educational institutions, internal FM providers, general FM providers, consultants and planners, as well as real estate trustees. A business unit coordinates the overall development of FMA while the rest of the network members have honorary functions.

In 2006, one of the authors was asked to work with the managing board to set up and implement a new strategy for the network with the help from experts in the field of Facility Management. The expert's project elaborated an interesting framework for a new strategy, including suggestions for new products and network restructuring. However, the paper lacked acceptance and commitment among the key players of FMA. These circumstances compelled the managing board to develop a more vivid strategy for the association which posed a positive and widely accepted future and a defined action plan on how to accomplish the goals with the help of the external consultant.

Step 1: Diagnostic Phase (April)

First interviews in the consulting process indicated that internal disagreements and conflicts blocked FMA's implementation of a consistent strategy for the coming years. The internal segmentation of the network into market-oriented substructures was very attractive to some members of FMA, while it at same time also led to disagreements and conflicts among various groups. Competitive relationships were exposed between the groups of internal and external providers and between consultants and service providers who also heavily questioned the being together in one organization.

Reflecting this diagnosis, the consultants' main consideration in choosing the model for that process was that associations like FMA are dependent on the voluntary commitment of their members who are truly dedicated to the organization's goals.

Therefore, three specific principles were important in shaping this goal-setting process:

1. A high level of process orientation: the association's value is determined by its development as well as its final results. Who takes the initiative? What do the managing board and other committees contribute? How are the members involved? How are the different interests being resolved?
2. As much participation as possible: associations are dependent on the exchange between and commitment of people in many different role and relationships. If an association is interested in encouraging lively exchange, it should open the possibility of participation, especially in shaping future goals.
3. Stringent coordination: this sort of process requires a manager who coordinates, and supports the process, continuously informs the managing board, and fulfills general management duties.

Step 2: The Planning Workshop (May)

Following the diagnostic stage, a workshop was held with the managing board's spokesperson, the director of the coordination unit, and the consultant. The purpose of this first workshop was to agree upon the process principles, to define the goals, plan milestones, and specify next steps. Especially the discussion about the basic principles for the strategy process led to a trusted and solid relationship between the parties involved, necessary for applying an effective and straight forward consulting process. The busy schedule had the aim of presenting the strategy at the coming members' convention by developing a conceptual rough draft by the next gathering, eight weeks later.

TABLE 8.8. The Main Topics on of the Strategy Project

- Define content and goals of FMA
- Develop members and member rules
- Identify services (for members)
- Map association's internal structures
- Develop public relations/lobbying strategies
- Develop alliances and partnerships

Step 3: Kick-off Workshop (May)

At the kick-off workshop board members and persons with more coordinative functions of the network as chairs of working groups and committees, were invited. At the kick-off workshop the general project was defined, working groups were initiated, the working formats were discussed and the milestones were set. On the content level, six topics were chosen by individual ratings and subsequent discussion (see Table 8.8) and task forces were nominated by the participants to stimulate targeted work and guarantee maximum participation. To foster wide participation as well as straightforward work, the consultant invented a special model for the task forces. It set cross-sectional teams at the center of the activities, and defined internal roles to secure connectedness to the overall network (see Table 8.9).

Step 4: The Task Force Meetings (May—June)

After the kick-off workshop, the mentors invited the task forces to meet several times to conduct work. The consultant was not directly involved in the task force meetings but provided a checklist with tasks and points to reflect the working phase (which was presented at the kick-off meeting). Tasks included the following topics:

1. Goal elaboration

TABLE 8.9. The Task Force Model

- A mentor chairs each task force to guide the group and keep them on track. Board members could only take on the role of mentor for one group.
- At least one other person from the managing board joins the task force
- The managing board's spokesperson and the chair invite at least one other person from FMA which is not in an official function to join the task force
- All syndicates should be actively involved.
- A minimum of four people work together.
- The COO helped to coordinate and document the task force's work.

2. Diagnosis of the status quo
3. Developing a need to change the current situation
4. Developing first solutions and suggesting appropriate work methods

Step 5: Review Meeting (June)

The extended managing board hosted a review meeting where the task force mentors presented the results and the participants together evaluated the task force results. The main part of the agenda was to test the results of the six task forces and examine them in terms of what they could contribute to the future of FMA The discussions were widely constructive: most of the suggested proposals included commitment by the board as well as the other participants, while others were sent to a deeper analysis phase or for further clarification. As the task forces' results brought a rough image of the future, the consultant asked how this could be achieved. The task forces then met to develop a draft action plan for reaching the intended goals, which again was exposed to feedback.

At the end of the meeting, the consultant helped the board to plan the milestones for preparing the member's convention and to decide upon the central issues to be communicated as the strategy of FMA or to be left as invitations for further clarification and feedback at the convention.

What did we learn from this project? The consulting process design proved to be quite suitable to this type of network:

- In a short period of time, many stakeholders were involved in discussing problems and developing solutions.
- The coordinating unit provided sound project management which helped the network members to see tangible results.
- A trusting relationship between the consultant and the managing board helped to proceed quickly and with big steps.
- Hands-on work tools made it possible not only to come up with a strategy proposal in time but also with a committed piece of work were most relevant key persons were actively involved in contributing to the association's future.

Meeting the Internal Requirements for Cooperation: The MedTogether Project

The project MedTogether was already presented in an earlier part of this chapter. In the following pages we will discuss the internal components of the cooperation, as well as the organizations' involvement and collaboration capacity. Participation in a cooperative venture has both positive effects and potential repercussions on participating organizations. So-called peripheral cooperative efforts only consist of a few autonomous subsystems that can make their own decisions. One example would be institute-based research cooperative ventures at universities. Research teams are able to cooperate in transorganizational settings without irritating their home organization too much. Unfortunately, in many cases repercussions are often underestimated or even neglected, as organizations tend to focus on the organizations' internal communication and procedures as well as on the relation to external partners. Yet the development of a cooperative venture has the potential to bring about enormous organizational changes.

The MedTogether project established regional task forces including hospitals and other providers of health care services in a regional setting to optimize the interfaces between various participating organizations (responsible for, among other things, diagnosis, treatment, rehab, etc.). The project's development and implementation affected many people and areas of activity in the partner organizations and led to additional changes there, which took a toll on their workmanship. Although the potential for change existed, inflexibility in the organizational structures and the participants' perceptions could not be overlooked.

The consultants recognized that a successful cooperative effort was dependent on clear cost-benefit analysis and strong support by the management in charge of the collaborating units. The criteria for admitting hospitals and regional partners to the project included the ability to cooperate and to apply given project management rules. For those reasons, the coordinators developed a concept that required applicants should fulfill certain conditions including previous cooperative experience (see Table 8.10).

The consultants and project coordinators introduced the project concept and the participation criteria in informational meetings. To help the applicants to prepare for what might happen, a set of prerequisites had to be met so the application process could occur:

- A commitment statement from the hospital—which included the head of the participating department and hospital management—that says that the hospital management fully supports the participating unit's cooperation.
- A letter of intent from external partners.
- The nomination of an internal project coordinator.
- The nomination of an internal coordinator/consultant.
- The signatures of the department heads on the application.
- The signature of a representative from hospital management on the application.

The hierarchical selection process provided an initial view of the cooperative effort's subject matter, ideas for its optimization, as well as associated processes. This selection process yielded the following results:

TABLE 8.10. Criteria for Participation in MedTogether

- Within the hospital, have at least two departments nominated because of their commitment to project tasks.
- Commitment to project support and implementation as well as commitment to the overall cooperative effort.
- Involvement of external partners that could guarantee a high level of care.
- Supply the necessary project structures.
- Willingness to participate in project benchmarking.
- Commitment to learning as an important project goal.
- Willingness to conduct surveys with interface partners (to enhance the quality of the cooperation).
- Commitment to the project's methodology (tools and approaches, benchmarking, project management, etc.).
- Supplying resources to assist with time management.
- Commitment to delegating project staff (workshops, regional task groups, and hose within their own institutions).
- Willingness to provide resources for optimizing or changing processes and structures in the organizations.

Source: The summary criteria are from a presentation on "Interface Management between Ambulatory and Inpatient Care," by Eva Maria Baumer, Heinz Ebner, Michael Haas, and Hubert Lobnig.

- A relatively small number of applications because potential nominees viewed participation as too complicated and too challenging. Only a minimum number of applications were received.
- Ultimately, qualified and experienced hospitals that applied were interested in enhancing organizational quality management.
- Certain "ambitious" departments applied to enhance their reputations in the diagnostic groups.

From the participant's point of view, the nomination concept also had its disadvantages. The internal procedures to form opinions, make decisions, and delegate the work were as different as the various cultures of each partner organization. However, some applicant organizations were not able to minimize the various differences concerning expectations and resources between the hospital department heads and other participants, since other applicant organizations were already experienced in such projects and later on also achieved positive outcomes. The selection process therefore supported not those who were motivated to improve, but those, which already were on a good way towards on their efforts to collaborate. Some hospitals just signed in, chose certain people as project coordinators and sent them to the workshops with little knowledge about the project. Accordingly, the latter group was quickly eliminated from the project since their project coordinator had too little information about the regional structures for which they were responsible and saw themselves overstrained in a context for which they were unequipped.

For those taking roles and responsibilities in the local projects, the design of the cluster workshops provided training and coaching to strengthen necessary skills for inter-organizational process management. In consequence, establishing and reinforcing the cooperation system took center stage in the first phase of the project. After the regional projects and working schemes were set up, various differences between the organizations surfaced, and the consultant team developed solutions to overcoming these differences through project analysis and coaching in the cluster group workshops.

As one of the tasks, the regional task force delegates were invited to analyze the first phase of the regional implementation based on the following set of questions:

- How should we rate the project's success and its ability to become sustainable within our organizations?
- What progress have we made? What progress have other participants made?
- Where are there deficits and problems? What could be enhanced?

As the second step, various regional coaching groups were formed and subdivided by the diagnostic groups of medical discipline. These groups discussed analyses, provided feedback, and developed possible solutions to any the problems surfaced in the analysis. This procedure revealed that some project groups had not taken the necessary steps to introduce change measures for the following reasons:

- The organizations did not show enough interest in the project.
- The organizations expected their delegates to solve problems themselves and not ask for support from others.
- Management showed increasingly less interest over time, as it had already turned its attention to new projects.
- Nevertheless, certain positive factors for long-term success also became apparent:
- The organizations initiated smaller internal projects to stimulate the main project's success.
- Highly qualified and motivated project coordinators with the necessary authority stayed in touch with their management and made a great contribution to solving problems.

- Project leaders with high positions in their home organizations were mainly responsible for implementing change measures because of their managerial functions and experience.

MedTogether did not provide the regional task forces with any direct counseling. Instead, the project placed value on strengthening the project coordinators' skills through professional training in change and cooperation management. This approach was particularly helpful in providing support to those organizations experienced in cooperation management. On the other hand, organizations with less experience—and especially their project coordinators—received less assistance than necessary to fully explore the potential of better regional collaboration.

THE ZURICH COUNTY PROJECT (KANTON ZÜRICH): A COOPERATIVE VENTURE WITH RISKY PARAMETERS

The project "outcome" aimed at implementing a quality measurement system (patient outcomes) for hospitals in the county of Zurich. One of the authors, together with an Austrian consulting group, was invited to consult to the project. For our purpose, the case serves as practice example on the key issues of "establishing a cooperative steering system," "meeting the internal requirements of cooperation" and to the role of learning, evaluation and reflection for collaborations. This section describes some of the experience we gained about success factors in these areas.

Organizing a Cooperative Effort as an Independent System

This project with Zurich County was a quality measurement initiative of the health department of Zurich canton, Switzerland, and took place from 1996 to 2000. The regional administration financed the project to monitor the implementation of various local hospitals' outcome measurement systems.

On the part of the politician responsible for the project and her reform team,[1] it was a drastic intervention in developing countywide hospital policy. The introduction of the performance-oriented control and funding models was accompanied by both positive and negative comments of stakeholders involved, such as an increase in efficiency vs. the danger of "double class medicine."[2] This project also served to demonstrate the importance of performance-oriented control and of enhancing transparency in hospital services. The responsible politician and the health administration of Zurich invited all the hospitals in the county to participate in this project. The initiators, assisted by an Austrian consultancy, also realized the importance of involving experts in medicine, nursing and hospital management to add credibility to the project.

A Precarious Principal-Agent Conflict

Initial issues that were of interest to potential participants and leadership included:

- The hospitals were worried that health administration would adjust the amount of funds to the results of the project so poor results would result in less money.
- Politics and administration were focused on simultaneously streamlining and safeguarding the quality of hospital care.
- Many hospitals were in competition for funding and their regional position in the medical care sector.
- The above-mentioned circumstances forced hospital staff and management to increase transparency of quality of all their services.

It was clear to both project management and the consultants that the project's success would depend on trust between the partners and quality tools for measuring results.

Initially, three hospitals took part in the project and one year later, six other hospitals were included. These first nine partners helped to test the criteria and tools for measuring outcomes and to refine the project concept. The consultants organized this self-reflective process with the aid of project management. During the beginning phases, it became clear that outcome measurements would continually have to be developed over a long period of time. Social insurance agencies, ambulatory and inpatient service providers, health administration, and experts on quality measurement also participated in this process. The quality measurement team and the consultancy group took a series of steps to establish a cooperative system (see Table 8.11).

In our experience, an application procedure to join a project makes it easier to define the criteria for success, as it requires a voluntary decision from each partner organization based on a formal process.

A workshop was the first basis for a possible cooperative venture in which interested hospitals could familiarize themselves with the project, including its risks and opportunities. At this stage, we emphasized on building relationships and trust, as this provides a basis for collaboration. The workshop offered the consultants the opportunity to introduce themselves as consultants for all collaborating parties and most importantly for the underlying idea. The workshop also allowed both interested institutions, as well as consultants, to have a chance to experience the inter-professional and trans-organizational approach to cooperation from the beginning.

TABLE 8.11. Steps in Establishing the Cooperative System

• Developing a work schedule and project's philosophy
• Holding information meetings for the invited hospitals
• Announcing the project and calling for applications for participation
• Holding a workshop for the representatives of interested organizations
• Entering a cooperation agreement with three pilot hospitals
• Establishing a control system and organizational structure

Organizing a Cooperative Control System

In the second stage of the project's development, the decision was made to develop a cooperative venture. Though an important step, it was not the only definitive prerequisite. Cooperative efforts generally owe their definitive existence to a dynamic process of agreed-upon goals, the definition of basic rules, and practical operation. This project exemplified this type of dynamic development process. During this formation phase, the steering group held three all-day meetings in which the joint consultant and project coordinator's project plan had to be continually adjusted and refined.

The First Steering Group Meeting

In its first meeting, the steering group worked diligently on goals and the business case. As new players were on the stage, many questions concerning the clarification of the business case ("what exactly are we here for") had to be addressed again. The consultant facilitated the subgroups, which were divided up according to hospital, health administration, and project coordinator. Reflecting on the outcomes of the project, assessment focused on such questions as:

- What did we learn from this project?
- What could we do better next time?
- What should be excluded from the project's content?
- As the steering group, what could be our overall learning?

The representatives from the hospitals had important concerns which included: 1) defining a binding application and review of measurements; 2) promoting the interdisciplinary cooperation between hospitals through training; 3) developing standards of quality management in the hospitals; and 4) fostering a spirit of openness and universal support. Both the consultants and health administrators considered the applicability of the indicator model in practice as the most important outcome of the project.

The steering group discussed issues of entering a commitment to the project, stressing that the network is based on the partners' relationships and the project's anchoring in the practice of the participating hospitals. Consequently the steering group defined the requirement that each participating hospital needed to send in directors to be able to make binding intra-organizational decisions.

Concerns formulated as answers to questions three and four (mentioned above) surfaced possible conflicts—such as power struggles, lack of group solidarity and punctuality and/or reliability in participation, unprofessional argumentation, concealed self-interests and lobbying, and a lack of joint responsibility, among other issues.

An interim evaluation indicated that the motives and expectations of the partners were very different. That is why the consultants suggested concentrating primarily on the main concept behind the project rather than on a set of indicators and tests. Also, the first steps in developing an organizational structure were postponed until the end of the meeting. At that particular time, the most important task was to develop a joint decision about work schedule adaptation.

Towards the end of the meeting, participants once again held a discussion about the possibility of participating in the network. They finally developed a set of minimum conditions for participation in the steering group. They included: no nomination of deputies; having consistent representation by at least one person in meetings (otherwise there would be penalties); and engaging intensively with hospital services.

The Second Meeting of the Steering Group

Managers of all the participating hospitals took part in the second meeting. It was commonly stated that the steering group had assumed an optimal organizational and interdisciplinary form. The criteria for documenting the work schedule were defined, which proved to be important for the project's transparency and potential future plans. In addition, all of the partners made a commitment to continuity and presence at meetings. Missed meetings would lead to penalization or cancellation of participation. Penalties could reach up to 9,700 euro as the working time of all participants, expenses for consultants rent for rooms were summarized.

The steering group also made decisions about the terms of collecting data and utilizing knowledge that included conceptual framework and joint policy for external communication and media. After this discussion, the consultants asked the partners if they were ready to start the project. The answer was unanimously positive, although some representatives wanted to confer with their own management before signing the contract. After some deliberation, they finally agreed to sign a modified contract. The consultants could finally draw attention to establishing the indicator test and providing guidance for work methods.

Founding the Cooperation by Defining its Tasks

Steering groups of inter organizational projects such as those of the Outcome project have many tasks to accomplish, which need to apply different work methods for the steering group:

- Working on the content: it is particularly important that existing professional resources were put to good use.
- Coordinating the overall process: defining workmanship and assignments, dividing the work into sequences, tasks and portfolios of activities
- Analyzing, evaluating, and reflecting on preliminary results: circular feedback loops help to correct course and stay on track with current internal and external realities.
- Decision making: ability to make binding decisions which not only affect the cooperation system but also the rest of the hierarchy of their home-organizations.

The ability to switch between the different levels and approaches of work methods form an effective precondition for collaboration. The success of the steering group increased when all the groups involved in the cooperative effort were convinced that their work methods functioned properly (Grossmann 2002, p. 49).

Creating the Internal Requirements for Cooperation

All the members of the outcome project were aware that the success of their network would be largely dependent on the internal structures, quality management processes and the cultures of the partnering organizations. First, it was imperative to align the quality management processes in the hospitals and their control systems to the requirements of the outcome indicator measurement procedures. Since hospital representatives were aware of this as a possible area of tension, they asked for support for internal organizational development and the enhancement of quality management.

As the business case of the network clearly focused on the definition and piloting of outcome criteria intra-organizationally, organizational development within hospitals was not part of the agenda. However, this focus on the collaboration was crucial to the success of the whole project. At the same time we realized that the network's business case had not taken center stage in all of the partner organizations. Fortunately, the hospital manager's decisions helped to secure enough commitment and participation in most hospitals, although some of the partners did not extensively coordinate the transfer of the collaboration project to the quality management processes of the local hospitals.

Nonetheless, the consultants' partners made repeated efforts to discuss questions concerning internal project organization in the steering group meetings, since this was one of the requirements for participation. However, in some cases it was not a criterion that quality management be present or even developed along the way.

Learning, Reflecting, and Researching Cooperative Processes

In the outcome project, consultants and project coordinators invested much effort in documentation and assessment. During the project, a number of assessments were carried out using innovative forms of organizing the discussion and reflection. Continuous observation and reflection and the stakeholders' perspectives were also taken into account, as evaluations of various groups of people involved in different roles in the hospitals also addressed the levels of process and culture. Using staff questionnaires, the project coordinators surveyed the personal opinions about the outcome project of staff members. However the most innovative approaches were the established observation groups in the partner organizations. Their tasks included:

- Using continuous observation and critical reflection during the testing phase
- Providing continuous feedback to project management and the project coordinators in the hospitals
- Conducting a final evaluation on the practicability and implementation of the indicator sets (see Gesundheitsdirektion des Kantons Zürich, 1998)

The steering group assembled and discussed the results.. Discussions led to a final opinion of the steering group which was presented as interim reports to the regional health administration.

Although the steering group extensively discussed the results, they were not used systematically for inter-organizational learning purposes. Because reflection processes were not shared with representatives from non-participating management, the individual organizations could not sufficiently learn from the project.

The internal project coordinators also offered supplemental evaluation workshops for discussing the stakeholders' various perspectives. However, the focus of those evaluation workshops remained on those inner-organizational structures which were relevant to the cooperative effort. As the partners might have had the duty to reveal their organizational and decision-making structures, as well as their quality management procedures, some momentum for the participating organizations to learn was missed.

Different Approaches to Cooperative Efforts

The contrasts between the interests of health care policy and those of cooperative partners were repeatedly a topic of discussion. If these differences could be handled properly, the effort would grow in trust and security. The preoccupation with these contrasts surfaced in all different project phases, and the partners constantly worried if the politicians would leave current policies intact.

The topic of trust also was often dominated by how project data would be used and whether it would form the basis for the government's funding decisions. The steering group the project coordinators, the health administration, and the various groups concerned also dealt with this stress factor which resulted in a solid foundation of trust. On the other hand, the possibility that representatives from the health administration would order a drastic reorganization in the partner hospitals was threatening to existing relationships.

On the positive side, the success of the joint project maintained its stability over a long period of time and still exists after some amendments. However, project participants did not take advantage of the cooperative effort to enhance the collaborative capacity of the participating hospitals. It may be that a number of high leverage instruments and creative ideas to enhance the relation between the collaborative system and the local hospitals were missing. Yet the question remains open about how organizations can improve their internal capacity to change and prosper through external cooperation or how cooperative projects can help organizations to develop.

NOTES

1. Reform Project LORAS: Leistungsorientierte Ressourcenallokation im Spitalsbereich in der Verwaltung.
2. See Gesundheitsdirektion des Kantons Zürich [Directorate of Health of the county of Zurich], (Ed.), 1998, Chapter 2, p. 5.

CHAPTER 9

COLLABORATIVE MERGERS

Klaus Scala and Michael Stadlober

On our research journey through the vast field of collaboration in the public service sector, we stumbled upon an astonishing number of mergers between organizations. A public hospital owner seeks to reduce the overcapacity of hospitals in a specific region with the goal of combining the four existing hospitals into one. In order to accomplish this merger, the hospital owner cancels the contracts for two of the locations), defines the minimum number of necessary beds, recommends a merger and leaves the rest of the downsizing process to self-policing and market forces.

Two state universities located in the same area are considering a collaborative effort to build their reputation. A merger is proposed and the idea is pursued, although the process falters because common goals are unclear. The ministry of science, research and technology as owners of both universities come up with a plan to dissolve both universities and found a new one (made up of the previous two), appoints a new principal to manage the new project and instructs him to implement the merger.

Trade unions perceive their differences that are oriented to industries which are traditionally oriented around different industrial branches find that this fragmentation weakens their political power. A joint venture is discussed, many similarities and differences are revealed and the idea of

Facilitating Collaboration in Public Management, pages 157–185

a merger evolves. This establishes a whole new dynamic into the process because some unions are combined, others drop out and eventually four unions merge to create one new, large union.

Two neighboring municipalities discover parallels between their various facilities and responsibilities and consider a merger which they have to discuss with their citizens. A first merger vote among them has a negative outcome. But the initiators are persistent and an information-gathering and opinion-forming campaign ensues. Four years later, a public referendum decides to move forward with the merger.

Two traditional conglomerate energy corporations merge to prevent a hostile competitive takeover. Subsequently they sell most of their industrial holdings. Through more sub-mergers and active hostile takeovers, they develop into a very strong global energy enterprise.

In all the examples listed above, the subject of a merger is recurrent. However, the examples in their respective objectives, roles, processes and successes vary so greatly that one must consider a more in-depth examination of mergers—which means developing a "merger phenomenon" map.

In this chapter, we focus on a special type of merger—the *collaborative merger* as a feasible and yet not an absolutely necessary final stage of a collaborative process between organizations. For this purpose we use some of the case studies mentioned above in order to describe the key elements of successful collaborative merger management. In conclusion, we then reflect on whether the results are transferable to the management of all types of mergers.

The following questions will be covered in this chapter:

- What types of mergers are currently observed?
- How can merger processes of independent organizations be managed and structured?
- To what extent are merger processes of independent organizations instructive models for other types of mergers?

THE ROADMAP

For our purposes, the diversity in the types of mergers can be best differentiated by: 1) the goals, motives and the difference in the level of required participation; and 2) the ownership and decision-making infrastructures.

Goals, Motives and Fears: Is Merger Always the Right Solution?

The first central category to be considered with mergers includes assessing the goals, sources of motivation and fears involved or might eventually arise. These would include questions such as: "To what end?," "Why?" and "Why not?" are we considering a merger? The questionable track record of mergers suggests that decision-making based on alternatives is not a consistent standard (see Porter, 1987). The merger concept is often hastily chosen as a solution to many business problems, although considering the chances of success, other possibilities of collaboration might be more promising. Mergers often already fail at this step of goal-clarification: potential adverse side effects do not receive enough attention, or the decision is misguided because the merger is chosen as a solution for goals that it simply cannot attain.

These dynamics require a critical look at the objectives of a merger. There are four distinguishable objectives that have a different impact on decisions and success (Huber, 2004: Jansen, 2004a): efficiency, quality, market presence and influence, and fear and needs for security.

Efficiency

One expects to economize on eliminating duplicated responsibilities, to utilize synergies and to thereby obtain more resource efficiency. In institutions with public investors, austerity programs as well as cost-reduction programs are on the agenda. Mergers may promise greater efficiency and therefore savings.

Quality

Technology development and innovation of new products and services can be carried out or implemented more easily by "bigger players" who can also better focus on the increasing differentiation of customer expectations and the associated expansion of their range of products and services. For instance, a large company can afford a larger research department, whereupon a large hospital has a broader range of specialists, and might therefore offer better quality. A large trade union can care for its members in a more efficient and goal-oriented way, especially in the constantly changing and differentiated professional environment.

Market Presence and Influence

Growing domestic and international competition forces companies to expand their market presence and reduce competition through a merger of former competing enterprises. Similarly, through mergers, organizations such as trade unions or municipalities can increase their political influence and power and reduce competition "in their home base."

Fear and Security

Often the fear of marginalization or being taken over by other companies is present. This also explains the strong emotional components of mergers: the fear at the top of being brought down by economic and political competition, and not being able to take appropriate action on time to prevent that from happening.

This special motivation to merge is based on the underlying assumption that large organizations have a safer position in the market, are not so occupied with internal competition, and therefore can take more powerful action in their markets. The formula "security plus strength through size" is based on the often ill-fated assumption that size also means an increase in competitiveness. Collaborations between organizations in the form of alliances, strategic partnerships, joint ventures and networks (see Chapters 4–6) are of vital future importance if organizations are to compete effectively. In addition to the for-profit sector, the principle of competition also affects the public sector (such as the competition between different locations for schools and hospitals).

A merger is a very particular form of collaboration in which the independence of organizations is sacrificed for the benefit of one new organization. It is worthwhile, however, to critically examine whether the benefits of collaboration can be achieved using a simpler means than a merger, so that problems associated with mergers can be prevented (Lohmer & Lohmer, 2005). We often think that the decision to merge is influenced by the supposed magic of the security-providing large organization—but that "magic" often cannot stand a critical evaluation of the advantages and disadvantages.

Given the poor track record of mergers (Jansen, 2004a), one can assume that not enough attention is paid to the adverse effects of creating large organizations. These disadvantages were the very cause that in the 1990s, many corporations and businesses were restructured into extensive autonomous and independent business segments. The diagnosis is as follows: most large organizations lack proximity to customers as well as differentiated market monitoring; they are unable to respond quickly to changing market conditions and the great gap between specialists' expertise and the responsible managers diminishes entrepreneurial commitment. Also, the "old" functional arrangement of the organizational structure increased the autonomy of the individual departments (research, production, finance, personnel) which made control very difficult for top management.

An undirected enthusiasm for mergers (*Merger Mania*, Hackett, 1996) risks the re-emergence of all aforementioned deficiencies in new organizations. For the providers of public goods and services, a public discussion of these issues on a political level are feared, as mergers are often associated with the elimination of jobs and the reduction in the supply of services.

Ownership and Decision-Making Structures

In addition to the objectives of mergers, the public and private ownership structures are vital, since all owner(s) are accountable for the decision to merge: Who is being involved in the decision-making process and how? A traditional distinction exists between various ownership relationships, including the difference between the state (government-owned) and market (private owners), recently expanded by the third sector (non-profit organizations) (see Chapter 1). The development that has been increasingly observed over the last few years outdates the preciseness and usefulness of this distinction. The state intervenes in the market with subsidies, seeks new forms of organization for its tasks, and re-formulates its range of duties.

Due to economic pressure, the attempt is made to create more efficiency and, to an extent, more quality and customer orientation in the public organizations, as well as in the delivery of public services. This is accomplished with the help of different models such as outsourcing, public private partnerships, privatization, mergers, and administrative reformation (see Chapter 1).

Mergers are *one* prominent "solution variant" in the currently observable organizational experimental field of the public sector. From an organizational development perspective, the following assignments have to be sought: to evaluate in the case, and to establish appropriately complex know-how so management can understand the benefits of mergers. By understanding the process, the success of a merger both largely depends on who made the decision to merge and when that decision was made. Here, the range of variations in the degree of participation ranges from the "hostile takeover"—where the owner decides on a merger without disclosure to the managers, employees and customers—to a referendum for merging two municipalities, where all citizens are involved in the decision-making process.

The merger initiator and implementer fundamentally determine the management of a merger style. Furthermore, it is important to understand whether the ownership relationships will change in the market because of the merger. One can distinguish between three types of "merger logic," each determined by the ownership relationships, which are highly relevant to the merger process:

- Mergers by acquisition based on the *market model*
- Mergers of organizations based on decisions of the *hierarchical owners*
- Mergers by *autonomous decisions* of the organizations involved

In the first two cases, the owner decides and carries out the merger either through a sale or a hierarchical decision and the implementation is put into practice in a "post-merger" process. In the third case, the "horizontal merger" (Jansen, 2004b), or the "merger on one level" (Plamper, 2004, p. 41), the decision to merge does not come from outside (the owners), or from above (the sponsors), but from within the organizations.

The incidental responsibilities related to the merger are essentially the same, but roles and implementation process are filled and conducted differently. In particular, the formation and timing of decisions vary, particularly the fundamental decision whether or not to merge. Occasionally, cases occur where a merger of two organizations is initiated from within the organizations (for instance, from the top management) but the merger somehow comes to a standstill and outside owners then take over and drive the process.

Market Model: Merger as "Merger & Acquisition"

The first group concerns mergers of companies that are bought and sold as commodities, corresponding to market logic. This market phenomenon of buying and selling receives much attention, whereas the implementation happens in the "post-merger process" and illustrates significant variations in scale, depending on the specific objectives of the purchase. A real merger with the goal of replacing the old identity by a completely new one is just one of many possible variations in the degree of consolidation (Krusche, 2000).

Mergers and acquisitions have long been an integral part of constantly changing economies, although lately, the trend is slightly declining. However, the merger boom continues to take place despite the fact that mergers and consolidations have a surprisingly low success rate. Different studies reveal a success rate of less than 50 percent—measured by the intended objectives, and usually related to economic effectiveness and efficiency. It is argued that this poor outcome is caused by shortcomings in "pricing" (mostly overpayment) and the lack of attention paid to post-merger management (Jansen, 2000, Nguyen & Little, 2003, Porter, 1987).

Hierarchical Model: Mergers from Outside

The second group concerns mergers of organizations in the public sector joined by sponsors and owners—for instance, mergers of universities, hospitals and social insurance companies. Public sector mergers are currently being pioneered and reveal a strong upward trend (Jansen, 2004b). However, they are not primarily determined by market logic or by the purchase of one by another. Instead of the market logic that is based on the "purchase negotiation, purchase contract," the sponsor or investor decides on a merger using hierarchical logic.

When non-autonomous organizations are merged, for example, the municipal sponsors or owners restructure the hospital facilities in a particular region and, within this context, two hospitals are consolidated. This type of merger constitutes the triangular orientation in which a parent body—mainly a political institution—is faced with two or more merging organizations.

Decision-making and management in this type of merger is complex because two contradictory forms of management logic have to be controlled simultaneously: For the organizations involved, the merger is basically based on an external decision. Although they didn't want to merge, they must find common ground in order to realize the actual implementation of the merger and to achieve the desired benefits.

Until now, professionals have not had much discussion about mergers in the public service sector. The professional knowledge about relevant issues and complicated tasks that should be addressed in such mergers is not very deep. This often leads to at best semi-professional management and suboptimal outcomes.

In our research process, this took us by surprise. While we looked for examples of collaboration between organizations in the public sector, we "discovered" a surprising number of specific merger processes—without the players having been prepared and supported with the counsel of experts.

One can hypothesize that the logic of public sector politics in particular is affected by the negative connotations of mergers: downsizing, decrease in supply due to facility closures, and job loss. Politically, it is feared that this would trigger a public discussion about these issues because the debate itself could cause "potential resistance" against seemingly necessary restructuring. However, this defensive approach has a number of drawbacks. Turning the issue of merger into a very "sensitive" theme which one shouldn't discuss stokes fears, and therefore directly mobilizes the "resistance potential" that would preferably be avoided (Huber, 2004, p.59). Mergers therefore can be negatively emotionally charged and the chances of finding and conveying their positive aspects remain undefined. This, in turn, has a negative effect on the merger process.

Among other things, the lack of open discussion leads to the broad dissemination of conventional, linear merger models. Mergers traditionally are differentiated from one another by phases, including the pre-merger (vision)—and the decision to merge at the end of the pre-merger phase—the merger (design, implementation), and the post-merger (integration).

In these models, the convoluted paths which merger processes tread disappear. The chronological order (above) makes a distinction between (1) the political environment, (2) the merger, and (3) integration management. However, this model misses the opportunity to support the integration by means of a collaborative merger. With "mergers from within," a different approach is used (see Table 9.1).

Collaborative Models: Merger from Within

In a "merger from within,"[1] autonomous organizations independently proceed to create a new organization through a merger. This is typically the case in organizations where the members have a say in the merger de-

TABLE 9.1. Phases of a Merger

	Pre-Merger	Merger		Post-Merger
Question	What are the advantages and disadvantages of a merger?	What are the goals of the merging organization and how will they be achieved?		How was the merger realized and accepted?
Topic	Merger initiation and decision	Strategic planning and implementation of the merger		Deepening, securing + monitoring
Main activity	Political management	Merger management		Integration management
Phases	**Vision**	**Concept**	**Implementation**	**Integration**
Typical tasks	Preparation of political environment	Implementation planning (detailed goal formulation, strategy selection)	OD: Reorganization of the design and operational organization	Acceptance management
	Feasibility study & SWOT (evaluating Strength, Weakness, Opportunities and Threats)	OD, HR and IT concept BCS and controlling	HR: Incentive systems, compensation/ lay-offs, MA development & training	Cultural change, team- and trust building
	Goal formation (centrality /de centrality)	Internal PR: Increasing employee's acceptance	IT: Adaptation of functional and technical support	Public relations (internal and external)

Source: Huber (2004, p. 79)

cision-making process (e.g. unions, municipalities, associations). The final decision to merge is not made at the start, but at a much later stage in the process. Prior to this decision, a discussion is required about the necessity, the objectives, the new organizational and legal structures, the procedures, the rules and the transition from the "old" organizations to the "new" organization. Mergers of this type are not characterized by purchasing logic or hierarchy, but by a negotiation logic whereby the partners have to first define "prices" and "costs" in the course of the process.

The currencies here are diverse, often difficult to quantify and are always political. However, they are still involved with goods and services intended for the general public. The mode that leads to a merger of several organizations is not the acquisition, but the collaboration of organizations. This particular type of merger requires a special design which is not the process of an actual purchase, but developing a collaborative relationship between the various organizations and establishing a collaboration system. This system, paradoxically, must end the collaborative relationship and dissolve the individual organizations when the merger is completed and a new organization emerges.

Some pragmatic paradoxes exist at the inception of such a merger process: Organizations fundamentally *always* have their own "eternal" survival as their main goal while at the same time, the survival of a company can be secured more easily through the abandonment of its past identity. Power and equity are to be managed and continuously developed in the merger decision-making process.

Mergers from within characteristically distinguish between the decision and integration process, yet these processes cannot necessarily be differentiated socially or chronologically. Pre-mergers, mergers and post-mergers are timed and organized differently than "mergers from outside." Before a merger decision is made, many aspects of the post-merger phase are taken into consideration. Political, merger and integration management must be synchronized.

The decision to do a merger is a product of the process that essentially guides it. What started as partial co-operation later culminates into a merger. The final decision to merge has a long lead-time, and the final formal decision to merge concludes a long process in which integration has already taken place in some areas. A merger from within must overcome the paradox of having to create –through decisions—a stable and binding structure for the decision-making process. This must be done for a very open and far-reaching change process using pre-existing autonomous systems. A bridge between openness and commitment over a long period must be built and maintained.

The case study examples we examined clearly illustrate that creating the decision-making structure is the bottleneck for most merger processes. Where openness concerning the outcome is lost, the fundamental strategic questions, as well as the discussion of how the joint future will appear, cannot be exhaustively addressed. Unsolved problems will then emerge at a later time and hinder the process. However, if the decision-making process lasts too long, there is the risk of losing credibility. In this case, joint actions on a very practical level (e.g., merging customer databases, cooperating in PR activities) can drive the decision process "from the bottom up."

MERGER AND COLLABORATION

This section focuses on merger in the form of "collaboration between organizations." This type of merger is both the result and the end point of a collaborative effort. Without adequate cooperation, a collaborative merger would not be set in motion, and at the same time, the implementation of the merger would cause the end of collaboration between the participating organizations. We are therefore mainly interested in the "merger from within," because this type of merger clearly and solely is achieved by collaboration. The requirements here—in terms of participation and joint decision-making—are more comprehensive than in market-conforming mergers & acquisitions, or in mergers initiated by owners. If these requirements in the decision making process are not met, there will be no merger.

With the other two types of mergers mentioned above, the decision to merge is not based on a collaborative process between the participating organizations. However, this idea radicalizes the question about the degree of significance that collaborations and participation have in merger processes. If the main goal of a merger is to eliminate the competition between two companies and to create one new company that has a larger market share—without changing the existing company infrastructures and operating procedures—minimum cooperation is required.

If, however, in the interest of minimizing costs and improving quality, the merging organizations are completely integrated into a new unit while the existing structures, processes and working relationships are dismantled and restructured, the question is intensified about how the implementation process should be managed and to what extent the principles of collaboration and participation could be of assistance. In this case, collaboration represents a merger from within. A decision to merge on the top-level or from "outside" brings in a directive management-based logic, which conflicts with the principles of collaboration and participation.

How is it possible to intervene to make changes on a grand scale from outside the company and ensure that a high performing, organization will be created? This presupposes that the organizations concerned accept their own "deaths" and can assume a more attractive future and identity in the new joint organization. In this triangle, the combination of hierarchical decision-making and horizontal collaboration is a particularly difficult challenge for all parties involved. Success can only be obtained by first answering the most important question: when and how the organizations will be merged. Based on the existing decision-making structures, the answer to this question cannot be assumed and must be answered.

As is our central thesis, "mergers from within" serve as a model from which merger management can learn—especially regarding the pre-merger phase. Critical evaluation of mergers confirms the thesis that the poor track record of mergers is generally due to inadequate communication management and insufficient attention paid to the pre-merger management phase (Jansen 2004a). The recommendations of these evaluations are in accordance with the recommendations unions and municipalities must employ if they want to negotiate a merger agreement. The same concept applies to mergers decided by the hierarchical owner. The decision from the outside takes some of the weight off of the organizations concerned, yet it creates difficulty in transforming this external decision into a future shaped by the organizations themselves.

For this reason, the next section uses a separate section to outline the process of a "merger from within" based on some case studies. We then will formulate theses for the management of mergers from outside based on the market or hierarchy model.

Mergers from Within: Illustrative Cases

A merger from within is necessarily a result of a collaborative process and the ideal example of a co-operation-oriented merger. Throughout this process, the paradox must be overcome where a relationship between organizations is constructed which will eventually lead to the dissolution of the participating organizations themselves. One collaborates at the cost of giving up one's own organizational identity and creating a new mutual one. The second paradox arises from the fact that the decision to merge is not dogmatically made at the beginning of the process, but is itself a result of the collaboration. The merger isn't the solution a priori, but emerges as a possibility in the wake of the collaboration. It is considered, discussed, partially tested, evaluated and then a decision is made, implemented or discarded.

To illustrate the emergence of this process, below we will outline, examine and evaluate the case of a merger of unions. We will then describe the various foci of a merger from within, using selective examples.

UNIA

UNIA refers to the collaborative merger of five Swiss unions into a "union for all"[2] (see Figure 9.1). The two largest trade unions in the Swiss industry, SMUV (Trade Union of the Machine and Watch Industry) and GBI (Union of Construction Workers & Industry), were dealing with declining membership in the mid-1990s. Because of the existing employment market, a reversal of this declining trend was not expected in the near future. The keyword for this trend was "growing services—declining industries." As a first response, GBI and SMUV jointly established their own service union—"unia."

This move, however, failed to increase membership in the big industrial unions, whereas in the small service unions like the VHTL (union for sale, trade, transportation and food) and the newly founded "unia" a strong membership influx ensued. At the same time, it became clear that these small unions did not have the necessary infrastructure and organizational requirements that a workers' union needs to grow and effectively position itself in the market.

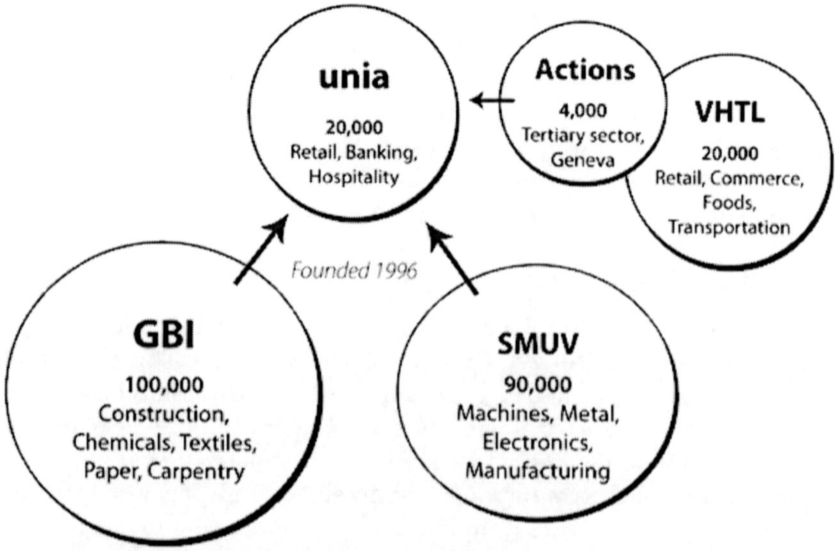

FIGURE 9.1. The Beginning: The Five Founding Unions
Source: www.unia.ch/Gruenderinnen.584.0.html

As a reaction to socio-economic pressures, the big trade unions began to look for other, deeper solutions outside their organizational borders and began to consider collaboration with potential partners, who were often also competitors.

A Collaborative Beginning

In joint discussions between the big unions, the idea was formulated to cooperate more closely, and so they founded a common "House of Unions" to join parts of the infrastructure. The unions' differences were less evident in the objectives, but more so in their identities. For example, the GBI was considered more militant, while the other unions (SMUV, VHTL) were labeled as "open to negotiation." These differences in culture, however, were not serious obstacles to developing a collaborative effort.

The individual unions pursued the idea of utilizing their individual strengths and addressing their weaknesses by increasing collaboration, as well as serving as a united and effective employee union. Furthermore, cooperation occurred in other areas, such as the unification of IT and member administration, and later a common newspaper also was added.

These projects were jointly managed. In one of the meetings, participants discussed whether the collaboration should only remain on a singular, project-based level, with every new project bearing new questions, new interfaces and the creation of new negotiation processes. Another question addressed was the consideration of how and in what form a complete merger of the unions would be possible. With these considerations, the spirit of the "House of Unions" merger emerged.

The transition to the House of Unions let to the establishment of a management team where representatives included the presidents and the finance managers of the three largest unions, GBI, SMUV and VHTL, and two persons from the political field of the trade union. While one person was responsible for the "main support of the process," the group as a whole made the main decisions and pushed the merger process forward. An external consultant also aided the group.

Project Phase

The management team launched a project phase in which pros and cons about the merger were discussed in working groups and workshops internally and between the individual unions (see Figure 9.2). The results of the discussions were then communicated to the management team through data that underpinned both opinions.

The project structure stipulated one management team participant would always be in charge of one of the several project groups along with the associated project manager. The project groups dealt with the main merger issues, for example: human resource management, contract drafting, or IT. The management team discussed and decided on common procedures for the project groups on which participants in the original organizations' committees and meetings eventually agreed.

To provide feedback on the results of the project groups, a "sounding board" was set up which consisted of corporate representatives and voluntary members of the trade unions. In planned intervals, this large group met and discussed the findings and proposals of the project groups, for instance, regarding the merger of the different IT-Systems. Apart of that expert role, the "sounding board" also managed to effectively broaden the entire discussion by disseminating knowledge throughout the company, which was further supported by an internal newspaper.

Clarification Phase

In the third phase, a big picture was developed and strategic issues were worked out to address the following questions: What could a merged union look like? How could one label the branches? How would the responsibilities be divided? How would the legal structure be determined? What would the cash flows look like and what would be the new structure of the organization?

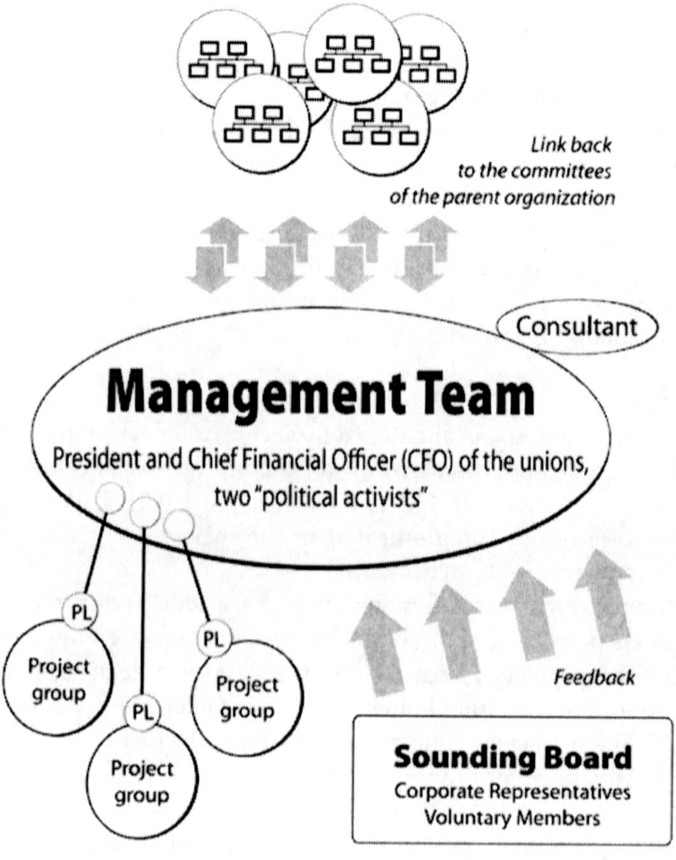

Figure 9-2 The Project Organization

Decision-Making

In December, 2003, the core question in the management team eventually was whether or not to implement a merger. After external experts helped to clarify the trade unions' legal and economic situation, the management team decided on a merger. Because the union members had to be asked if they even wanted a merger, they were integrated into a rapid, clear and intense discussion process which had to be finished before the next delegates' meeting in June, 2004. The delegates and the central management boards of the SMUV, GBI and VHTL adopted the "founding congress" for the decisive event, and worked out the central founding documents of the UNIA including the merger agreement, as well as statutes and regulations.

TABLE 9.2. The Merger Process: From "unia" to "UNIA"*

1996	GBI and SMUV jointly founded the service union "unia." Eight years later "unia" enjoys 20,000 members.
1998	GBI and SMUV establish the "Associated Union House". They gradually develop collaborative projects (a joint newspaper, computer center, common software and the first joint office staff).
2000	The congresses of SMUV and GBI give the order to prepare the foundations for co-operation or integration of the trade unions.
2001	GBI and SMUV launch own newspaper, "Work".
2002/03	The special congresses of SMUV, GBI, VHTL and "unia" decide on the integration into an inter-professional union. In 2003 the project phase of integration of all areas takes place.
2004	The 5 merging unions hold internal assemblies to inform of and solicit future structures; Appointment of responsibilities
June 2004	Delegates of all merging unions assemble. The central board of SMUV, GBI and VHTL adopt the founding documents including merger agreements, as well as statutes and regulations.
10.15. 2004	Last congresses of GBI, SMUV, VHTL and "unia."
10.16. 2004	Founding congress of UNIA (discussion and resolution of goals for the first 4 UNIA years).
1. 1. 2005	Start UNIA. Implementation of integration in the majority of areas.
Until 2006	Integration in the remaining areas.
Until 2008	Consolidation of the structures and budget

*Source: http://www.unia.ch/Meilensteine.583.0.html?&L=0&0=

In October 2004, the actual founding of the new merged union, UNIA, happened in two phases. Initially, in a voting process, each union had to individually secure a majority so that the merger could be carried out. Until that day, the decision to merge was still based on the desire of the management team and nothing had yet been agreed upon. The following day, the founding congress of the new joint union, UNIA, took place where roughly 1,100 delegates from all unions participated. The merger was decided on in January 1, 2005, and the new UNIA emerged with 200,000 members and about 900 employees.

New Management Structures, New Appointments

As a result of the merger, it was obvious that there would be job losses, especially among the executives, since fewer management positions would be needed regionally. The central issue of appointing senior positions had to be solved quickly to avoid long power struggles among the candidates. The management team's quick decision on new regional managers was very helpful in solving this delicate issue. For employee recruitment, a project management group developed a procedure to compile job profiles of the necessary positions and subsequently match them with employee competency profiles. The reduction of executives from the pre- to the post-merger phase resulted in the departure of some union executives because they would have been being demoted to lower levels. Others secured different positions in the new union.

Implementation Phase

During the implementation phase (post-merger integration), the existing cultural differences again emerged. Much time and effort was invested in the integration and restructuring of personnel while the merger itself was no longer questioned. After a relatively short time, the merged organizations could focus on the future and membership also was kept stable. An overview of the merger process is provided in Table 9.2.

Foci of a Merger from Within

We consider the described merger above as a success, even if cost and duration clearly show the great investments of time, expertise and energy needed. These efforts, however, do not have the merger as their sole result. Due to the diverse clarification and work conducted during the process, the course for the future collaborative effort was already set which greatly benefited the performance and viability of the new organization. "Many agreement processes developed, and with that, the foundation for the new joint venture was laid," says the key person responsible for the merger process. Based on this case study as well as the experience with other mergers from within, the following foci necessary for a successful merger are listed below.

Business Case: Common Goals

Mergers from within mostly concern organizations that have to involve their members in making decisions about a merger—such as unions, associations and municipalities. This requires an in-depth discussion about the organization's goals and whether they realistically can be achieved. To manage this participation process, it is necessary to consider and adopt a sufficient framework for live discussions and communication (e.g., workshops, meetings, gatherings) and for information dissemination through appropriate media. The absence of decision-making pressure in these discussions helps to avoid fruitless blockades and opposition. Yet it is still important to keep attention focused on future goals to maintain internal energy and future orientation: discussions on the "how" of the merger tend to breakdown if the questions about long-term objectives remain unresolved or if people are sidetracked. Putting too much focus on the cultural differences between the merging organizations instead of developing a common future vision also strengthens the skeptical side of the people involved.

For these tasks, mergers from within bring along some strengths: The reality check to determine if the merger is the best solution continues and is more critical and involves a greater diversity of perspectives. It entails noting the mergers' consequences from various internal (and external) interest groups by examining possible advantages and disadvantages, profit- and loss opportunities, success criteria and the traps of a merger in comparison to other alternatives. It is easy to assume that the "public due diligence" (Huber, 2004, p. 73) is sufficiently and broadly dealt with and doesn't just conform to particular interests (e.g. the owners') either internally or externally. It is more likely that a well-elaborated merger model fulfills expectations.

In the context of a forthcoming merger decision, the discussion of goals is closely linked to the decision-making process. It is worthwhile to debate the goals and base the decision on a solid goal-clarification process. Nevertheless, the goal discussion ('consultation') and the decision-making should be separated steps in the process, for reasons described above.

Joint Management and Control in an Own Social System

For the management of a merger, a jointly structured steering system is needed. Even in organizations like unions or municipalities where "bottom up" participation rights are well established, a steering system with highly equipped authority is essential to design and monitor the process. An intelligent and mutual decision-making process does not just arise automatically, but must develop through a sophisticated procedure that sufficiently prepares the content of the pending issues, communicates transparently and works in appropriate, communicative settings. Both the objective quality of the decision as well as its acceptance by the people depends on the quality of the foregoing process. The success of a steering system depends on several conditions, including:

1. *Authority and membership*: a management team can meet these requirements if, along with authority and mandate, they also have a high level of acceptance from the participating organizations. At UNIA, the management team consisted of the top executives (the president and the head of finance) of the merging unions, as well as of leaders of political action groups.
2. *Ability to work and trust*: With mergers from within, it is necessary that the development of an intensely collaborating control group can debate and provide conflict resolution. Only if there is success at this level will mergers have a chance to succeed by focusing on a joint future, gaining each other's trust, developing an interest in

each other, creating room for negotiation and moving the process forward together.

At the same time, the members of the steering structure have to take both the participating organizations' common and the individual interests into consideration. Much has to be invested in these relationships and the ability to work in the new group without the perception of alienation from the original organization. The mutual trust is as important as the trust obtained within the members of their own organizations.

Individuals who carry out a solid function and build confidence are of great importance. Considering the future, one must take a stand and be convinced of the merger, work toward this direction, continue collaborations within daily routines while *at the same time* a credible discussion process with *open* results has to be organized. A member of the UNIA management team summarizes that:

> A key success factor was the loyalty and the commitment of the managers in the management team, who worked together to develop a common vision and a common strategy, and who also displayed mutual respect and understanding, and maintained a high degree of openness. Most important was the hard work of the presidents of the organizations and the executive boards of trade unions, who were all personally convinced of the merger and who had such an intense relationship of trust towards one another that they were also able to convince others to come on board. The 'Yes' from the union eventually only succeeded because this group really believed in its vision, and was ready to implement it.

Reports from a different case study left a similar impression, the merger of the Swiss municipalities, Jona and Rapperswil: Uncensored communication is common in the steering committee. One could think of the steering committee as a kind of future workshop." The following explicitly formulated rules of conducting supported this performance of the steering committee:[3]

- Define the framework of the decision process instead of deciding by ourselves
- Encourage diverse opinions (all opinions are considered equal) as well as an open attitude to new suggestions
- Focus on solutions instead of problems
- Do not focus on past issues
- Find common ground instead of celebrating conflicts

Small-scale Collaborations, Mixed Teams

Mergers from within start as collaboration efforts. At first, collaborations on a small scale are observed and the attempt is made to collaborate within the boundaries of the existing organization, to have the experience of working together and to move the process forward (Huber, 2004, p. 66). The first successful collaboration and mutual learning experiences serve as a good entry point into a "trust building loop" (Huxham & Vangen, 2003b) by taking others' interests into account for long-term benefit. An initial collaboration process builds up "trust capital," which helps in coping with the difficulties and conflicts that arise with mergers at later stages. Even if contracts and committees secure collaborations, trust is needed for the sustainable development of the organization. Again, this trust only can be built through real action and a series of honored commitments and should not be confused with psychological attitudes.

Collaborations on a small scale can help to test the other's real commitment to merge and provide answers to the following questions: 1) Are the partners willing to engage in a collaborative relationship? 2) Will they succeed in balancing the power in spite of great differences in size and resources? and 3) Will these collaborations fulfill their strategic purpose, will working together add value?

Both successful collaborations on a small scale as well as those that do not fully meet their goals can lead to a following merger process: In the first case, one wants to proceed, in the second case one realizes the limitations of the partial cooperation, and urges that "We have to collaborate even more strongly!" In the UNIA Case, the joint founding of a new union (unia) by the two big unions didn't stop the membership decline of members—so they decided to take further steps.

The test of trust and the construction of a collaborative merger system are as vital as the tangible results that are achieved by partial forms of collaboration. In this way, the "Associated Union House" established by GBI and SMUV had a far greater impact than was originally intended. Bottom-up collaboration can reach such a stage that the decision-making process is "overtaken from the bottom" by operational, actual partial mergers. In the merger of the Swiss municipalities (see below), the administrative bodies mutually tackled numerous tasks before the final decision was made via a public ballot.

For instance in the school sector, one of the communities' most important fields, the issues were addressed as if there were already a joint community, although the final merger decision was not yet made. In the IT sector, the municipalities also organized joint activities and the garbage collection was carried out according to a common waste disposal plan.

These examples illustrate that the common linear "blue print" approach with carefully divided subsequent stages of decision-making, implementation and integration are often not well suited to the social dynamics of mergers. Following the tracks of decision making and practical collaboration simultaneously will help reach the goal of merging. At the same time the chance that the new merged organization will "get into gear" more quickly may increase since they have already set up internal collaborative structures and connections.

Swiss Films: A Merger with Exit Option

An illustrative example of the dynamics discussed above is "Swiss Films."[4] In Switzerland, at the beginning of the decade, the promotion of Swiss film products was seen as a task of the state, but was highly divided among miscellaneous independent and subcontracted organizations.

Several fruitless attempts to merge these organizations were made before the Federal Office for Culture developed the plan of founding a joint venture in form of an association, which would acquire assignments from the Federal Office. Subsequently, the four main organizational players started "Swiss Films" as a temporary collaborative project with the task of promoting Swiss films in internal and external markets. But the Federal Office also required that the founding organizations should be able to draft and execute a joint merger process and that the emerging organization would maintain a certain degree of independence.

To motivate the four organizations, the Federal Office of Culture conceded an "exit-option" to them. In the aftermath of the merger, this turned out to be a decisive success factor. The four founding organizations weren't forced to close down after the setup of the new "Swiss Films," but were allowed to maintain a partially organizational structure. If the new organization would fail to meet its goals over the course of time, the founding organizations could have been reinstated.

In the following preparatory phase, the project was put on the track. At the management level, the four participating organizations set up a pilot group with all the responsible decision-makers from the participating organizations, as well as a representative of the Federal Office of Culture. They managed to decide very early on the top manager of the new "Swiss Films," which was important for fostering independency because it soon created a counterpart with whom to deal.

Parallel to the setup at the management level and long before a final decision about a merger was reached, the four organizations jointly worked on merging their organizational processes. They built up four mixed subteams who worked on merging the core processes of domestic representation, representation abroad, communications/PR, technical work. These four sub-teams also met three times a year to reflect on mutual progress.

Apart of these organizational challenges, it was also necessary to find a location for the new organization. The chosen site was the former residence and "home" of one of the participating organizations. The physical adaption of the building to the needs of the new Swiss films was a great opportunity to "grow together" because the mixed teams set up their future workplaces together.

The management organized the transition of the staff from the old to the new organizations as a ritual: At a collective party of 70 people, they said goodbye to their former organizations and were then escorted to the new site. At this farewell and welcome, the directors of the participating organizations also gave speeches. Such rituals are very powerful methods of marking and facilitating transitions on an emotional level.

In the meantime, Swiss Films is well established and an important and successful player in the current market. Some of the parental organizations still exist and are charged with other tasks, while others exist only formally without being active or have completely vanished.

The Jona-Rapperswil Case: Setting up the Merger Process as a Project

One of the main management tasks is to set up a project for processing the merger. Projects are the preferable social form when implementing changes within and between organizations. They can serve as laboratories of (inter) organizational innovation (Grossmann & Scala, 1996). Work in the form of a project enables and supports open consultation and decision-making processes: One has "extra space" to make inquiries, formulate objectives and design the new joint organization, as if the merger is already reality, but without pre-empting decisions ("As if"—character).

In a merger project, one must work on the content of the future merger, as well as anticipate the common future by setting up a socially autonomous system between the systems that the parties concerned jointly manage (see Chapter 5). In this way, social forms, like mixed working groups, workshops, and sounding boards, are possibly helpful, as the UNIA and Swiss Film cases have shown. But setting up of these social structures isn't enough: they must also come to life. If the people involved get in touch with each other and work together on common results they can realize their integrative potential. In the merger case of the two Swiss municipalities Jona and Rapperswil, the project organization was especially sophisticated and the crucial success factor (see Table 9.3).

At this stage, the main challenge of the process design is to separate the content-based project work from the decision-making processes while at the same time connecting them. The conceptual work needs decisions (e.g., on the themes to be worked on) as a framework on which to rely), and the decision-makers need conceptual results (e.g., a proposition for the new distribution of school funds) as basis for their decisions.

Decision and Transition

In depicted collaborative merger, the decision to merge only is made if:

TABLE 9.3. Project Organization of the Merger of Swiss Municipalities Jona and Rapperswil

- An administrative conference where members from both councils are represented is responsible for the strategic decisions, the merger process (not the outcome) as well as the products of the project groups.
- The steering committee develops the foundation for the administrative conference, implements its decisions, gives orders to the project leaders and is responsible for communication, hearings and formal discussion stages. The steering committee is a transitional government.
- The conceptual work for the merger is conducted in mixed work groups with eleven subprojects. The subprojects "contracts", "government and administrative structuring" and "municipal code" deal with the basic and most important questions. Other topics include: computer science, pension funds, buildings and rooms, contracts and agreements, as well as age and health.
- The project manager coordinates the work of the sub-projects and is a member of the steering committee.
- The interest syndicate is composed of parties, government and public bodies, trade representatives, neighborhood associations and groups. Opponents are also invited. The members represent the opinion of their respective organizations. The syndicate serves as a partner of the authorities, is invited to discussion stages and hearings, submits proposals and suggestions, and is a key information hub.

1. On a business level, the strategic advantages and disadvantages, legal and financial conditions, a concrete view of the future joint organization (its functions, strategies, structures, management relationships, regulations, economical- and legal situation and constitution), and the union contracts and founding documents have been worked out and various services (IT and administrative systems) have been integrated.
2. On a social level, the merger is extensively tested in a collaborative setting, to integrate a number of services, and implement intensive communication and PR activities as well as a detailed decision-making process.

The decision-making level is about designing a process that is: 1) result-oriented; and 2) takes the original organizations' formal decision-making structures into account; and 3) beyond the formal level, allows the organization's members in participate informally but appropriately depending on the members' involvement.

A UNIA merger executive involved with the process noted that: "A determining factor in the project was also the fact that intense work was performed on the project for one and a half years, while the situation was held in extreme suspense. The biggest challenges were: the decision-making process, the balancing the going back-and-forth, the Yes and No and the issue of not merging but cooperating."

Although it is necessary to conceptualize the new organization, it is also essential not to take a preliminary decision to merge because plenty of room must be made available for pros and cons and various ideas about the future. Sufficient time has to be allocated for this process (Jansen 2004a, see thesis 6). The process must also be planned accurately and repeatedly adapted and reshaped to maintain the iterative nature of the process. Interim steps and results must be communicated to the partner organizations and the process steps should be formally delegated one at time. Crucial decisions must always be made at the collaborative level (e.g., the merger management team), and at the level of the individual organizations which latter secures the ongoing commitment of the participating organizations.

Often the full range of decisions is cut down into several steps, including: considering the merger and to testing it as a future alternative; pressing ahead with the merger (or not); and developing a design of the future joint organization (tasks, strategies, structures, regulations, economical and legal situation, and constitution). Based on this design, the participating organizations can decide to enter into a formal decision-making process (or not) and to agree on the regulations for the transition (founding documents, contracts). Only on the basis of these agreements is the formal decision to merge (or not) made (see Figure 9.3).

Attempts to shorten this sophisticated multi-staged path could lead to failure, as the Jona-Rapperswil case demonstrates (see Table 9.4). At a very early stage in the case of the Swiss communities' merger, the top politicians made the attempt to reach a quick decision on merging the two municipalities through a referendum. Because of economic imbalances one of the two communities was rather skeptical, so the public vote was negative. However, instead of feeling defeated, the municipal leaders chose to learn from the experience. Four years later, they initiated a new, more open process and after 1 1/2 years of thorough debate and hard work that resulted in a positive vote for the merger.

The Swiss villages' merger's project structure included various elements of "opening" (fostering open debates) and "closing" (reaching decisions). For example, the project structure allowed for a "interest syndicate" (IS), which involved various organizational stakeholders as an important sounding board; at certain points in the process the IS had the opportunity to discuss the interim results of the project groups, provide feedback, suggest changes, and submit proposals, which included further work.

The citizens on the other side were involved in various informational meetings ("opening") as well as in the formal instruments of participative decision making ("closing"), which are part of the county's constitution. In addition to lively debate within the local media, the citizens were regularly

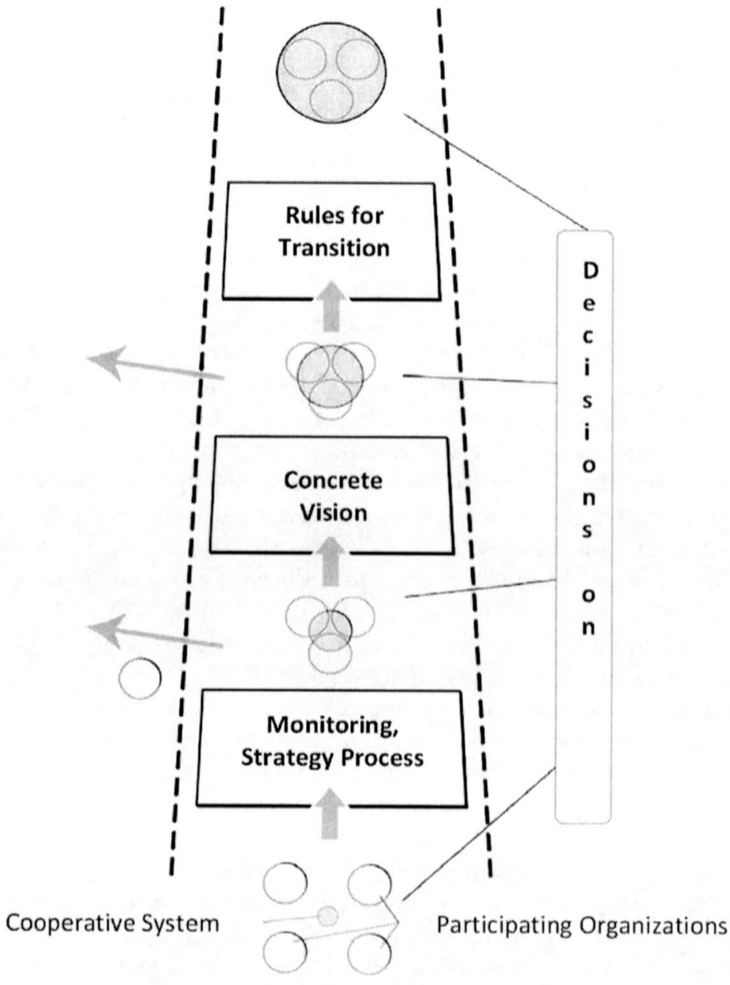

FIGURE 9.3. Decisions in Collaborative Mergers

informed of the merger process by their own newspaper ("Zäme," meaning "Together").

Immediately after a long, public decision-making phase, it is important to carefully create context for closure and set the stage for future activities. Public events support that. During this transition, the new reality comes to life through founding congresses and elections and rituals can be used in these transitional situations where big events involve the whole system.

TABLE 9.4. The Process of the Jona-Rapperswil Merger: Second Phase

11. 30. 2003	The citizens approve the initiative to merge the municipalities Rapperswil and Jona.
12. 8. 2003	The authorities (city council of Rapperswil and municipal council of Jona) develop the project organization in a conference
7. 2. 2004	The merger project is launched with workshops using the following themes: expectations, role of the authorities, agreement on rules and strategic goals.
4. 27. 2004	The Interest Syndicate (IS) Rapperswil and Jona conducts its first meeting, where they share informations and formulate expectations.
6. 1. 2004	The IS conducts its second meeting discussing strategy documents and action guidelines.
6. 21. 2004	The conference of authorities adopts the final strategy documents, action guidelines and the financial model
June 2004	Publish ZÄME 1
Sept., Oct. 2004	The IS discusses in three meetings the coalition agreement (procedural matters) and the unification treaty and formulate written modification
Nov. 2004	Publish ZÄME 2
End 2004	The authorities present the strategy documents, the action guidelines and other documents to the public, according to the constitutional rules
1. 31. 2005	The conference of the authorities adopt the coalition agreement and design the unification treaty
March 2005	The authorities present the coalition agreement and the unification treaty to citizens in five evenings of public information sessions. The steering committee runs a student Q&A session
May 2005	Publish ZÄME 3
5. 1. 2005	The citizens vote positively on the coalition agreement and the deconstruction of the school districts. The vote on the unification treaty, which is the real foundation of the collaboration, on constitutional causes has to be made later, although the text is already available.
8. 8. 2005	The internal department of the county of St. Gallen approves the unification treaty. It authorizes the municipal authority conference to implement the assembly of the citizens.
Aug. 2005	The steering committee holds a joint Information event at the schools for teachers.
Oct. 2005	Publish ZÄME 4
12. 1. 2005	All citizens of Rapperswil-Jona get together at a constitutive assembly. They approve the above mentioned unification treaty
12. 8. 2005	The citizens of Rapperswil-Jona hold a regular assembly
Feb. 2006	Publish ZÄME 5 (Special edition - master plan of the settlement and region)
April 2006	Publish ZÄME 6
5. 21. 2006	The citizens elect the new authorities for the joint municipality (mayor, principal, city council, school council, control committees)
6. 16. 2006	The citizens of Rapperswil-Jona hold a regular assembly
Sept. 2006	Publish ZÄME 7
12. 18. 2006	The city administration moves to the town hall Rapperswil-Jona in Jona
1. 1. 2007	City festival and official opening ceremony
3. 1. 2007	The city administration starts to work

In many ways, the new organization is a result of the quality of the merger process. Not only do concrete solutions emerge into the organizational design, but the new organization must be equipped with the ability to continue collaboration, including concrete solutions, new contracts and the ability to draw on previous collaborative experience.

REFLECTIONS ON THE FORMATION OF MERGERS FROM THE OUTSIDE

Mergers from within emerge from collaborations and continue as collaborations between organizations. As suggested, they bear many requirements and are time-consuming as well. Until recently, they are exceptions to the norm. The public service sector more commonly experiences mergers that political stakeholders, financers and top managers initiate though hierarchical decisions.

When reviewing the different merger models, the processes seem quite different. While in a collaborative merger many integration steps are anticipated, mergers from the outside only tackle these steps in the post-merger phase. With closer examination of the public sector, a particular difficulty exists with the exclusion of employers, customers, and citizens in the stakeholders' decision-making process, creating much criticism and skepticism. From these differences, we can speculate that the diverse mergers models also require very diverse management.

However, we finally want to examine what can be learned from mergers from within for the management other mergers. Are there any hints and clues among the presented success factors which could prove helpful in the post-merger management of hierarchical or market model mergers?

Integration Requires Collaboration and Participation

Different mergers have different objectives. For performance improvement that includes quality and efficiency (and not just a matter of eliminating competition or closing a particular site), a high level of integration is needed and expected. Our fundamental thesis is that integration greatly benefits from collaboration and participation. The logic of a successful integration process corresponds to the logic of collaboration. In that aspect, mergers from the outside do not differ from mergers from within, which is illustrated in the merger of the two universities at the University of Duisburg-Essen.

After the two universities Duisburg and Essen failed to merge from within, the state government of North Rhine-Westphalia legally closed the two universities on January 1, 2003, and established one new, merged university. This caused great resistance and turmoil at both universities. The universities proposed a founding rector, who would be responsible for the merger process management, and the regional government approved and appointed him. He was put in charge of the merger management and decided to follow a three-phase-plan to conduct the merger (in 2004, gross structural decisions; in 2005, strategy development in the sub-units; in 2006, evaluation and quality development).

Through information and discussion, the merger management team (founding rector together with his assistants) made great efforts to properly communicate these procedures and to involve the deciding leadership bodies, as well as the employees. In the various fields and disciplines, the merger management team set in motion often difficult negotiation processes to create a solid design of the future university structure. These processes were driven by the knowledge that collaboration could only take place if the concerned parties conducted the implementation.

The rector, the presidency and the department leaders guided the process along the hierarchy, without a project structure. Looking back, the rector now would process the merger as a project, resulting in higher transparency and involving all concerned parties.

This example demonstrates that the decision-making authority (i.e. regional government) can establish a framework for collaboration. It is not sufficient to merge subordinate units under pressure in order to economize (for example, with shortened working contracts) and leave the rest of the decision-making to the involved organizations. These self-organized work processes with politically determined cuts promote destructive competition.

In such a context, entering into a collaborative process can be difficult and probably is not deliberately intended. In the case of some mergers, hierarchy can only develop an enabling role if decisions are made that take the following into consideration:

- Commitment of the (often varying) regional and local political stakeholders and institutional management affected by the merger, which can be diverse and time consuming.
- The decision to merge must simultaneously provide a viable framework and leave room for its formation. Over the course of a pre-merger, it is advisable to decide on the merged institutions' top-level management, the main structural framework for the merger and the most fiercely disputed issues. If one wants encourage collaboration, conflicting issues have to be resolved to unburden the affected organizations. At the same time, too detailed specifications of the future organization must be avoided.
- The decision makers (e.g. politicians) must provide resources, such as external expertise and process consulting.

Communicating Decisions and Procedures

In the political field, mergers are always risky projects because resistance must be expected. Clear decisions become difficult, which in turn makes the merger difficult.

Finally, it is fundamental to consider important issues *before* a decision is made, taking into account the interests of all concerned parties. It is also important to actually make the necessary decisions, advocate the "case for action" with the help of persuasion, and to achieve commitment if a merger is the best strategy.

Establishing an Independent Social Control System

With mergers from the outside, a stringent, yet flexibly managed process is a key success factor. It is helpful to set up an independent control system, such as a steering committee, and to invest in the development of collaboration and conflict management (see Chapter 5). As mentioned previously, one should however, distinguish between stakeholders and the new management. If the authority on "how to process the merger" is in the hands of the organizations, this will influence the organizational structure that is "in the shadow of the hierarchical preliminary decisions." This dynamic can impose limitations on a flexible, innovative process.

Similar Tasks for Mergers from Within and from the Outside

In the management of the merger process mergers from within and from the outside do not differ in the sense of *what* has to be done. The goals from a merger from within can also provide lessons for a merger from the outside, including: a joint steering system, gradually implementing collaboration, designing different areas with mixed teams, defining new management positions and quickly and transparently recruiting qualified leaders.

Here the conflict between hierarchy and collaboration has to be managed through different forms of participation. Active and efficiently designed involvement of the parties concerned creates appreciation and generates a high level of integration.

Mergers can be Used to Resolve Other Problems

Within the scope of the new organization, mergers can be used to address changes already needed in the original organizations. By focusing on topics that have clear benefits for the employees, the new organization enhances its attractiveness.

Use of Consulting

Using external consultants on a merger can be very helpful since neutral parties can help to address conflicts, facilitate the collaborative process, and support the development of a new organizational framework (see Chapter 5 & 6). Stakeholders can significantly support mergers if they provide consulting resources. However, public sector mergers often do not use consultants. In many areas there is still little (though growing) experience with different forms of consulting (Grossmann, 2004b).

NOTES

1. Mergers from within are ideal examples for mergers, which are oriented on a collaborative process between the merging organizations. However, the other types of mergers (market-oriented, hierarchical) can also contain some collaborative aspects.
2. The sources for the UNIA case (1995–2005) consist of an interview with a member of the management team and document analysis.
3. The sources for the Jona-Rapperswil case consist of an interview with a member of the steering committee and document analysis.
4. Sources for the Swiss Films Case include an interview with the CEO of Swiss Films and document analysis.

APPENDIX

The Research Context

This book originated within the iff-oegd research group "Collaboration and New Public Management," which has run since 2004. Its subject matter includes the procedural development of relations between organizations for the provision of public services with the following focal points:

- New Public Management in practice: The design of the governance relationship between political decision-makers, financing organizations and service providers
- Collaboration of organizations as well as subsystems of several organizations in service cooperatives, networks, reform processes, development partnerships and merger processes
- From hierarchy to the internal network: The internal management and organizational development of decentralized organizations.

These three development perspectives within and between organizations are analyzed in their necessary interdependencies. The aim of the research program is to develop process models of collaboration between organizations within the scope of the public sector and to logically disseminate the findings.

Facilitating Collaboration in Public Management, pages 187–189

METHOD AND BASIS OF DATA

Our findings presented in this book stem from the following sources:

1. Long-term OD consultant projects on organizational collaboration and networks
2. Thirty-three further case studies of collaboration in the field of public service
3. Discussion of these case studies at the expert conference "The process makes the difference" (in Zurich, 25.–26.11. 2004)
4. Theses and dissertations developed within the context of our master's program of organizational development (MSOD) and our PhD program (Dr. OD)

Gaining knowledge through practice is dominant in all of these sources.

Chapter 1 describes the historical development of our practical field work. Furthermore, in the past few years, the authors worked as consultants in a variety of OD projects in Austria, Germany, and Switzerland, including the fields of federal-, state- and local government, hospitals, schools, universities, research institutions, social services, churches and other NGO's. This researcher-like reflection and analysis of fieldwork based on the "practitioner's model" is the most important information source for this book. Examples can be found in Chapters 5–6 which represent the core empirical findings of our study.

To obtain a broader basis of data and to validate our findings, an additional 33 case studies relating to cooperation, networking and mergers were examined in two rounds through face-to-face interviews of executives and staff and supplementary materials analysis. These case studies originate from the fields of health care, education, science, culture, politics, administration and social affairs. Examples can be found in the following chapters, covering a wide range of topics that include regional employment pacts, research networks, nanotechnology, e-learning platforms across universities, hospital mergers, universities, unions, municipalities, collaboration between hospitals in introducing digital X-ray, and a network of residential physicians.

Overview Case Examples

Field	No.	Subject	No.	Land	No.
Health Care	15	Network	7	Austria	11
Education, Science	6	Collaboration	15	Suisse	20
Politics, Administration	6	Of these: Governance	7	Germany	2
Social Work	3	Amalgamation	11		
Culture	3				
Sum	**33**		**33**		**33**

Interviews averaged two-hours and were supported by guidelines and carried out in a semi-structured format. Data was collected on the perspectives of the practitioners regarding history and context, the development and process of cooperation, significant intervention cases, success factors and obstacles, as well as consequences for the people involved and the individual roles that they played. The research team then transcribed and analyzed the data. Some of these cases are examined more closely in Chapters 4 and 8.

Experts Conference: "The Process makes the Difference"

This conference (Zurich, 2004)—itself a result of collaboration between the iff-oegd-alumni-network and public service enterprises from various social fields—was held to discuss case studies originating from personal experience and from the first round of the interviews mentioned above. Approximately 100 practitioners (managers, staff employees, consultants) from different organizations participated. This started with an interim analysis of the existing research on cooperation. After that, data in the form of four case studies was presented for discussion. Intensive data processing was carried out in workshops and plenums, dovetailed between other lectures. Subsequently, we identified a number of key findings about collaboration between organizations. On the basis of these results and the questions that emerged, the focal points of the second round of case studies (see above) were determined.

Since 1999, as part of our Master's program entitled "Organizational Development" (see Chapter 1), participating practitioners have written some 110 master theses, primarily dealing with the public service sector and others more closely addressing the construction and design of cooperative relations between organizations. These works arose out of intensive discussions between the participants with their own practical case studies in which they, as managers, internal change agents, or external consultants, operated as OD practitioners. They provided content-rich case studies from an insider's perspective, and thus, valuable data based on the practitioner's model.

In contrast, the iff-oegd PhD program entitled "Dr. OD" focuses on a *researcher-based* analysis of individual OD cases. Again, this is a matter of processing case studies combined with practical OD experience. However, the reflections and findings are presented more strongly in the context of existing OD research discourse. Since 2003, students have written 28 dissertations, supported by in-depth discussions with Ralph Grossmann and Klaus Scala, of which several explicitly deal with collaborative relationships and networks in the public sector, and whose findings are presented in this book (Mayr, 2003; Payer, 2003; Schmidt, 2006; Wabnegg, 2006).

BIBLIOGRAPHY

Alber, J. (2000). *Recent developments in the German Welfare State.* Paper presented at The Changing Landscape of the Welfare State. Rockefeller Foundation Study and Conference Center, Bellagio, Italy, August 5–11.

Argyris, C., Putnam, R., & Smith, R. M. (1985). *Action science, concepts, methods and skills for research and interventions.* San Francisco, CA: Jossey Bass.

Austin, J. E. (2000). *The collaboration challenge: How nonprofits and businesses succeed through strategic alliances.* San Francisco, CA: Jossey Bass.

Auth, A. (Ed.) (2003). *Neue medien in der lehre: Erfahrungen der ersten Etappe* [*New media in teaching: Experiences of the first phase*]. Vienna, Austria: Bundesministerium für Bildung, Wissenschaft und Kultur.

Bahle, T., & Pfenning, A. (2001). Angebotsformen und Träger-strukturen sozialer Dienste im westeuropäischen Vergleich [Types and organizational structures of social services in Western Europe]. *Observatorium für die Entwicklung der sozialen Dienste in Europa* [*Observatory of the development of social services in Europe*]. Arbeitspapier Nr. 4, Frankfurt am Main, Dezember.

Bateson, G. (1973). *Steps to an ecology of mind.* New York: HarperCollins.

Bateson, G. (1980). *Mind and nature: A necessary unity.* New York: Bantam Books.

Brandenburger, A., & Nalebuff, B. (1996). *Co-opetition—kooperativ konkurieren: Mit der Spieltheorie zum Unternehmenserfolg* [*Co-opetition—compete collaboratively: Game theory for success*]. Frankfurt: Campus.

Facilitating Collaboration in Public Management, pages 191–199

Breitwieser, U., Donauer, B., Elsigan, G., & Grossmann, R. (1991). *Gesundheitsförderung: Appelle sind zuwenig! Beispiele regionaler Bildungsarbeit* [*Health promotion: Pleas are not enough! Examples of educational efforts in the regions*]. München-Wien: Profil.

Buono, A. F. (1997). Enhancing strategic partnerships: Intervening in network organizations. *Journal of Organizational Change Management, 10* (3): 251–266.

Buono, A. F. (2005). Consulting to integrate mergers and acquisitions. In L. Greiner & F. Poulfelt (Eds.), *Handbook of management consulting: The contemporary consultant—Insights from world experts* (pp. 229–249). Cincinnati, OH: Southwestern/Thompson.

Buono, A. F., & Bowditch, J.L. (1989). *The human side of mergers and acquisitions: Managing collisions between people, cultures, and organizations.* San Francisco: Jossey-Bass.

Buono, A. F., & Nurick, A. J. (1992). Intervening in the middle: Coping strategies in mergers and acquisitions. *Human Resource Planning, 15*(2), 19–33.

Burchardt, T. (1997). *Boundaries between public and private welfare: A typology and map of services.* London: Center for Analysis of Social Exclusion, London School of Economics.

Chisholm, R. F. (1998). *Developing network organizations: Learning from practice and theory.* Reading, MA: Addison Wesley.

Ciompi, L. (1988). *The psyche and schizophrenia: The bond between affect and logic.* Cambridge, MA: Harvard University Press.

Ciompi, L. (2003). Reflections on the role of emotions in consciousness and subjectivity, from the perspective of affect logic. *Consciousness and Emotion, 4,* 181–196.

Collins, J. (2005). *Good to create and the social sectors: Why business thinking is not the answer.* New York: HarperBusiness.

Cummings, T. G. (1984). *Transorganizational development.* In B. M. Staw & L. L. Cummings (Eds.), *Research in organizational behavior* (Vol. 6, pp. 367–422). Greenwich, CT: JAI Press.

Cummings, T. G., & Worley, C. G. (1997). *Organization development and change* (6th ed.). Cincinnati, OH: South Western.

Cummings, T. G,. & Worley, C. G. (2001). *Essentials of organizational development and change.* Cincinnati, OH: South Western.

Davoine, E. (2003). Building effective innovation networks: Enhancing cooperation in public-private partnerships. In A. F. Buono (Ed.), *Enhancing inter-firm networks and interorganizational strategies* (pp. 187–206). Greenwich, CT: Information Age Publishing.

Dillenbourg, P., Baker, M., Blaye, A., & O'Malley, C. (1995). The Evolution of research on collaborative learning. In P. Reimann & H. Spada (Eds.), *Learning in humans and machines: Towards an interdisciplinary learning science* (pp. 189–211). London: Pergamon.

Drucker, P. (2001). *The essential Drucker.* New York: HarperCollins Publisher.

Ecker, A., & Grossmann, R. (2001). Die Initiative: Neue Medien in der Lehre an Universitäten und Fachhochschulen als Best-Practice-Modell für e-Government [The initiative: New media in teaching at universities and colleges as a best-practice model for e-government] *Verwaltung heute. Zeitung für Führung-*

skräfte im öffentlichen Dienst [*Administration today: Journal for CEOs in public services*], *44*, 14–16.

Ecker, A., Pflichter, F., & Weilguny, A. (2000). *Neue Medien in der Lehre an Universitäten und Fachhochschulen: Handbuch* [*New Media in teaching at universities and colleges: A manual*]. Vienna, Austria: Bundesministerium für Bildung, Wissenschaft und Kultur.

Evers, A. (1992). Megatrends im Wohlfahrtsmix: Soziale dienstleistungen zwischen Deregulierung und Neugestaltung [Megatrends in welfare: Social services between deregulation and reform]. *Blätter der Wohlfahrtspflege* [*Papers of welfare services*], *139*(1), 3–7.

Evers, A. (2002). Auf dem Weg zu einem neuen Wohlfahrtsmix? Pflege im Alter und der mögliche Beitrag der Bürgergesellschaft [A new mix of social services on the journey? Care for the aged and its contribution to civil society]. In BAS (Ed.), *Grundsatzthemen der Freiwilligenarbeit* [*Basic issues of voluntary service*] (pp. 85–100). Stuttgart, Marburg, Erfurt: Verlag Peter Wiehl.

Gesundheitsdirektion des Kantons Zürich (Ed.) (1998). *wif!-Projekt LORAS: Outcome-Projekt Schlussbericht / wif!* [*Project LORAS: Outcome-project final*]. *Public 2.* Zürich: Kanton Zürich.

Giddens, A. (1984). *The constitution of society: Outline of the theory of structuration.* Cambridge: Polity Press.

Gilbert, N. (2005). The 'enabling state'? From public to private responsibility for social protection: Pathways and pitfalls. *OECD Social employment and migration working papers*, No. 26, OECD Publishing.

Gray, B. (1989). *Collaborating: Finding common ground for multiparty problems.* San Francisco: Jossey-Bass.

Gray, B., & Schlesinger, M. (2002). Health. In L. Salamon (Ed.), *The state of nonprofit America* (pp. 74–75). Washington D.C.: Brookings Institution.

Gray, B., & Wood, D. J. (1991). Collaborative alliances: Moving from practice to theory. *Journal of Applied Behavioral Science, 27* (1), 3–21.

Grossmann, R. (1984). Arbeitsbelastung und Gesundheitsverschleiß, Gesundheitserziehung zur Prävention arbeitsbedingter Erkrankungen [Work loading and deterioration of health, health education for prevention of labor-induced diseases]. *Europäische Monographien zur Förderung in der Gesundheitserziehung* [*European monographs for promotion of health education*] (pp. 199–219). Bd 6., Edinburgh, .

Grossmann, R. (1995). Das Krankenhaus auf dem Weg zur „lernenden Organisation": Zum Verhältnis von Qualifizierung und Organisationsentwicklung [The Hospital Becoming to a "Learning Organization: The interdependence of HR training and organizational development]. *Gruppendynamik* [*Group dynamics*], *26* (2), 203–222.

Grossmann, R. (2002). Auf das Ergebnis kommt es an. Die Verankerung von Outcome-Indikatoren als Entwicklungsprozess in und zwischen Organisationen [The results count: The implementation of outcome-indicators as development in and between organizations]. In R. Grossmann & K. Scala (Eds.), *Intelligentes Krankenhaus* [*The intelligent hospital*] (pp. 32–60). Wien-New York: Springer.

Grossmann, R. (2003). Das Öffentliche organisieren—Die Beziehung zwischen gesellschaftlichen Sektoren und Organisationen managen [To organize public goods: managing the relationship between sectors and organizations]. In H. Lobnig, J. Schwendenwein & L. Zvacek (Eds.), *Beratung in der Veränderung [Consultancy in change]* (pp. 33–54). Wiesbaden: Gabler Verlag.

Grossmann, R. (2004a). Die Reform des Öffentlichen in einer Gesellschaft von selbständig agierenden Organisationen [The reform of public services in a society of independently acting organizations]. In R. Grossmann & K. Scala (Eds.), *Das Öffentliche organisieren [Organizing public goods]* (pp. 115–120). Wien-New York: Springer.

Grossmann, R. (2004b). *Organisationsberatung in der Reform öffentlicher Leistungen: Auf den Nutzen kommt es an [Organizational consultancy for the reform of public services: The benefit counts].* Wien: Springer.

Grossmann, R. & Heintel, P. (2000). Vermittlung von Organisationskompetenz [Teaching organizational competence]. In P. Heintel & L. Krainer (Eds.), *Weiter Bildung? Beiträge zur wissenschaftlichen Weiterbildung aus Theorie und Praxis [Further education? Articles on science-based further education in theory and practice]* (pp. 49–60). Wien-New York: Springer.

Grossmann, R., & Lobnig, H. (2003). Die Initiative NML als Beispiel der „neuen Steuerung" zwischen bm:bwk und Organisationen der Wissenschaft und Bildung aus Sicht der Organisationsberater [The initiative NML (new media in teaching) as example for a new type of governance between the ministry of higher education and organizations of science and education in the view of consultants]. In A. Auth (Ed.), *Neue Medien in der Lehre. Erfahrungen der ersten Etappe [New media in teaching: Experiences of the first phase]* (pp. 33–34). Wien: Bundesministerium für Bildung, Wissenschaft and Kultur.

Grossmann, R., & Mayr, F. (2005). *Organisationsentwicklung öffentlicher Leistungen. Strategische Steuerung von Organisationen und Management von Netzwerken [Organizational development of public services: Strategic governance of organizations and management of networks].* Presentation at the conference X-Organisationen Berlin, October.

Grossmann, R., & Scala, K. (1996). *Health Promotion and Organizational Development: Developing Settings for Health.* 2nd ed. European Health Promotion Series, No. 2.

Grossmann, R., & Scala, K. (2002). Veränderungsfähigkeit macht die Intelligenz einer Organisation aus [The capability of change is the intelligence of an organization]. In R. Grossmann & K. Scala (Eds.), *Intelligentes Krankenhaus [The intelligent hospital]* (pp. 179–199). Wien-New York: Springer.

Hackett, M. C. (1996). Are there alternatives to merger? *Health Manpower Management, 22* (5): 5–12.

Heintel, P. (2005a). Grundaxiomatik der Interventionsforschung [The basic axioms of the intervention-research]. In P. Heintel, L. Krainer & I. Paul-Horn (Eds.), *Klagenfurter Beiträge zur Interventionsforschung [Articles from Klagenfurt on intervention-research*]. Klagenfurt: Klagenfurt: IFF-Abteilung für Weiterbildung und systemische Internventionsforschung.

Heintel, P. (2005b). Prozessethik und Mediation [Ethics of process and mediation]. In A. Bammé, P. Baumgartner, W. Berger & E. Kotzmann (Eds.), *Klagenfurter Beiträge zur Technikdiskussion [Articles from Klagenfurt on the debate about technics]* (pp. 5–9). Klagenfurt, Graz, Wien: Fakultät für Interdisziplinäre Forschung und Fortbildung, Abteilung für Technik- und Wissenschaftsforschung.

Heintel, P., Krainer, L. & Paul-Horn, I. (Eds.). (2005). *Klagenfurter Beiträge zur Interventionsforschung [Articles from Klagenfurt on intervention-research]*. Klagenfurt: IFF-Abteilung für Weiterbildung und systemische Internventionsforschung.

Heintel, P., & Krainz, E. E. (1990). *Projektmanagement. Eine Antwort auf die Hierarchiekrise? [Project management. An answer to the crisis of hierarchy]*. Wiesbaden, Germany: Gabler.

Huber, A. (2004). Public Due Diligence. In A. Huber, S. A. Jansen, & H. Plamper (Eds.), *Public Merger* (pp. 57–89). Wiesbaden: Gabler.

Huber, A., Jansen, S. A., & Plamper, H. (Eds.) (2004). *Public merger.* Wiesbaden: Gabler.

Huxham, C. (2003). Theorizing collaboration practice. *Public Management Review, 5* (3), 402–423.

Huxham, C., & Vangen, S. (2002. *Enacting leadership for collaborative advantage.* University of Strathclyde Business School, Working Paper Series Paper No. 2002-19R.

Huxham, C., & Vangen, S. (2003a). Ambiguity, complexity and dynamics in the membership of collaboration. *Human Relations, 53* (6), 771–806.

Huxham, C., & Vangen, S. (2003b). Nurturing collaborative relations: Building trust in interorganizational collaboration. *Journal of Applied Social Behavior, 39* (1), 5–31.

Huxham, C., & Vangen, S. (2005). *Managing to collaborate: The theory and practice of collaborative advantage.* London: Routledge.

Jacobs, R. W., & McKeown, F. (2007). Real time strategic change. In P. Holman & T. Devane (Eds.), *The change handbook* (pp. 295–311). San Francisco: Berrett-Koehler.

Janes, A., Prammer, K., & Schulte-Derne, M. (2001). *Organisationen von innen verändern [Transformations-Management].* Vienna, Austria: Springer.

Jansen, S. A. (2000). Thesen gegen (Post Merger Integration Management) [Theses against (Post Merger Integration Management)].*Organisationsentwicklung [Organizational Development], 1*, 32–47.

Jansen, S. A. (2004a). *Management von Unternehmenszusammenschlüssen: Theorien, Thesen, Tests und Tools [Management of mergers: Theories, theses, tests and tools].* Stuttgart: Klett-Cotta.

Jansen, S. A. (2004b). Public merger management. In A. Huber, S. A. Jansen, & H. Plamper, (Eds.), *Public merger* (pp. 3–37). Wiesbaden, Germany: Gabler.

Kickbusch, I. (2005). Gesundheit als globales öffentliches Gut: eine politische Herausforderung im 21 Jahrhundert [Health as a public good: A political challenge for the 21st Century]. *Politorbis: Zeitschrift zur Aussenpolitik [Politorbis: Journal of Foreign Affairs], 39* (3), 12–18.

Königswieser, R., & Hillebrand, M. (2005). *Systemic consultancy in organisations.* Heidelberg: Carl-Auer Verlag.

Kotter, J. P. (1996). *Leading change.* Boston: Harvard School Press.

Krusche, B. (2000). *Perspektiven der Beratungsarbeit [Merers and Acquisitions].* Presentation at the conference of GWS, 24. 2. 2000, Wiesbaden, Germany.

Lewin, K. (1951). *Resolving social conflicts.* New York: Harper & Row.

Lewis, J. D. (1999). *Trusted partners: How companies build mutual trust and win together.* New York: The Free Press.

Littmann, P. & Jansen, S.A. (2000). *Oszillodox: Virtualisierung—die permanente Neuerfindung der Organisation* [*Virtualization—the permanent reinvention of organizations*]. Stuttgart: Klett-Cotta.

Lohmer, M., & Lohmer, M. (2005). Room to move: Die Psychodynamik von Fusionen [Room to move: The psychodynamics of mergers]. In *osb reader 2005* (p. 174 et seq.). Berlin: osb international Consulting.

Luhmann, N. (1979). *Trust and power.* Chichester: Wiley.

Luhmann, N. (1992). Organisation. In W. Küpper & G. Ortmann, G. (Eds.), *Mikropolitik—Rationalität, Macht und Spiele in Organisationen* (p. 174 et seq.). Opladen: Westdeutscher Verlag.

Luhmann, N. (1997). *Die Gesellschaft der Gesellschaft [The society of the society].* Frankfurt, Germany: Suhrkamp.

Lundstrom, T. (2000), *Non-governmental Actors, Local Administration, and Private Enterprise: New Models in Delivery of Child and Youth Welfare?* Paper presented at the International Conference on Playing the market game. University of Bielefeld, Germany, March 9–11, 2000.

Malkin, J., & Wildavsky, A. (1991). Why the traditional distinction between public and private goods should be abandoned. *Journal of Theoretical Politics, 3*(4), 355–378.

Mayr, J. (2003). *Implementierung einer kontinuierlichen Direktkommunikation mit den VertragsärztInnen der OÖ Gebietskrankenkasse zur Beeinflussung der Veranlassung von medizinischen Leistungen mit Schwerpunkt auf das Heilmittelverordnungsverhalten durch Organisationsentwicklung* [*The implementation of a direct communication with the contracted physicians with the health insurance of Upper Austria in order to influence the medical service, focusing on prescription behavior through organizational development*]. Ph. D. Thesis. Klagenfurt: Alpen-Adria University of Klagenfurt.

Nagel, T. (1986). *The view from nowhere.* New York: Oxford University Press.

Nguyen, H., & Kleiner, B. H. (2003). The effective management of mergers. *Leadership and Organization Development Journal, 24*(8), 447–454.

Novak, P., Lobnig, H., Krajic, K., & Pelikan J. M. (1998). Case study Rudolfstiftung Hospital: Vienna, Austria-WHO-Model Project 'Health and Hospital.' In J. M. Pelikan, M. Garcia-Barbero, H. Lobnig, & K. Krajic (Eds.), *Pathways to a health promoting hospital.* (pp. 47–66). Gamburg: G. Conrad, Health Promotion Publications.

Odenthal, S., Säubert, H., & Weishaar, A. (2002), *Strategische Partnerschaften. Mehr Erfolg mit dem neuen Partnering-Ansatz.* Wiesbaden: Gabler.

OECD, *Economic Outlook* 79, Online resource Database. http://stats.oecd.org/OECDStat_Metadata/ShowMetadata.ashx?Dataset=EO79_MAIN

Orton, J. D., & Weick, K. E. (1990). Loosely coupled systems: A reconceptualization. *Academy of Management Review, 15*(2), 203–223.

Payer, H. (2003). *Wie viel Organisation braucht das Netzwerk? Entwicklung und Steuerung von Organisationsnetzwerken* [*How much organizing does a network need? Development and management of networks of organzations*]. Ph. D. Thesis. Klagenfurt: Alpe-Adria Universiy of Klagenfurt.

Pechar, H. (2004). Über Veränderungen im Verständnis "öffentlicher Güter" [On changes of meanings of "public goods"]. In R. Grossmann & K. Scala (Eds.), *Das Öffentliche organisieren [Organizing public goods]* (pp. 9–16). Wien-New York: Springer.

Pelikan, J. M., Garcia-Barbero, M., Lobnig, H., & Krajic, K. (Eds.) (1998a). *Pathways to a health promoting hospital.* Gamburg: G.Conrad, Health Promotion Publications.

Pelikan, J. M., Krajic, K., & Lobnig, H. (Eds.) (1998). *From projects to networks: Feasibility, effectiveness, efficiency and sustainability of health promoting hospital projects.* Gamburg: G.Conrad, Health Promotion Publications.

Pelikan, J. M., Lobnig, H., Krajic, K., & Dietscher, C. (1998b). Structure, process and outcome of the European Pilot Hospital Project: A summary. In J. M. Pelikan, M. Garcia-Barbero, H. Lobnig, & K. Krajic, K. (Eds.), *Pathways to a health promoting hospital* (pp. 17–44). Gamburg: G.Conrad, Health Promotion Publications.

Peter F. Drucker Foundation for Nonprofit Management. (2001). *Meeting the collaboration challenge workbook: Developing strategic alliances between nonprofit organizations and businesses: Workbook.* San Francisco: Jossey-Bass Wiley.

Plamper, H. (2004). Politische Voraussetzungen einer Fusion [Political conditions for mergers]. In A. Huber, S.A. Jansen & H. Plamper (Eds.), *Public Merger: Strategien für Fusionen im öffentlichen Sektor* [*Public Merger: Strategies for mergers in the public sector*] (pp. 39–55). Wiesbaden: Gabler.

Porter, M. (1987). From competitive advantage to corporate strategy. *Harvard Business Review,* (May/June): 43–59.

Ripperger, T. (1998). *Ökonomik des Vertrauens: Analyse eines Organisationsprinzips [The economics of trust: Analysis of a principle in organizations].* Tübingen: J.C.B. Mohr.

Roschelle, J., & Teasley, S. D. (1995). The construction of shared knowledge in collaborative problem solving. In C. O'Malley (Ed.), *Computer-supported collaborative learning* (pp. 69–97). New York: Springer-Verlag.

Salamon, L. (2001). *The third sector and volunteering in global perspective.* Presentation at the 17th Annual International Association of Volunteer Effort Conference, Amsterdam, The Netherlands, January.

Salamon, L. (2003). *The resilient sector: The state of nonprofit America.* Washington D.C.: Brookings Institution.

Salamon, L., Hems, L. C., & Chinnock, K. (2000). *The nonprofit sector: For what and for whom?* Working Papers of the Johns Hopkins Comparative Nonprofit Sector Project, no. 37. Baltimore: The Johns Hopkins Center for Civil Society Studies.

Salamon, L., & Sokolowski, W. S. (2005). Nonprofit organizations: New insights from QCEW data. *Monthly Labor Review,* (September), 19–26.

Salamon, L., Sokolowski, S. W., & List, R. (2003). *Global civil society: An overview.* Baltimore: The Johns Hopkins Comparative Non-profit Sector Project.

Scala, K. (2000). Wissenstypen und ihre Verknüpfung [Types of knowledge and how to connect them]. In P. Heintel & L. Krainer (Eds.), *Weiter Bildung? Beiträge zur wissenschaftlichen Weiterbildung aus Theorie und Praxis* [*Further education? Articles on science-based further education in theory and practice*] (pp. 31–38). Wien-New York: Springer.

Schauer, R. (2000). Betriebswirtschaftliche Überlegungen zu den ,Kernkompetenzen' öffentlicher Verwaltungen [Business reflections on core competencies of public administations]. In R. Schauer & D. Budäus (Eds.), *Public Management, Arbeitsberichte und Forschungsergebnisse [Public Management, reports and scientific results]* (pp. 28–40). Forschungskolloquium Linz-Hamburg: Johannes Keppler Universität Linz.

Schein E. H. (1987). *The clinical perspective in fieldwork.* London: Sage Publications.

Schein, E. H. (1995a). *Kurt Lewin's change theory in the field and in the classroom: Notes toward a model of managed learning.* Invited paper for a special issue of *Systems Practice edited by Susan Wheelan, March, 1995.* www2.tech.purdue.edu/Ols/courses/ols582/SWP-3821-32871445.pdf.

Schein, E. H. (1995b). Wie können Organisationen schneller lernen? Die Herausforderung, den grünen Raum zu betreten [How can organizations learn faster? The challenge to enter the green room]. *Organisationsentwicklung[Organizational development]*, *3*, 4–13.

Schmidt, A. (2006). *Erfolgsfaktoren für die Entwicklung und Steuerung von interorganisationalen Kooperationen in Unternehmensnetzwerken [Factors of Success for the development and the management of international collaborations in networks of enterprises].* Ph. D. Klagenfurt: Alpe-Adria Universiy of Klagenfurt.

Seidl, D., & Becker, K.H. (2006). *Niklas Luhmann and organization studies: Advances in organization studies.* Copenhagen: Copenhagen Business School.

Simon, F. B. & CONECTA-Authorgroup (1992). *Radikale Markwirtschaft* [*Radical Free Market Economy*].Heidelberg: Carl-Auer-Systeme.

Simon, F. B. & CONECTA-Authorgroup (2004). *The organisation of self-organisation: Foundations of systemic management.* Heidelberg: Carl-Auer-Systeme.

Simsa, R. (2003). Nonprofit-Organisationen und der Staat: Eine langjährige Liaison wird brüchig [Non-Profits and the state: A long-term relationship decays]. *Juridikum [Juridicum],* 3, 134–137.

Simsa, R., Schober, C., & Schober, D. (2004). *Nonprofit Organisationen im sozialen Dienstleistungsbereich—Bedeutung, Rahmenbedingungen, Perspektiven [Non-Profits in social services: Importance, general conditions, perspectives].* Studie des NPO-Insitutes im Auftrag der BAG Freie Wohlfahrt. Gekürzte Version [Assignment of the BAG Freie Wohlfahrt: Study of the NPO-institute]. Abbreviated version. Wien: NPO-Institut.

Statistik Austria (2007). *Jahrbuch 2007 [Annual 2007].* Wien, Publisher: Central Office of Statistics.

Sydow, J. (2004). Network development by means of network evaluation? Explorative insights from a case in the financial services industry. *Human Relations 57* (1), 201–220.

Sydow, J., & Windeler, A. (2003). Reflexive development of interfirm networks: The role of managers and consultants. In A.F. Buono (Ed.), *Enhancing inter-firm networks and interorganizational strategies* (pp. 169–186). Greenwich, CT: Information Age Publishing.

Tichy, N. M., & Bennis, W. (2007). Making judgement calls. *Harvard Business Review, 85*(10). 94–102.

v. Foerster, H. (1973). On constructing a reality. In F. E. Preiser (Ed.), *Environmental design research,* (Vol. 2, pp. 35–46). Stroudberg: Dowden, Hutchinson & Ross.

Wabnegg, H. (2006). *Das Öffentliche verantworten: Zur politischen Steuerung des Öffentlichen [Responsibilities for the Public Sector: On managing of the public sector]*. Ph. D. Klagenfurt: Alpe-Adria Universiy of Klagenfurt.

Weick, K. (1969). *Social psychology of organizing.* Reading, MA: Addison-Wesley.

Weick, K. E. (1985): *Der Prozess des Organisierens.* [*Cognitive processes in organizations*]. Frankfurt A.M.: Suhrkamp.

Weick, K. (1995). *Sensemaking in organizations.* Thousand Oaks, CA: Sage.

Weick, K. (2001). *Making sense of the organization.* New York: Blackwell.

Weisbord, M. R., & Janoff, S. (2000). *Future search: An action guide to finding common ground in organizations and communities.* San Francisco, CA: Berrett-Koehler.

Willke, H. (1991), *Systemtheorie: Eine Einführung in die Grundprobleme der Theorie sozialer Systeme [Systems Theory: Introduction into the basic problems of a theory of social systems]*. Stuttgart, Jena: Gustav Fischer Verlag.

Willke, H. (1994). *Systemtheorie II: Interventionstheorie: Grundzüge einer Theorie der Intervention in komplexe Systeme [Systems theory II: Intervention: Basic theory of intervention into complex systems]*. Stuttgart, Jena: Gustav Fischer Verlag.

Willke, H. (1995). *Systemtheorie III: Steuerungstheorie: Grundzüge einer Theorie der Steuerung komplexer Sozialsysteme [Systems Theory III: Theory of governance: Basic theory of intervention into complex systems]*. Stuttgart, Jena: Gustav Fischer Verlag.

Willke, H. (1997). *Supervision des Staates [Supervision of the state]*. Frankfurt: Suhrkamp.

Willke, H. (2007). *Smart Governance: Governing the global knowledge society.* Chicago: University of Chicago Press.

Wimmer, R. (1995). Die permanente Revolution: Aktuelle Trends in der Gestaltung von Organisationen [The permanent revolution: Current Trends of Designing & Managing Organizations]. In R. Grossmann, E. Krainz & M. Oswald (Eds.), *Veränderungen in Organisationen, Management und Beratung* [*Change in organizations, management and consultancy]* (pp. 21–41). Wiesbaden: Gabler.

Wimmer, R. (1999). Wider den Veränderungsoptimismus: Zu den Möglichkeiten und Grenzen einer radikalen Transformation von Organisationen [Versus the optimism of change management: Chances and limitations of a radical transformation of organizations]. *Soziale Systeme: Systemtheorie für Wirtschaft und Unternehmen. Zeitschrift für soziologische Theorie [Social Systems: System theory for the economy], 5,* 159–180.

Zimmermann, A. (2000). Nonprofit-Organisationen im Wohlfahrtsmix—Konfliktlinien, Trends und Perspektiven in Münster [Non-Profits in welfare—Conflicts, trends and perspectives in Münster]. In A. Zimmer & E. Priller (Eds.) (2000), *Der deutsche Nonprofit-Sektor im gesellschaftlichen Wandel. Zu ausgewählten Ergebnissen der deutschen Teilstudie des international vergleichenden Johns Hopkins Projektes [The German non-profit sector in change: Selected results of a German study of the international comparative John Hopkins project]* (pp. 65–72). Münsteraner Diskussionspapiere zum Nonprofit-Sektor—/ Paper of Münster on the discussion about the non-profit sector. Nr. 3, Münster.

Zulehner, P. M. (1999). *Wege zu einer solidarischen Politik: Unter Mitarbeit von Anton Pelinka, Hermann Denz und Reinhard Zuba [Paths towards a solidary politics: Together with Anton Pelinka, Hermann Denz and Reinhard Zuba]*. Innsbruck: Tyrolia.

ABOUT THE CONTRIBUTORS

Anthony F. Buono, series editor, has a joint appointment as Professor of Management and Sociology at Bentley University and is Founding Coordinator of the Bentley Alliance for Ethics & Social Responsibility. His many books include *The Human Side of Mergers and Acquisitions: Managing Collisions between People, Cultures and Organizations* (Jossey-Bass, 1989; Beard Books, 2003) and *A Primer on Organizational Behavior* (Wiley, 7th ed., 2008). His current research and consulting interests focus on organizational change and interorganizational alliances, with an emphasis on mergers, acquisitions and strategic partnerships, and developing organizational change capacity. He holds Ph.D. with a concentration in Industrial and Organizational Sociology from Boston College.

Ralph Grossmann is Professor for Organizational Development and head of the Department of Organizational Development and Group Dynamics at the Faculty of Interdisciplinary Studies at the University of Klagenfurt, Austria. He is also scientific director of the Master Program Organizational Development (MSOD) at the University of Klagenfurt. Dr. Grossmann has been an organization and management consultant for more than 20 years.

Facilitating Collaboration in Public Management, pages 201–202

He has specialized in the consulting of public institutions and non-profit organizations. As a founding member (1973) of the Austrian Association for Group Dynamics and Organization Consulting he still acts as teaching consultant for this professional association. His current research and consulting interest focus on organizational change and transorganizational development, the learning in management and organisation, responsible leadership, organization development in Asian countries, e.g., Mongolia, China, Vietnam. He holds PhD in law from the University of Vienna.

Hubert Lobnig is co-founder of Lemon Consulting, specializing in consulting and research in organization design, strategy, interorganizational collaboration as well as training for executive managers and OD professionals across industries and in multinational companies. He is a member of the Alpen-Adria University Klagenfurt (Faculty for Interdisciplinary Studies—Department "Organizational Development and Group Dynamics"), and teaches in the Group Dynamics and Master in Organization Development programme. He has a doctorate in organizational psychology from the University of Vienna (AT) and Habilitation (State Doctorate) for "Organization Development and Group Dynamics" at the University of Klagenfurt (AT).

Klaus Scala is the Founder and Head of the Center for Social Competence at the University of Graz, Austria. He also is engaged as a Permanent Guest Professor at the Department for Organization Development & Group Dynamics of the University of Klagenfurt, Austria. He conducts master's and PhD level classes in Organization Development. His main area in consulting and research is the development of cooperation between public service organizations (education, public health, health care, traffic). He is a member of the Austrian Society of Group Dynamics and Organizational Consulting and holds a Lectureship there. He has taught at universities and academic institutions in Austria, Kyrgistan, USA (Stanford) and Zimbabwe.

Michael Stadlober is managing partner of MelangeC Sustainable Consulting. He works as trainer and consultant, mainly in the areas of organizational development in public-sector organizations and non-profit organizations. He has facilitated change processes in a variety of organizations and branches in Austria and Germany. As a researcher, he has worked as scientific assistant at the IFF department of Organizational Development and Group Dynamics, with responsibility for overseeing research projects and publications. His main areas of interest focus on organizational and inter-organizational change processes in the field of public goods. He is currently finishing his PhD thesis on "How to organize change: Outsourcing in public management."

CPSIA information can be obtained at www.ICGtesting.com
Printed in the USA
LVOW13s1314060814

397727LV00007B/91/P

9 781617 358869